A Family Apart

Sleuthing the Mysteries of Abandonment, Adoption and DNA
A Memoir

Craig A. Steffen

Nanette:

Thank you for your personal
interest in this story.
" Endings Beget Beginings "

GA Steffen

10-5-15

First Printing - Hardcover : 2014

ISBN 978-0-996-3642-0-1

Published by Cognoscente Publishing Spring Valley, OH

Acknowledgments

I realize I've been AWOL for much of the last two years, either literally absent traveling about doing research, or emotionally absent as I've tried to internally process the results of that research.

Cindy, my wife, has taken the brunt of my absenteeism. And she has done so with amazing grace, understanding and support – "MOSTLY," (an inside joke).

Thank you my dear Punky" for standing with me and alongside me throughout most of my life. We've been acquaintances, friends, best friends, and lovers for 72.9% of my life to date, a clear majority.

Cindy, I have no way to express my deepest gratitude for your true companionship (Cue Mark Cohen's song of similar title at this point). You are simultaneously a rock and a soft spot. You are both supporter and motivator. You are, at the same time, a wise counselor and a tender friend. We are truly "one flesh."

It is my hope that these many words, assembled into a book, will provide "completion" and healing to me, to us and to all who venture inside its pages to share this journey with us.

It is my sincere hope that, should I live to be 90, you will have shared 81.11% of my life with me at that point. As I promised in 1984, "Cindy Steffen, I'll love you till the day I die."

***

To my sister, Theresa, who has literally been a part of my life every single day of it. We've shared DNA since day one, and your willingness to share it again for the lab in July of 2012 set my life's story on a new course. You will always have a very special place in my loving heart.

***

To my adoptive families, the Steffens and the Gardiners, I am eternally grateful for the rescue and normalcy you provided me at a critical juncture in my early life. I cannot imagine what alternate and inferior path my life may have taken without your intervention, acceptance and dedication to the task of providing for children who were not your own. Our lives were far from perfect, but despite some frustrations I've mentioned herein, make no mistake that I loved you all and, deep within, I knew *your* love too. I wish we had all known how to communicate our love with more grace and frequency.

***

To all my brothers and sisters in faith, I am honored to call you friends. I cannot possibly name each of you without doubling the number of pages in this book – but you know who you are and you are loved. You may find yourself disagreeing with some of my statements about human traditions inside religion. I'm not trying to be obstinate or provocative, just honest about my own experience. I couldn't be where I am today without having walked that part of the journey. In places I may be wrong, please show me the patience of Jesus – and I'll endeavor to do the same with you. May we learn better each day to walk in the way of Jesus and to cherish the multifarious diversity we find in him and each other.

***

To my many friends who have been engaged by my story for years and who lovingly prodded me to write – Thank You. In our many discussions I've learned that we all have a unique story – tell yours. I hope you're not so weary of hearing my story that you no longer want to *read* it.

***

To my writerly friends, many of whom were with me at the Antioch Writers Workshop and the McCoy Book Club. Thank you for your invaluable feedback, suggestions and, most of all, your time. Your sage advice helped me to keep putting words on the page. And if any of those words resonate with readers, it will be in no small part due to your tireless hours of coaching this doe-eyed rookie.

***

To my hands-on bookish friends with "red pens," Greg Belliveau, Connie Clark, Kerry Leibowitz, Frances Barber, Dan Fouke, Lee Martin and Brian McLaren, thank you so much for your invaluable insights, stellar editing and warm mentoring. All of life is about relationships – and I'm SO pleased to have them with each of you.

***

To the many mentors I've had at various stages of my life – Thank YOU. I recognize that nothing I have achieved in life, however modest, could have been done without the care, wisdom and foresight of the dozens of folks who "took me under their wing." It truly made all the difference.

***

And for all of my "new family" who will be revealed within these pages, I am so grateful for each of you. I am grateful not just for the good parts of our family history, but also for the bad and the ugly – for it is the WHOLE story that has given me life and made me what I have become – and what I will ultimately be.

***

And to Cindy, my wife, I STILL love you. Everything begins and ends with you. ☺

Dedication

To my beloved wife Cindy. And to all those I've encountered in life who have dared be "mother," "father," or "family" to this once lost little boy.

Author's Note

This is a *piece* of my story. I tell it to the best of my memory.

What you find here is memoir, not fiction. I have painstakingly researched the facts to the extent that the facts are available. In the few places where I cannot possibly know the exact nature of what happened, either because I was not there, was too young to remember, or could not interview witnesses, I have painted scenes that I think are most plausible based on a myriad of supporting data that I *can* apply to the situation. But in these few cases, I have been careful to preface the section with statements such as, "I can imagine ..."

There are two places within where I have changed the names and/or places of events in order to honor the privacy of the people involved. The events themselves, however, are just as I recall them.

This memoir was written *as the story unfolded for me.* Therefore, there are facts that exist in later stages of the book that I literally did not know when writing earlier parts of the book. I made this structure choice deliberately so that I could invite you to travel the journey *with* me.

I journey forward without fear.

Craig A. Steffen

Part One

A Journey for Identity

The human estate is precarious indeed. As Pascal noted we are but a fragile reed, and yet a thinking reed capable of writing the Brandenburg concerto, creating a concentration camp or imagining our own demise. No one escapes pathology, for no one remains unwounded. 'Pathos'... derives from the Greek word for suffering. Psychopathology may then literally be translated as 'the expression of the soul's suffering.' It is not whether or not one is wounded, but how deeply, and, more important, what adaptations we have made as a result.

James Hollis
The Eden Project, In Search of the Magical Other

Stanchion

It is three months after the disappearance.

The stanchion rises before me like a cruel monolith. It is at least three of me high and two of me wide. It is made of old, ugly, unfinished wood. It is like a coffin stood on end, divided into three uneven sections. The middle section is big enough for more than two of me. I am sad.

The base of the stanchion sits on the floor, and above the floor is a drawer that comes up above my knees. At the top of the drawer is a piece of wood that serves as a seat, on which I must sit during morning instructions. I get splinters in the backs of my legs. I sit quietly, facing out into the room. I feel alone.

There is an important shelf far above my head. More than my arm's length above that shelf is the dusty, spider-webbed top of the stanchion. There are many of these stanchions lining the walls of this small, linoleum-tiled room. Now, there is a kid in each stanchion looking blankly out into a room of strangers. I am frightened.

Big people talk at us. They say words I do not understand. They speak rules I don't know how to keep. They do not smile. Are they mad? I am accused.

The shelf above my head is impossibly high. My face is hot and red with anger and physical strain. I'm stretching as far as my little two year old body can reach without disassembly. I'm wearing nothing but yellowish-white underwear fitting loose around my short, chunky legs. I've climbed atop the stanchion drawer. I'm on my barefoot tippy-toes, but I *still* can't reach my clothes on that shelf. I am helpless.

No one sees me.

Every face is unfamiliar. I have no idea where I am, or what has happened to all the people I once knew. Everyone else seems to know what to do. I am lost.

My hair is disheveled from a night of fitful sleep in the upper room of this cottage. I attempt slumber alongside row after row of strange, orphaned kids in ancient, steel army cots no longer fit for soldiers. The only light comes from a single, naked bulb glowing dimly in the center of the large, open loft, like a tiny moon above vast, ominous waters. I am adrift.

Every few seconds a random noise jolts me back to an awakened state of terror in a sea of shadows. Each movement of a restless kid sends the rejected cots into convulsions that sound to me like the groanings of monsters. Sobs from a kid in the corner. Whispers from the bigger kids over there. Blanket shadows dance wickedly across the plank floor. An unbefitting, solitary laugh from somewhere in the room. The utter absence of an adult, a tender word or a soft touch. I am left behind.

I CAN'T reach my clothes! Tears of frustration run down my cherubic, white cheeks. Anger turns to rage as I collapse onto the floor, legs crumpled under me, with my head buried in my arm which rests atop the stanchion seat as I scream till my empty belly aches through my uncontrolled sobs. The cold, tiled floor beneath me warms and yellows until I am jerked to my feet by an adult – male or female … I cannot tell – who shouts commands that I must get my clothes and dress myself. I am discarded.

No one will help me.

This is my earliest childhood memory. It has lurked in the shadows of my conscious mind for decades. The nature of this fragment is so foggy, so surreal, that I have never been certain if it is a true memory. Some have suggested that it may be a scene from a disturbing movie that got stuck and owned inside my head. The personal nature of it has always led me to consider it a memory. But the fact that I could not be more than two or three years old would seem to indicate it could not be real. I've always wondered.

Ending

It is forty-eight years after the disappearance.

I sit in an Iowa nursing home in front of a ninety-year-old man in a wheelchair. Tiled floors act like piano keys, sending every heel strike echoing. Odors of disinfectant, medicine and excrement co-mingle in my offended nostrils. Hopelessness is apparent on every face I encounter. I know it is the last time we will ever see each other alive. There are important words gathering in pressurized clumps at the back of my throat. These words long to be untangled and released into this moment.

In all our years on the planet, neither of us has ever said "I love you" to the other and we have never hugged; even though I have called him "Dad" for 47 years.

After three days of searching for a moment appropriate to share the life-long silence of my heart, I have procrastinated as long as the journey will allow. Tomorrow morning, before the sun will rise, I must begin the 700-mile journey back home. It's now or never.

We sit and talk about anything else. The weather; my drive here; the car I bought and how he saw one like it a few weeks ago.

Time in this place is from a different dimension entirely. Clocks spin at a third the speed of time-pieces in the outside world. The collective will of the residents conspires to slow the passage of time. Knowing that the means of exit are predestined, no one, it seems, is in a hurry to leave.

I sit before him for what seems like days, but only a few more hours have passed. The pressure in my heart and throat continues to expand like a water balloon snapped onto a leaky, warm tap. I am urgently aware that each topic of conversation ticks away the few remaining minutes he has on this earth and guilt rises within me that I am stealing them from him.

His eyes are growing heavy. If silence lingers for more than a minute, his head drops, in slow motion, to his chest and bounces off of its force-field. The interval between bounces shortens as I gather my courage.

Finally, choking back tears, I manage to form the words I had practiced on a greeting card a few hours earlier, hedging against my possible failure to actually vocalize them.

"Dad." I catch his drifting attention and our eyes reconnect. When I am sure that the fog of drowsiness has lifted and his eyes are clear and focused, I continue.

"I want to thank you for being my dad. I know that, for you, it was a choice. I am grateful."

Tears begin to stream down his sagging, barely recognizable face. After he attempts to wipe them away, our eyes meet and lock and, with a brightness I'd rarely ever seen in his life, I received slow, halting words from him that puncture me like a syringe.

"Well, thank YOU for being my SON ... I ... love ... you."

As the words pierce and spread through me, I stand and approach him. He extends his feeble arms, limited by recent fractures. We embrace and weep together. It is the longest sustained physical contact we have ever had with each other.

The entire scene consumes about fifteen minutes of our lives, but I don't believe its brevity diminishes the eternal significance for either of us.

I will come to find out I have five parents.

This is the first and only time, in my fifty-something years, I have ever heard any parent call me "Son" or speak the words, "I love you," or offer a hug. These few quiet moments give birth to a powerful declarative triumvirate.

Faces still wet, we say good-bye to one another. We both know it is for the last time. Reluctantly, I return down the tiled halls, my veins pumped full of adrenaline, sadness and a strange and unfamiliar kind of joy.

I am "Son."

I turn right at the nurse's station and proceed toward the exit. I pass the community room, occupied by a dozen or so residents, most in wheelchairs. The cheap boom-box in the corner of the room pipes out a squelched, ancient version of a hymn, "*It Is Well With My Soul.*"

When peace like a river, attendeth my way,
When sorrows like sea billows roll;
Whatever my lot, Thou hast taught me to say,
It is well, it is well, with my soul.

The residents sing along ...a beat or two tardy. I flash back to the dozens of times my youth group sang this song during special events at church, Dad and Mom always present.

It is one of my father's favorite hymns. At this moment, I long for it to be my soul's true condition. But copious new waves of tears betray me.

I fight my way to my car as if trying to swim in a dream. My vision is blurred from self-inflicted waters. My chest aches with the pressure of the sadness of a life about to end; from the thoughts of what was and never will be again; from the knowledge of what could have been, but is now forever lost.

It is finished.

I sit in my car for an hour. I pray and weep uncontrollably in the dark – as if I'm the lone inhabitant of the universe. Finally, I conclude that I will never sleep tonight because of a cocktail of emotions, like gallons of caffeine shot directly into my heart. I start the car and drive through the night toward Ohio and home.

One week later, I return to Iowa to officiate Dad's funeral.

Alone with him after the funeral, I remove the photos from his coffin and the rings from his waxy fingers. And at that moment, a protective layer around my heart begins to melt away. A tiny tongue of curiosity begins to whisper questions from my DNA. From whence did you come? What is your gene pool? Who is your tribe? Are any of *them* still alive?

Retro

❧

I grew up in rural Southwest Iowa, working on farms and attending a tiny Plymouth Brethren church, whose building and leaders hadn't visibly changed since the 1920s. Behaving, working hard and 'gathering' in church were, it seemed to me, the sole valued virtues of my family's existence.

Flora Steffen was 43 when she and Morris adopted my sister, Theresa, and me in October of 1964. Our revised birth certificates were finalized on my sister's seventh birthday. I was four.

When I think of my mother in my childhood, I see her sitting short in the front seat of every car Dad ever owned. Her hair is permed plump and starched crisp into a scrub pad. A plain black purse, large enough to transport a fortune in gold bars, lies restrained across her lap, gripped tight with both hands.

All her dresses are polyester, pastel and floral. On Sundays and Wednesday nights, she wears hats and rouge.

She stares straight ahead, always statuesque in solitude, except when spooked into sudden fear by alleged road-danger. At those moments, more frequent than warranted, her right hand would shoot to the roof to save herself.

But when I was small, I sat to her left – third child. She was different then. In those days, perceived roadway peril would send *both* hands toward salvation; one across my chest. Then, the purse would fall.

When I think of my father, I see him, head down, at the kitchen table. Every meal is taken there, and every family member is present – always. I think of him there because I rarely saw him stationary anywhere else. To him, life is about work and responsibility and duty, and he never wavered from it – ever.

His head is down because he is an introvert – an unquestioned introvert.

His head is down at the beginning of every meal with his massive hands intertwined to form a flesh visor over his eyes, softly and deeply mumbling the same prayer of gratitude for every meal. For years, I believed that the prayer started with the words, "ninety favor." I was in high school before I realized it began, "Thank you, Father." And even though I heard that rote prayer thousands of times, I never heard it clearly enough to be able to recall it here.

He rarely looks up during the meal, head down to focus on the task at hand – fueling the body – as worn out as his overalls – from the rigors of farming 320 acres "alone," even when he has help. On the occasion he does make eye contact with any of us, it is nearly always to correct our slightest straying into "foolishness," as he called it. Anything loud or silly or talkative or worldly or accompanied by a smile is in danger of being squelched by his fear of foolishness and our fear of his harsh correction.

At the end of the evening meal, he turns silently to a thick wall calendar, *Our Daily Bread*, hanging head-high on the wall to his left, a date and a devotional on every page. He begins our after-meal reading ritual by tearing off yesterday's page and reads it, head down, in a slow throaty staccato.

And his head is down at the end of his recitation of the calendar as he reaches under the toaster for five worn and tattered Scofield Bibles that he distributes clockwise around the table. We had started in Genesis at some distant point in the past. And now, after each meal, we read a chapter – a verse for each of us in turn – until it is consumed. I am all but certain that he never read any other book in his life.

Dad had not yet learned to read at age 31 when he married for the first and only time. It is quite likely that he was dyslexic, though that was never formally diagnosed.

When they married in 1951, Mom taught Dad to read through years of lessons from their Bibles. She told me that she sat beside him in their early childless years, grasping his meaty, cracked and wounded hands—these working hands often reeking from yet another application of *Cornhuskers Lotion*. In those days she had guided his index finger along countless scriptures, pausing at each word to instruct. Eventually, embarrassed, like a child imitating, he learned to read in this halting, deep-voiced style that was uniquely his.

Grateful, Dad had tried to return the gift of instruction. Mom had never driven in her 35 years before marriage. In his later years, he told me how he had taken her to the field once in the early days of their union. He was certain that the plodding pace of the tractor would remove her fear of driving.

After having her sit beside him on the tractor fender for several laps around the field, pausing at each curve to instruct, he determined he'd taught her all of the necessities. Mom watched him with trepidation as he dismounted the John Deere 'B' and allowed her to drive alone. At his coaxing, she slowly eased the hand-clutch forward and the tractor lurched ahead in what Dad called "creeper gear." Dad stood in the half-plowed field, hands on his hips, straw hat upon his head, and watched the distance between them grow.

Mom sat short in the seat, moved the steering wheel this way and that, like a child imitating, eyes staring straight ahead. But when she came to the end of the row and a full turn must be maneuvered, she did nothing. The rogue tractor proceeded, unguided, through the fence, into the ditch, across the road and into the neighbor's field on the other side. Dad fled after her, straw hat lost into the wind, caught up and mounted the tractor from behind, rodeo style.

He brought the runaway beast to a halt, no real damage done, and did a poor job of consoling his trembling and sobbing bride. From that moment on, I would only ever see her sitting short in the passenger seat of every car Dad ever owned.

My mother died in 2003 after a long and frightful battle with dementia. But rarely do I choose to call up memories from her last four nursing home years – her mind stuck in a distant past memory loop like an ancient phonograph record.

My father soldiered on for eight more years until prostate cancer, dormant for 20 years, reemerged to claim his bladder and then marched through his bones. His once imposing 6' 1" 250 pound frame shriveled to an assortment of paper skin, brittle joints and broken bones. But, unlike Mom, his mind remained sharp till the end.

When I would visit him at the nursing home where he spent his final year of life, I would retrieve that same after-meal Bible, now barely hanging together by its sinews, and I would read to him. My voice, trained from years of public speaking, glided over the passages with attention to punctuation and inflection, properly paced to fit the time of life in which we both found ourselves.

When I would complete a chapter, he would always say, "You've become such a good reader," as if I were ten. And in each of those moments, I felt hopeful that my dad had finally noticed and verbalized some virtue in me.

And then, I would think how much I longed to hear his monotone staccato just once more – and I would turn away, head down, hiding my tears.

Home

It is 13 months after the disappearance.

Something is different in the cottage today. Big people are all around me. I didn't have to sit in the stanchion this morning. A woman washed my face and is helping me get dressed, but I don't need her help. Where was she last year?

I'm wearing clothes I have never seen before. They feel scratchy on my skin. They are not play clothes. The woman tells me I need to keep them clean. Why is everything different today?

I see Theresa this morning. Big people are all around her too. They are brushing her hair. She yells when they hit a snag. I want to help her, but I'm in the next room. Sometimes Theresa and I catch each other's eyes as they dress us. I can tell she doesn't know what's happening either. Now they are sticking colorful clips in her hair. She has a pink dress on. She won't get to play today either. Where is Ricky?

When we are dressed, the two women who have been dressing us take us by the hand and out the cottage door. We walk two-by-two toward the big building at "The Home." Theresa and her woman are in front of us. We go slow. I want to run, but my new black shoes are heavy and stiff and the woman holds my hand tight. Have we been bad?

It is so hot. I want these strange clothes off me. I want to have shorts on and run barefoot in the cool grass. I want to talk to Theresa

15

without the big people. I want someone to hold me and talk to me. What is happening?

We go into the The Home's big building. The big people take us to a room I've never seen before. An old man sits behind a big table thing. The two women leave us alone with him. He talks to us. He does not smile. He says something about "going away." He tells us about a place called "a farm" where there will be animals and big tractors – like my toys. He says, "If you are good," we won't have to come back to the cottages ever again. Where are we going?

We sit for a long time. The man stops talking and pushes paper around on his table thing. I want to get out of the big wood chair and look at the books and things on the shelves. I am hot. My sweaty pants and shirt peel from the chair when I try to move. Theresa does not talk. Is she afraid?

My butt starts to hurt from the hard chair. Everything in me wants to talk – to anyone. Then three big people come into the room with the old man and us. They are dressed funny with hats on. There is an older woman who starts talking to us right away. I don't know who she is. I've seen the other two people before. They were here looking at us weeks ago. These two people are younger than the woman who talks to us. They talk to the old man. I can't figure out what their words mean. The younger man and woman scribble on paper, then the old man scribbles on paper. They push paper back and forth and scribble lots of times. Is this a game?

The older woman talks to us and pinches our checks. I think she likes us. When the paper game is over, the younger man and woman talk to us too. They talk about a "long ride in a car," and going to "a place with animals" far away. They take our hands and lead us outside into the sun, where it is even hotter than in the old man room. We walk toward a big car the color of sky. But, where is Ricky?

We get into the car. The younger man and woman are in the front. The older woman gets in the back between Theresa and me. Everyone talks at the same time. Everyone wears hats. The car starts. Are we going without Ricky?

Fear. I can't stay quiet. "Where's Ricky?" I blurt.

No one seems to hear me. I look at Theresa. We both say it again, together, louder. "Where's Ricky?"

The younger woman turns around and looks at us. She says lots of words. I don't think Ricky is coming with us. I cry. Theresa cries. Why don't these people like our brother, Ricky?

We drive and drive. It is hot; the windows are down and it is noisy. I can't hear the big people talk. The back seat is covered with clear plastic that has little triangle bubbles all over it. When I push the bubbles in, they pop back out. Theresa and I fall asleep. Our arms and faces stick to the big back seat. Does Ricky know we are gone?

We stop at a place that feeds us. It is like a kitchen, but not in a house or The Home. I have never been to a place like this before. We sit quietly and try to be good. We try hard not to get our clothes dirty. We get back in the hot car. We drive and drive some more. We sleep some more. When will we see the animals?

We turn onto a noisy road. There is lots of dust. I can't see out the back window anymore. We turn again, and then we stop. All the big people say "We're here, we're home." We must have been bad. Are we back at The Home?

We get out of the car. I am wet with sweat. This is not The Home. I don't know where I am. It is a big white house. It is much bigger than the cottages. There are no other houses. Across the dusty road there are big buildings. I hear strange noises. I smell strange poopy smells. Are these from animals?

We walk up steps and into a long room. The younger woman calls it a "porch." An old man and a big boy they call "Kinny" come into the porch. The big boy does not smile. Is he mean?

It has been a very long drive. The younger woman takes me to the bathroom. I stand in front of the toilet. She does not leave. She extends a hand toward my pants zipper. I reflex away. I don't want her help. I take out my peepee. She reaches down to hold it. I yell, "I can do it myself." I turn to look at her. Pee goes everywhere. I pee on her. She yells at me. Will we have to go back to the cottages now?

Love

There was nothing quite like Grandma Steffen's pot roast. Though I have never been able to duplicate the taste, I can still see her working in her primitive kitchen creating her signature dish.

The first vestiges of late autumn light begin to reveal kitchen contents and the roosters announce morning's presence from the barnyard. I sit six and drowsy at the weary oak table that soldiers on under the double kitchen windows. I watch her glide across the drab and damaged linoleum with the rote predictability of a music box ballerina. Nearly 70, her feet are clad in manly, black leather shoes that are scuffed, cheap and orthopedic. The front of her long, plain dress is concealed under a once-white, muslin apron. Her impossibly long chestnut hair is truncated into an artful bun, stuck full of hair pins and cloaked in a nearly invisible net.

She slips in and out of the tiny pantry at her back to retrieve secret containers of ingredients. A pinch of this, a handful of that, a dash of something else all tossed together with fist-sized produce into a vast, thick, cast-iron kettle. The black, gnarly kettle looks as if it has been salvaged from an ancient battle field, sporting a strap of flat steel hooped from side to side like a bucket handle. Ingredients all accounted for, she repeatedly dips a long-handled, aluminum ladle into the creamery can of fresh well-water, until the crimson beef is nearly submerged. The lid, so heavy it cannot be lifted with a wet hand, clanks into place obscuring the evening meal for its day-long metamorphosis.

Grandma then grips the flat steel hoop with both hands and lowers the kettle from the counter, staggers bent under its load, shimmies to the adjoining room, swings it backward between her legs, and hoists it with a grunt atop the coal-burning heat-stove. The tiny house echoes with a cast-iron to cast-iron percussive thud.

There the kettle sits all morning and all afternoon – ignored. It would be forgotten altogether if not for the expansive aroma so insistent that the lid's girth must occasionally yield to its swelling and rise to release it, filling our nostrils with its steaming glory. Settling back into place, the lid chimes its metallic Pavlovian bell – subconsciously we salivate.

On one such day, Theresa and I wile away the time in the barnyard, anticipating dusk and the return of Grandpa from picking field-corn – by hand. Then we can partake of the feast in the kettle that assails our noses even out here. Our patience for waiting grows thin.

Theresa returns to the house and comes back a few minutes later with jaws masticating and moans of the glorious taste of Grandma's pot roast.

"Grandma gave me a taste of the roast – its SOOO good, mmmmm. Maybe she'll give you a taste too."

Without a word, I bolt for the house, leap upon the porch, throw open the screen and march through the door to find Grandma.

"GRANDMA?"

Her voice comes back to me from a back room, "I'm here, little one; what is it?"

"Can I get a taste of the roast?"

"No, honey, it isn't ready yet."

"But Theresa got some," I protest, and turn around angry, running out the door. I stomp past my taunting sister in the barnyard and march animated down the long, steep gravel driveway. When I get to the newly paved road that runs in front of Grandpa and Grandma's house, I indignantly turn to the right, fully intent on running away from such injustice forever.

I huff right past the neighbor's house where my little friend Pam lives, now a half mile from Grandma. Then I hear a short blast from a car horn behind me. Startled, I turn to see my grandparents' light green Rambler – but then I turn defiantly and sulk onward.

Grandma drives slowly past me, window down, trying to coax me into the passenger seat. I don't even turn to look at her and never lose stride. She pulls over ahead of me, opens her door, and walks back toward me.

Her voice is calm, winsome and full of compassion. She does not shout or demand or show anger. She simply walks toward me, speaking soothing words I do not now remember. She asks questions and seeks to understand what wrong has been done to me, so that she may seek to correct it.

By the time she reaches me, I want again to be with her, to watch her mysterious ways, to be spoken to as if I am one of her kind. She leads me off of the road and into the car, pulling me close so that our hips touch.

She drives us back to the house, up the driveway and into the barn where the car is always kept. Once we are safely in the barn, she coaxes my perspective from me, and I tell her of the great injustice I have endured – being denied pot roast when Theresa was granted her similar request.

Grandma explains that this is *not* what happened. Theresa's request for pot roast had been denied exactly as mine had been. The food was not yet fully cooked and would not be good, despite the hunger-inducing aromas that tempted us. Theresa was playing a trick on me.

"She LIED to me?" I ask in disbelief.

"Well yes, Craig, Theresa lied. But she wasn't trying to be mean, she was just having fun."

"Well it ISN'T fun." I pout.

We talk a while longer sitting in the car in the barn. Then she takes me by the hand and together we walk across the barnyard, past Theresa (without uttering a word) down the sidewalk and into the house. We warm ourselves around the coal-stove, with the aromatic kettle still tempting us with its chime and smell. When we are warm, Grandma slips into the pantry for a moment, then comes back to the stove and hands me a molasses cookie.

"Now you mustn't tell your sister about the cookie. This will be our secret. Ok?"

I nod my head in agreement and hug her legs. She leads me over to the big brown chair that sits under the party-line phone by the front door that no one ever uses. We sit tight together in the chair and she tells me a story.

"Do you remember the cottages where you and your sister used to live, before you came here to be with us?"

I shrug and shake my head slowly from side to side – not knowing for sure.

"Your first mommy and daddy couldn't take care of you anymore, so you went to live at the cottages with lots of other kids who didn't have their own mommy and daddy anymore either. Those nice people at the cottages took care of you and fed you and gave you clean clothes to wear, but they couldn't be your mommy and daddy."

I listened to her story with vague recollection, but keen interest.

"Then Morris and Flora, your new mommy and daddy, went to the cottages to find you and Theresa and bring you back here to be their very own children. I remember going with them to the cottages to see you for the first time and being so happy to meet you and your sister. You were both so pretty and well-behaved. I knew right away that I was going to love you and raise you as my precious grandson. I'd never do anything on purpose that would make you want to run away from me. Do you believe me, honey?"

I shake my head up and down, with my lower lip protruding in front of me – tears and snot rolling down my red little face.

"Do you promise never to run away again?"

"Uh huh."

She hugs me tight for a long time. I nearly go to sleep in her arms. When she gets up, she lays me down in the chair to rest. I watch her horizontally as she walks toward the kitchen, and then she pulls a handkerchief from the sleeve of her dress.

Grandma Steffen was the only person in my childhood who truly knew how to love me.

Fishing

It was February 2011 when the man who had been my father for most of my life died. And though I can't describe our relationship as warm, I can say now that its stability and constancy meant more to me than I ever considered while he was alive. I don't say that because of regrets I have or because of things that got left undone or unsaid between us. We did eventually have those awkward and, for us, unnatural conversations, succinct as they were. Our relationship was what it was. Given Dad's background and mine, as dissimilar as tractors and baseball bats, I can't see how the relationship could have been markedly different.

I actually don't think either of us was happy with the tepid and shallow connection we had, but for most of our lives neither of us was equipped to affect change. Dad couldn't do it because he was a product of the financial and emotional poverty of the Great Depression, having been born in 1920. His relationship with his own father was volatile and sometimes abusive. I couldn't change it because, to him, I was forever "child," and one who had wandered far from home and spent my life and strange talents in what seemed to him to be incomprehensible pursuits. Dad never did understand what I do for a living. And, for both of us, change wasn't possible because we lacked the ability to manipulate the vague idea of a father/son relationship into anything tangible and actionable. It was as if neither of us could pick the other one out of the fog of our own woundedness.

We lived on a farm near Grant, Iowa in 1969 – a solitary existence on which my dad thrived and one which drove his family nearly to

25

despair. I came home from the fourth grade on the school bus, changed my clothes, grabbed a snack and went outside to goof around in the barnyard alone. After supper, my mother approached me, while I washed dishes with my sister, and asked me where I'd been after school. I shrugged and told her of my passing of time poking about amongst the several buildings, sheds and granaries out in the barnyard. "Why?" I asked.

"Because your dad came in from the field and wanted to take you fishing." She said this in a manner that made me feel that somehow I should have known this would happen. Yet, my dad and I had never heretofore gone fishing. Nor had there ever been any talk of doing so.

I recall a cacophony of confusing emotional voices in my head. First defensiveness: "how was I supposed to know?" Then a thrill, "Hey, my dad wants to hang out with me, groovy." (Yes, I used to say that.) Then distrust, "Geez I was just in the barnyard, if he'd have hollered for me I'd have heard him. How hard could he have tried?" And then sadness, "He talked with her about it, why didn't he talk to me? He never talks to me."

My dad never did mention that failed fishing trip to me. I never brought it up to him either. And, so far as I know, he never again attempted to go fishing – with me or anyone else.

That scene is emblematic of my relationship with Dad. Lots of emotions and questions, near zero communication and confusions left hanging in the air like dust in a coal mine.

Cottages

❤

I grew up knowing that I was adopted. So many adopted people I've met, or have heard about, tell of a moment in their teens when they were finally told the truth of their origins. I never had one of those events in my life where someone sat me down to tell me that my whole life had been a sort of lie. For this I am grateful. But having avoided that particular brand of trauma doesn't mean I escaped the wounds of abandonment. The wounds themselves have always been exacerbated by not knowing WHY I needed to be adopted.

I was two when I went to the orphanage, three when I went to foster care, and four when Theresa and I were adopted.

Adapting to the Steffen household was tricky. We'd just gotten used to the plethora of rules at the orphanage, and now there were all these new rules and new people to decipher.

One of the first adaptations was going to church. We hadn't been accustomed to going to church three times a week and we didn't know what church-behavior looked like. As the youngest, I didn't take to it naturally.

The coping mechanism I'd embraced was to be a pleaser. When I failed at pleasing, it crushed my spirit.

We always sat in the same pew at church… five rows back on the right side of the meeting room, just behind Harold and Leona Meyer. Dad's parents sat on the left side of the Meyer pew. The Sunday morning services would last over two hours without a break. Sunday night and Wednesday night services were one hour.

In the early church years, I'd often get fidgety, or distracted or be exchanging goofy faces with other kids in church, all of which seemed to be an embarrassment to the Steffens. I could see the blood of anger rise in their faces and I'd be harshly corrected via several specific methods. If I "had ants in my pants," as Dad would sometimes say, I'd get lifted off the seat several inches and slammed back down hard into the same spot, as if Dad were driving a fence post. If I was distracted, Dad would grab my thigh just above my knee cap with his massive hand and squeeze till he had my full and undivided attention. If I was caught making eye-contact with some other kid, Dad would grab my left ear and twist it hard as if trying to unscrew it from my head. This punishment was the one I hated the most.

In retrospect, I think the harsh discipline said more about how they wanted to be perceived by their church community, than about training excellent character into their children. How things *looked* to others seemed far more important than the reality itself. This deep desire to be accepted by their community was likely compounded by the presence of Grandpa and Grandma in the pew in front of us. Desire for acceptance and the fear of rejection are both powerful motivators for kids and adults alike.

On those Sundays that my behavior had embarrassed them, and they had subsequently embarrassed me through public punishment, I'd sulk all the way home. Apparently I thought that I was punishing them back by withholding my words and engagement.

Sometimes my internal anger would boil over and I'd loudly and indignantly shout out, "YOU don't even love me."

It was at these moments of unbridled emotion that my mother would often respond with an exasperated, "Well of course we do. If we didn't, why would we have gone to The Home to get you and bring you here? We drove all the way to Davenport, clear across the State of Iowa, and walked from cottage to cottage looking for children to bring home with us. And then we chose you and Theresa and brought you to our house to raise you as our own."

The adoption topic would come up in the middle of random conversations several times a year. Mom or Dad (usually Mom) would tell us, or some visitor, how they came to choose us in the adoption process. Each time, the story was more or less a variation of what I related above. It wasn't until decades later that I learned that this account of choosing was the dominant narrative of the time in adoption circles.

In 1939, Valentina P. Wasson wrote a children's book on the topic of adoption called *The Chosen Baby*. That book was revised in 1950 and became a widely used resource in adoption communities. The edition of the book I have promotes an early and positive method of communicating with adopted children; informing them that they are special because they were *chosen* by their new families. In the forward of the book, Sophie Van S. Theis, Secretary of the Committee on Child Placing and Adoption at the time, called the book "the story of every adopted child." Because of the book's wide acceptance and broad circulation, when the Steffens first engaged with the Annie Wittenmyer Home in the late 1950s when they adopted their first child, Kenny, it is likely that they were either given a copy of the book or briefed on its contents and message. Dozens of times in childhood I heard, or overheard, this *chosen* concept matter-of-factly proffered, mostly by Mom, as if it were a magic elixir that would heal all the adoption wounds of Kenny, Theresa or me.

But one night the narrative changed significantly.

We were on a summer vacation out West in the very early 1970s, visiting a relative of Mom Steffen somewhere in Utah. To this day, I have no idea who this person was; it was the first time I'd ever met her and it was the last. We were staying the night in her home. If memory serves, she was older than Mom and a widow. It was a small three bedroom house in a suburban development. One of the two guest rooms was granted to my folks, the other to Theresa; so I got the sofa in the living room. Dad and Theresa had gone to their rooms, but Mom wanted to stay up to chat with this relative. I had lain down on the sofa and was presumed sleeping – but I wasn't.

To my horror, the two women began talking about menopause and its various unpleasant symptoms. Frankly, I didn't really know what menopause was at the time; I was about 10, but I knew it was way more information than I wanted to know. How I LONGED for precious sleep at this point.

Eventually the conversation turned to this woman's adult children and then she asked Mom about why she "hadn't had any children of her own." There was the $64,000 question.

Here's where the conversation went from icky to interesting from my point of view.

Mom told this relative about a pregnancy she'd had early in her marriage. It had ended in a miscarriage and as a newly married couple they were devastated. After the mourning of the loss, they had decided that they were just too old to "have children of their own," so they began to talk about adoption. Mom explained that, decades earlier, one of the prominent families in their church community had adopted a boy from the Annie Wittenmyer Home in Davenport, Iowa. On their recommendation, Mom and Dad decided to pursue that place as a potential source for children.

Mom described Kenny's adoption process and the difficulties he'd had adapting. Eventually he required "nerve medication." She explained how his love of music and his beautiful singing voice had been attributes that won them over. I remember being astounded by this, since neither Mom nor Dad could carry a tune in a bucket.

Eventually she started talking about their decision, five years after adopting Kenny, to adopt again. I expected the same story I'd always heard, but she began this story differently than I'd heard it before.

"We really wanted a girl this time. So we went back to Annie Wittenmyer and asked if they might have a girl a little younger than Kenny, so that we could have a sister for Kenny. We talked to Kenny about this and he was so excited to have a little sister. In his natural family, Kenny had several brothers and sisters. He just wasn't used to being alone. He was from the city with lots of friends and family. Then he came to our farm and was alone, except for Morris and me. We could tell he was lonely. We really wanted to get him a sister."

"Wait. What?" My mind raced. "What about me?"

"When we got to The Home they had set aside several young girls that met our criteria and we went from cottage to cottage to see them. They let us spend time with each of them and watch them play with the other kids. Theresa was just so cute with that lovely smile, thick dark hair and those chubby cheeks. After spending the morning there, Morris and I went to lunch and talked about it, then we went back to tell them that we'd like to start the process of fostering with Theresa. If they agreed, we knew the process. They'd place her with us for a while to make sure she'd adapt, just like they'd done with Kenny, and then after several months, if everyone still wanted to move forward, we'd start talking about a formal adoption."

I was wide awake now, but was doing my best to keep the illusion of sleep going so as not to stifle this conversation. But to my consternation, the relative interrupted Mom.

"Would you like a cup of coffee? I'm going to have some instant."

"Do you have Sanka?"

"Yes, that's what I'll make."

"Can I help you?"

"No, I'll just put the tea kettle on and be right back."

Lying there on the sofa alone, with my mom five feet away as she harbored this secret version of a familiar story, was tough on a ten-year-old. Did I look sufficiently asleep? Would the story pick up where they'd left off? Would I have to listen to more icky women's stuff? When will that woman get back here so I can hear the rest of this story? It felt like a too-long Sanka commercial in the middle of *I Love Lucy*. What crazy antics will Lucy and Ethel be up to when we return from this commercial interlude?

What seemed like an hour was probably only a few minutes. The steaming Sanka appeared in tiny china cups, with matching saucers, and the conversation resumed.

"So, you were saying that you went back to Annie Wittenmyer in hopes of getting a sister for Kenny."

"Oh, yes. So we went back to talk with the administrator about our interest in Theresa and we were told that she had two younger brothers at The Home as well. They told us that they'd like us to consider taking all three, but that taking the youngest brother was required, as they didn't want to split up these two kids."

"Oh my. So what did you do?"

"Well, we really had to think about that; we never imagined having more than two children at our age. And we didn't go there to get a boy. We already had a boy. All we wanted was a girl."

"But, you obviously got a boy too, since he's sleeping right there. Craig is Theresa's little brother isn't he?"

"Yes, Craig is the youngest of the three children their mother had. We had to take him if we wanted to get Theresa."

"What happened to their other brother?"

"We were willing to take him too if necessary, but he was living in the little hospital they have right there on the grounds of The Home, not in the cottages like Theresa and Craig. He had some kind of medical problem, like epilepsy or something. In the end, they didn't really think he was ready for adoption because of his illness."

"What was his name?"

"They probably told us, but I don't remember."

"Why were these children in The Home anyway?"

"They really didn't tell us much. They had been abandoned by their parents. That's really all we know."

"Well, I think it's wonderful that you gave these kids a home, even if you did get more than you bargained for."

"We certainly did. It was a package deal – we didn't want another boy."

Something shifted in me. Things were different between me and Mom and Dad Steffen after that. This conversation confirmed all my childish suspicions about who was the least favorite kid. And the answer was, "We didn't want another boy."

Perhaps not coincidentally, *The Chosen Baby* told the story of a childless couple whose lives would be made happy by the adoption of a boy – and then later a girl – for the completion of a perfect little family. There was no third adopted child in the narrative.

Misfit

After about a year of fostering us, the Steffens adopted Theresa and me officially on my sister's birthday (October 16), in 1964. I was four years old at the time of the adoption.

Kenny, the boy who had been adopted from the same orphanage five years earlier than me, was almost exactly seven years my senior with a birthday one day later than mine. There was clearly a fair amount of jealousy in Kenny as the transition to acquiring two new siblings was anything but smooth for him or for me. On at least three occasions, Kenny premeditated mischief and carried it out in my name.

Once, while I lay in my crib sleeping in an upstairs room in the old Iowa farm house in which we lived, Kenny got a box of crayons and scribbled all over the wall paper above my crib and then left the crayons in bed with me. When Mom came up to wake me, I was caught with the evidence and a spanking ensued. I was, of course, completely mystified as to why I was being punished since I had nothing to do with any of it. Though I was only four, I remember the incident vividly to this day.

On another occasion, while I was supposed to be napping (a theme is developing here), Kenny and I snuck into my parent's bedroom, a forbidden part of the house for us kids, and he showed me a military hat that my father had received during his stint in World War II. Inside the hat was a collection of British coins and bills that Dad had brought back from the war. Initially this seemed like something that might allow a connection between my new brother and me – a little shared mischief sometimes has that effect. But after the nap, Kenny tattled to Dad that he'd seen me in their bedroom rooting through dresser drawers. When Dad went to investigate, he discovered the disheveled hat and all the money missing. Further investigation revealed the money stashed carelessly in a drawer in my own room; caught red-handed as it were. After loud accusations, producing of the evidence and severe disappointment from my new parents, another overly harsh spanking occurred and another vivid, life-long memory was established within me.

One wonders why I ever agreed to another nap but, being only four, I didn't have a lot of influence in the matter. Sound asleep again in the same upstairs bedroom on our farm near Elliott, Iowa, I was rudely awakened by a loud crashing, tumbling sound. I got out of bed, having graduated out of my crib by this time, and went to the top of the staircase where the sound seemed to have originated. Standing there alone, looking down, the door at the bottom of the stairs opened and my brother's coronet completed its tumble down the stairs and landed at the feet of my new dad, who was looking up at me with that increasingly familiar look of disappointment and anger. As I got another overly aggressive thrashing at the hands of my super-sized adoptive father, I heard my brother sniggering in his bedroom, and the proverbial light bulb went on for me. This little jealous deviant had been setting me up and getting his jollies from watching me get my ass whooped while I screamed, "I didn't do it; I didn't do it; I didn't do it!"

To be fair, many years later when we were both adults, Kenny confessed his pre-adolescent offences to me and sought my forgiveness. In the years since that forgiveness, we've sometimes talked about those childhood episodes and laughed uncomfortably.

By the time Kenny was 16, he'd learned to use his little brother for gain, rather than just sport. Kenny had a 1957 Chevy – still the best looking car ever made. We used to drive it into the tiny town of

Grant and stop in to a little filling station for a dollar's worth of gas. Kenny would engage the service station owner in chit chat about some phantom noise the Chevy was making, and I'd go into the station and steal packs of cigarettes and hands-full of cigars. Sharing these with Kenny and his friends gained me a bit of notoriety and, as a result, they tolerated me hanging around. As any nine-year-old might, I mistook this tolerance for affection.

Kenny rebelled hard against the strict control and legalism of the church that Dad and Mom had been a part of all our young lives. Mom and Dad Steffen were both second generation devotees to this little-known "non-denominational" denomination. If you're tracing the protestant Christian tree, you'll find the Plymouth Brethren emerging in the 1820s off of the evangelical trunk, down an Anabaptist branch, off onto a legalistic twig in the general vicinity of Conservative Mennonites and Unprogrammed Quakers.

As the little brother, I thought it cool to imitate my older brother in his rebellion through the use of bad language, hateful thoughts, theft and the aforementioned association with tobacco – all of which were strictly frowned upon and harshly punished by our parents. Eventually Kenny's rebellion resulted in him running away from home when he was 16, never again to live with the family. I was aware of Kenny's intentions to take his rebellion to this level far in advance of him actually doing so, and covered for him by not revealing his plans to Mom and Dad. I also recall pleading with Kenny to take me with him, which he said he would do, but then didn't. Being nine at the time, I immediately changed allegiance back to my parents as soon as he was gone, motivated by my survival instincts and a bit of revenge for all the crap Kenny had put me through over the years.

By the time I got to junior high school, I'd managed to get in a fair amount of trouble in my own right. It all started in kindergarten –

37

seriously. On my first-ever day of school, I missed the bus and my Grandma Steffen drove me to Elliott for afternoon, half-day kindergarten class. I recall getting there late and wandering in with all eyes on me after everyone else was already seated at their little desks. The teacher, Mrs. Anderson, shamed me publicly for my tardiness, as if I had anything to do with it. I was five, and as far as I can recall didn't have a watch or driver's license as yet. After the shaming incident, Mrs. Anderson droned on and on about something. I don't know exactly what, since I was now seething from public humiliation. I was also distracted by these perfect rows of desks occupied by silent little children sitting at attention with hands crossed and feet dangling above the floor. I don't recall any sort of preparation or communication about what school was going to be or what it would require of me. I just got driven there one day and dropped off. I was a sharp little kid, so I guess everyone thought I'd figure it out.

After what seemed like an interminably long monologue from Mrs. Anderson, I noticed that, at the back of the room near where I was sitting, there were two restrooms and a drinking fountain positioned in between them. Having seen this, I quickly became thirsty and decided I'd very much like to try out this fountain. Knowing no better, I simply got up out of my desk and walked to the back of the room and helped myself to the available drinking accommodations. Why were they there if they weren't to be used, I reasoned. As you might imagine, Mrs. Anderson was not keen on this demonstration of insubordination, as she interpreted it, and marched to the back of the room and yanked me away from the fountain and physically forced me back into my desk, verbally scolding and shaming me in the process. I'd been in school less than an hour and already it was clear to me that I was a bad kid – Mrs. Anderson had said so.

In first grade, I got paddled at school at least twice and my parents had to come in after hours to talk with my teacher, Miss Rubner. Dad had always said, "If you get in trouble at school, you're going to get in trouble again at home." True to his word, I got spanked again at home each time, as if one punishment for the crime simply wasn't adequate. One of the infractions involved hitting a kid in my class in the face with a rock at recess. By my way of thinking, he deserved it since he had just hit me for no apparent reason. Of course, the playground monitor, Mrs. Wagner, didn't see Jake's infraction, but she did notice the blood and his screaming after I threw the rock.

In second grade, Mrs. Eppelsheimer sentenced me to spend a fair amount of time in the coat closet in solitary confinement for infractions I don't recall, but probably associated with my propensity to talk too much.

In third grade, I remember refusing to learn how to write in cursive. Having recently mastered the art of printing, this new twist seemed redundant and a little bit "girly," so I defiantly said "no" to Mrs. Welsh's entreaties – hastily called parent-teacher conferences followed.

In fourth grade, after tolerating his bullying for weeks, I beat up a sixth grader, named Kelly, because he refused to stop picking on me at recess. He ended up having to leave school with a dislocated thumb, which I had used as a fulcrum to pull his arm up behind his back with one hand and repeatedly slam his face into a sub-zero-hardened snow bank with the other. I didn't get to go to recess for two weeks and had to write a thousand-word theme paper on why I shouldn't fight on the playground. Another redundant pearl of wisdom my Dad used to tell me was, "If you get into a *fight* at school, you're going to get into another one when you get home." I learned the truth of this statement when I also got a spanking at home, after this first ever fist fight.

In fifth grade, I had a crush on Mrs. Black who was a gorgeous young woman who may have been of Native American decent with waist-length straight black hair. My pre-adolescent infatuation kept my behavior pretty much in check as I recall.

Because we didn't own our own farm-land, we moved around frequently (seven times in 12 years). In the middle of my fifth grade year, we had moved to a new school and I got introduced to baseball. I wasn't any good at it initially, but was fascinated by the game. I got busted that fall trying to conceal a transistor radio under my shirt, so I could listen to a World Series game during class.

In seventh grade, a big, obnoxious freshman girl from my sister's class, JoLee, had been bullying me for weeks on the school bus. On one particular morning she sat behind me on the bus and kept jabbing pins from her home economics sewing project, into my neck and shoulders; dotting my shirt with blood with each pin-stick. After all the kids had been picked up from their homes, several buses would meet up out on a country road for what we called a "rendezvous." Kids would get off of one bus and onto another, and then each bus would deliver kids of similar age to a particular school building within the school system. On this same morning, I was walking in front of my destination bus, when JoLee shouted my name. When I turned to look back, she threw a chunk of gravel and it hit me in the face. I snapped. Fed up with weeks of abuse and humiliation, I dropped my books and charged her like an enraged bull, knocking her to the gravel, and kept hitting her till she passed out and rolled into the ditch alongside the road.

I spent that entire school day with the Superintendent of schools and the Principal, whose offices were in an entirely different building than where I had my classes. The Principal had come to my school to get me in first period and had driven me in his car across town to the high school building for these discussions. Initially they told me, in a rather knee-jerk reaction, that I would be getting kicked out of school indefinitely. By the time the day was over and the Superintendent and the Principal had heard my story and verified it with other students at various buildings within the school system, I was given no punishment at all. Apparently they'd come to the same conclusion I'd come to that morning: JoLee was a psycho bully and deserved whatever she had gotten. To most of the less popular kids, I attained near super-hero status for taking out one of the bullies. I never had any more trouble with JoLee, or anyone else at this school after this much talked about incident. This may have been a key step-forward in my propensity for negotiation. Given what awaited me at home for getting into both a fight and trouble, I was highly motivated to negotiate with the Principal and Superintendent with high-stakes passion.

In eighth grade we moved again, this time to a much larger school in Atlantic. I didn't know anyone at this new school and it was a tough adjustment. I got into several more fist fights in Atlantic, none of which was instigated by me and all of which took place after school hours and out of sight of authorities. I had learned that if I couldn't avoid the fight, I could at least avoid getting caught.

Always, I felt forced into these fighting situations by relentless bullying. And each fight ended the same way – with the other kid badly hurt. I HATED fighting. I really did. But apparently the thing I hated even more was being bullied. Once I had snapped and the fight ensued, I didn't stop hitting till the other guy stopped moving. One bully, whom we called "Coals," was out of school for two weeks after I left him unconscious on the practice football field. I guess there is some kind of honor among brawlers because, amazingly, I didn't get into trouble for any of these fights in Atlantic – until the end of the first quarter of my freshman year.

On that day I was goofing around in the cafeteria with a few friends, and we started snapping our fingers rhythmically and walking slowly toward a big, tall, quiet kid we actually liked, doing a poor imitation of *West Side Story* – which I hadn't even seen, but was aware of. Apparently the kid HAD seen it and was freaked out by what we were doing and charged us and a fight started with scores of kids yelling encouragements. In that setting, teachers are bound to notice and intervene, and we all ended up in the Principal's office. I got kicked out of school for a week. What the Principal didn't know, was that my parents were moving yet again, and I was changing schools for the sixth time in nine years. So I went home that afternoon and never went back to Atlantic High School. And I never mentioned any of it to my parents.

I went back to the Griswold school system at the beginning of the next quarter and continued to get into trouble. I was hanging out with kids who were doing drugs, drinking and seriously underachieving. I didn't do drugs or drink, but I was running my own little theft ring at the school. My parents would go into Atlantic most Thursday evenings – the only night the stores would be open late (till eight or nine o'clock). At school I'd ask around to see if anyone needed anything, making a list of stuff that usually fell into the categories of knives, electronics, lighters, sunglasses or other items small enough to shoplift. I'd steal the items on Thursday night and bring them to school on Friday for resale. It was my first foray into entrepreneurship. I made a tidy little profit and never got caught.

My grades were terrible – mostly Cs and Ds with an occasional F – but I managed to get through my freshman year. Before the last quarter, my parents moved again, this time into Cumberland and a completely new school system for me – the seventh and last school change. I complained loudly as this would be my third high school of the year.

I don't think my parents had any clue how difficult changing schools was. Dad had gone only through the 6th grade and Mom through the 10th. Finally they agreed that I could move in with my Dad's parents, who were in their mid-70s and lived in the little town of Griswold, so that I could finish out the school year in the same district. I'd never lived in the town of Griswold before, and being a social kid, I enjoyed being able to get together with friends after school to goof around, hang out or play some sandlot baseball – which had become a permanent part of my life by then.

Baseball

———————— ❦ ————————

I live a blessed life. There is a true companion, my wife Cindy, with whom I have shared this life for more than three decades. There is the company I founded that produces meaningful work that I enjoy immensely on most days. I have scores of very close friends for whom I would lay down my life and who, I am confident, would do the same for me. I have a relationship with the Creator that keeps me in awe and humble, at least when I am in harmony with that relationship. And, to paraphrase the Psalmist, I have enough in the temporal world so as not to be in danger of hunger, begging and dishonor, but not so much so as to be proud, hording and ungrateful.

I am not a famous person, or even particularly well known. It may seem to you hubris that I would even consider writing a book – especially one that would have *me* as the main character. But perhaps this is precisely why I must share this part of my story with you. You have heard of many people who have come from circumstances similar to what you'll read about here. Usually they are not famous, but infamous. The wounds they received in life have driven them to atrocity, crime and despair.

And such was the path on which I found myself.

How does an infant who is abused, abandoned and orphaned during the first years of life end up a church leader and advocate for non-violence?

How does a terrified child with abandonment issues who vomits when confronted with unfamiliar situations end up winning public speaking awards and co-owning a retreat ministry to help people through difficult life transitions?

How does a kid who bullied little girls on the playground, and beat one unconscious in junior high, end up teaching relationship techniques to married couples?

How does a pre-teen who has spent years selling his shoplifted loot to a clientele of classmates end up being a church deacon in charge of finances?

How does a vandalizing teen who once smashed every window of an entire fleet of vehicles, end up mentoring entrepreneurs as an adjunct professor in an MBA program?

I am convinced that I would have remained on these destructive paths until this very day – unless interrupted by early death or incarceration – if not for powerful and unlikely forces that tapped into my heart and had their transformative way with me.

Chronologically, the first of these forces was baseball.

I love baseball. The deep strategy that governs every aspect of the game, it's pondering pace, the mano-a-mano matchups and the fact that there is no clock are key attributes that wooed me to this love, and which have governed most other aspects of my life since.

But prior to the fifth grade, I didn't have a clue what baseball even was. I'd never played or seen a baseball game, I had no idea what the rules might be, and I certainly knew nothing of professional leagues.

During my fifth grade year, my parents moved … again. This was the third of what would eventually be seven school changes, all of them difficult.

When I arrived at Lewis Elementary in the late summer of 1970, there were a whole new set of strange faces, rules and processes to be confused by. The tiny rural Iowa school still smelled of summer's fresh paint and the aroma of cut grass breezing through the open windows. If Mayberry RFD had a scratch-'n-sniff, it would smell like this.

To my surprise, some of the boys in this new school were quite approachable and all of the friendly guys were rabid about baseball.

At the first recess on the first day of the new school year, a small band of boys, led by two guys named Kelly and Jim, approached me in the hallway. There was no small talk. There were no introductions nor formalities, just:

"Who's your favorite baseball team?"

"Uhh, baseball team?"

I searched their pre-adolescent faces for clues. What were they talking about? How could they be so enthusiastic about something I'd never even heard of? Desperation flooded my cranium. Think, THINK. I finally pulled a team name from deep in the archives of my heretofore dispassionate brain.

"Uhh, Idunno. I guess the Dallas Cowboys are ok."

As we huddled in the hallway outside our fifth grade classroom, Kelly, Jim and their posse looked at me like I had three heads. Their confused faces clearly indicated that they didn't know if I was just stupid, or if I had misunderstood the question. But in either case, it was clear to me that I'd better figure out this baseball stuff if I was to have a chance at friendship with these guys.

I really liked Kelly, and I soon learned that his favorite baseball team was the Baltimore Orioles. I resolved to make them *my* team as quickly as I could, however that worked. First, I discovered the school library. Then I discovered newspapers and I started scouring the sports pages for baseball news, learned how to understand box scores. I found out that these games were actually broadcast live on the radio in the evenings, so I began tuning in games on my (stolen) transistor radio every night before bed. On clear nights I could hear games from Chicago, Minnesota, Kansas City, Detroit and later Texas – all American League cities, like Baltimore. So I got to hear the Orioles play pretty often, even though I didn't hear an Orioles radio affiliate broadcast, nor see them play in-person, till the 1990s.

If you're wondering how a kid in Iowa becomes an Orioles fan while living 1200 miles from Baltimore, you'd be telling me *you* don't know much more about baseball than I did. It was 1970. When baseball historians ponder the greatest dynasties of all time, the '69, '70 and '71 Orioles are legitimately in that discussion. They went to the World Series all three years. They won the World Championship against Cincinnati's Big Red Machine in 1970 and were robbed by New York's Miracle Mets in 1969 and by the underdog Pittsburgh Pirates in 1971. Ask anybody, they *were* robbed.

We were fifth graders. We had no concept of "jumping on a bandwagon." We liked this team and their black and orange uniforms and their classic cartoon-bird logo. None of us were geography savants. *Every* major league baseball team was a long way from Iowa – we weren't calculating miles. To us every team seemed the same distance away in the newspaper or on Saturday television's *This Week in Baseball* and *Game of the Week*.

It was the best of times to be an Orioles fan.

Learning about the game by reading and listening proved to be far easier than learning it on the field. Kelly and Jim were universally regarded as the best players at Lewis Elementary, and as such were nearly always the captains of the hastily assembled recess teams. As soon as the bell would ring, or we had wolfed down our lunch, we'd all scramble to the one corner of the playground suitable for baseball. It was a mostly level tract with a piece of old fencing in one corner to serve as a backstop, but nothing else to distinguish it as a "ball field."

The first order of business was to choose up teams. Team Captains, Kelly and Jim, alternated their selections till every boy had been taken. My friend Mike and I were nearly always the last two picked. Mike and I were both from the country (strike one). Neither of us had brothers close enough in age to play ball with us (strike two). And though we both had older sisters, neither of them was inclined to hang out with their little brothers nor do anything athletic (strike three).

On one particular afternoon, I recall the selection process going something like this. Every kid had been taken and Mike and I stood there trying to look skilled, wondering which of us would wear the ignominious distinction of being last-one-picked. Reluctant to select either of us, Jim and Kelly conferred amongst themselves trying to find some virtue that would set one of us apart from the other.

Finally, Kelly said, "I'll take Craig, at least he can hit a little bit."

Now you might think that was a mean and condescending thing to say. You might have even thought or said, "awwwww" when you read it. But I will tell you categorically that what *I* heard was:

Selecting number one in the 1970 first year player's draft are the Baltimore Orioles. And with the number one pick overall, the Orioles General Manager, Kelly, selects outfielder Craig Steffen, out of Lewis Elementary, who can hit a little bit.

I had arrived. I was no longer last.

There are very few things that were a part of my life in the fifth grade that remain a part of my life today. Baseball has been a constant companion for more than 40 years. It has been the foundation that has served:

- As a hobby that has kept me out of (some) trouble
- As a tutor to teach me math and statistics
- As a mentor to instruct me in strategy
- As a personal trainer to keep me from weighing 300 pounds
- As a librarian to impart a love of reading
- As a friend who leads me to others of similar interest
- As a counselor to help me to deal with defeat and loss
- As a charmer to coax me out of my shy and fearful ways
- As a professor to teach me to negotiate, buy, sell and trade for value
- As an umpire to help me to reign-in the extremes of my emotions

All of these contributions from baseball have enriched my life in immeasurable ways. I'd even go so far as to say that in some ways, baseball saved me. I could write a book about it – someday, maybe I will. But in this book, let me just tell you one story about how baseball literally saved me.

It is July 13, 1976.

My parents are away on vacation, leaving me behind for a week so that I can continue my summer job at the Denham Veterinary Clinic. It is the night of the Major League Baseball All-Star Game. This year it is being held in Philadelphia.

I've been planning for this night for weeks. With Mom and Dad out of town, I can watch the game on the big console TV in the living room instead of the 9" Magnavox in my bedroom. Glory.

I come home immediately after work. I shower, get into my comfy baseball garb and rearrange the furniture in the living room. I'm determined to sit "in the front row," directly in front of the TV set, not off to the side and at a distance, as the chairs are normally arranged.

I've prepared some favorite snack foods and have arranged them strategically to my right and slightly behind my chair. The purpose of this placement is to accommodate my pre-game workout.

I sit on the edge of the recliner that is set on a swivel. My Cesar Cedeno baseball glove is on my left hand. My right hand holds a tennis ball. While I watch the pre-game shows, I fire the tennis ball at the base of the front door and scoop it with my glove-hand, calculating fielding percentage in my head after each "play." I do this hundreds of times throughout the evening hoping to amass enough "chances" to simulate an entire season by a major league shortstop. I pause occasionally, "between games" to grab some chips, cheese or Coke. Even MLB players have a post-game buffet in the locker room.

On this night, Bobby Grich, one of my favorite Orioles, is playing second base and batting eighth, and Detroit's Mark "The Bird" Fidrych is the starting pitcher for the American League squad. Fidrych is a national phenom, whose wacky antics and dominant games I often experience via WJR Radio.

Unfortunately, the American League gets behind early as the National League team, made up primarily of Cincinnati Reds players, score twice in the bottom of the first. I'm irritated before the game is even 20 minutes old.

Then the doorbell rings.

At first I think this may be a buddy who is coming over to watch the game with me, but when I look out I see it's a girl.

I've been building a relationship with a great girl, from another part of Iowa, who is two years older than me and has her own car. I like her a lot but, sheesh – this is THE All-Star Game.

We walk into the living room and I take my front row seat. I offer her some of my snacks and she takes a handful and sits in a chair to my left and slightly behind me, since my chair was out of its usual position. She tries to talk to me, but my eyes and attention are glued to the TV; Grich is coming to bat.

My girlfriend excuses herself and, presumably, goes to the bathroom. I watch the game. I put my glove back on and start firing the tennis ball against the door, trying to make up for the time I've lost socializing. Honestly, I forget that she's even there.

The game is a disaster. The National League scores twice more in the third. I'm really depressed now.

In about the fifth inning, my girlfriend comes stomping through the dining room, straight past my front row seat, mutters something in disgust and lets herself out, slamming the door behind her.

I have NO idea what *her* problem is, but I'm upset too, so I don't really pay much attention as I hear her car drive away, throwing some gravel as it goes.

The American League loses 7-1. Bobby Grich was 0-for-2, and grounded into a double play. Mark Fidrych was the losing pitcher. The whole thing was just SO disappointing; literally nothing to cheer for (obviously I didn't know then that he'd be a future Oriole, but

Fred Lynn hit a home run to account for all the American League scoring).

Two days later I get a letter in the mail (we used to do that in the old days) from my girlfriend. She wasn't shy about telling me why she was so upset when she left. Apparently, when she disappeared from the living room, she had gone back to my bedroom and had gotten into something a little more comfortable. She showed up intent on taking our relationship "to the next level." She'd even stopped on the way and purchased a box of condoms for the occasion.

I feel I need to say that I wasn't some eunuch. On any other night, I'd have been the stereotypical teenage boy having his girlfriend over while his parents were out of town. In fact, I was probably more interested in girls and sex than most of my friends. I thought about it all the time. All the time, that is, except when I was doing something related to baseball.

I'm pretty sure that if she had gotten her way that night, we'd have kept on having sex pretty much perpetually. We might not have stopped having sex until we died or, more likely, until we got pregnant.

When I look back at all the crossroads in my life, I always think of that night in the summer of 1976. Sex wasn't exactly on the approved activity list amongst the members of the church my family was a part of. Babies in high school have hamstrung the potential of better people than me. Teenage pregnancy is a great way to stay in one's hometown and out of college for the rest of one's life. And, it's a near-perfect formula for decades of shame and poverty – at least in that place at that time.

So, if we'd have had sex, I'm pretty sure my life would be VERY different today than it is. And since I really like my life the way it is, I can tell you for sure that, on that night, baseball truly saved my life.

So to my list of the ways that baseball has served me I guess I should add:

- As a sex education instructor, to keep me from generations of regret.

Heist

The only person I'd ever met that loved baseball as much as me, was my friend Kirby, who lived in another part of Iowa. Two weeks before school would be out for the summer of 1975, my folks went to a Bible Conference (which we often did) in Des Moines, at the church where my mother attended when she was single and worked at a meat packing plant. This was a much larger church than I was generally accustomed to, with seating for a few hundred folks instead of the 50-75 in the small town churches.

I mentioned that there were three things in my early adoptive life that had saved me. The first, chronologically, was baseball. You're about to hear the second – but perhaps not in the way you might expect.

While at the conference, I teamed up with my long-time friend, Kirby, who was in a rebellious phase of life much like me.

At fourteen years old, I was a year older than Kirby. Our shared love for baseball had been the foundation of our friendship. Like many Midwesterners, he loved the Minnesota Twins. I had few comrades, as I loved the Baltimore Orioles. A few years before, in 1969 and 1970, the two teams played each other for the American League Championship. The Orioles won both times. Kirby and I had been known to stay up all night asking baseball trivia questions of each other. I didn't know anybody at the time who knew more trivia than the two of us.

Kirby was quiet, a bit introverted, and was always looking for an adventure. Things at home were so routine and boring; Kirby compensated by being a thrill-seeker.

Though we both grew up in overly restrictive churches, his parents recognized his love for baseball and let him play on the organized teams. Mine did not. But my parents had a TV; his did not. As a result, we both had something for which to envy the other.

I ended up staying at his parents' house that night. We had been planning to "do a job" together for months and this weekend (a week or two before the end of my freshman year of high school) was going to be our opportunity.

Kirby had built a "fort" years earlier off of the barn and had constructed a secret room within the fort, where he kept stuff his parents didn't allow him to have.

We discussed the tactical details of our heist the following evening after his folks were in bed.

"Alright, Kirby, how far away is town from here?" I began.

"It's about five or six miles, but there's a neighbor up the road who has a pick-up he always parks out by his barn, and he leaves the keys in it. I've borrowed it before. We'll slip out my window tomorrow night and walk up the gravel and borrow his truck. Then we'll drive into town and break into the electronics store."

"So you've been in there a bunch of times, right? What kind of security system does the place have?"

"How should I know? I don't know anything about security systems; it's farm country, dude. What do we know about security systems? My neighbor leaves his keys in the truck at night. That's how we think about security here, man." Kirby sounded frustrated. "I suppose you got all kind of security systems in Cumberland, do ya?" Kirby's words dripped with sarcasm, since Cumberland was a town of just 300 people.

"Well no; but lots of places in Atlantic have cameras now and most of the stores have wired their doors and windows. Is your town that much different? Anyway, the reason you need me on this job is because I know how those systems work. They're really simple to defeat. We've just got to bring a flashlight and THIS," I said, holding out my secret weapon.

"What the hell is that and how's it gunna help us get past a security system?"

"It's a special magnet I made on Dad's grinder. It's some new kind of magnet that's really powerful. Our shop teacher brought several of them into class this past year to show us. He said they were developed by the military or something. He called them 'rare dirt magnets' or something like that. I stole one of them and filed it down so that it's thin enough to slip into a door jam. All we need to do is figure out which door or window is the most shielded from view, use the flashlight to identify whether it has a security switch and, if it does, we slide this magnet in between the contacts, and simply open the door or window. The alarm won't go off." I said all this as if I were some kind of expert – but, truth be told, I'd never actually done this. But in theory, I thought it should work.

"How can we be sure of that?"

"It's just how it works. It's a two-part contact switch; in one side is the switch itself with the electrical wires going into it. The other side of the switch is just a magnet like this one, but not as powerful and not as thin. We're simply replacing the magnet that's screwed into the door jam with this one, so that the security system doesn't know the difference."

Kirby looked at me with a confused and disinterested expression.

"What was YOUR plan?" I asked, getting annoyed.

"All right, we'll try it your way."

It was clear Kirby had no plan to deal with security, because he hadn't imagined that there would be any.

"Let's draw this whole thing out – get me some paper and a pencil with an eraser," I barked.

After several minutes of sketching out what we'd been talking about, I showed Kirby what I'd come up with.

"So, here's your house. We'll crawl out the window at midnight, and walk down this road to the neighbor's. It should take us about 20 minutes to get there and secure the pick-up. Then we'll put it in neutral and I'll push it down the driveway while you steer. I don't know how to drive a stick, so when we get to the road you can start it up, and I'll jump in, and we'll drive into town. That gets us there about 12:30. Does that all look about right to you so far?"

"Yeah, I guess. Why are we doing all this? We're just going to go to the store, steal a bunch of stuff, put it in the truck and drive it back here. It's not like we're a crime family."

"Hey, maybe we SHOULD be more like a crime family and less like a couple of stupid kids. If I'm going to be a part of this, I want to make sure I don't get caught. I don't want to screw up my whole life just because I didn't think this through."

"Does the place have a cop or a sheriff or someone who drives around town checking on things?"

"Not that I know of." Kirby shrugged. "Maybe the county cop drives through there, but I don't think that guy works all night or anything."

"Ok, I guess we'll just have to take our chances on that. Once we're in, you can go into the store, since you know the layout and there won't be much light, and carry stuff to the window and hand it to me. I'll load it up in the truck, while keeping an eye open for any cars driving by or lights coming on in the houses around the store. When we've got everything we want, or a truck load, we'll jump in the truck and drive nice and slow back here."

I jotted times onto the map as I rehearsed each step with Kirby. I sketched the route with a line and arrows and made corrections as we discussed alternatives.

"That gets us back here to the fort at about 1:15 by my estimate. We'll unload the truck and hide everything in the fort. Then we'll drive the truck back to the neighbor's driveway, push it down to where it was parked, wipe it down so we don't leave fingerprints, and walk back home. We should be back in your room by 2:30 without leaving a trail," I said while still pondering the plan. "If only it would rain after we're done, then even the tracks in the gravel would be erased … *that* would make this a perfect plan."

"Do you have any stocking caps?" I asked.

"It's not like it's going to be cold, dude." Kirby said with a snort.

"Duh. But we haven't talked about the possibility that there may be cameras." I said. "We can easily overcome them once we get to them, but we don't want to be caught on film as we get to them. We'll wear the stocking caps over our faces till we're sure about the cameras. Does your old man have any spray paint?"

"What for?"

"There's this TV show I used to watch called *It Takes a Thief*. I saw this professional thief guy use spray paint to spray onto security camera lenses so that they can't take pictures. It seems like a really fast way to defeat them if they're there."

"I'm pretty sure he's got some John Deere touch-up paint in the machine shed."

"Where's that flashlight? Let's crawl out the window and go check. It'll be a good way to test the first part of our plan." I was getting excited about our heist.

We slipped out the bedroom window and discovered that we made a lot less noise if we laid a pillow across the window seal first.

It was a cool, humid night with a bright, moon-lit sky. We didn't even need the flashlight till we got into the machine shed. We found several cans of paint and shook them up to see if any of them had enough aerosol pressure. We took one that felt almost full and had good pressure and hid it in the bushes behind the house near Kirby's bedroom window.

We walked around the barn yard talking in a stream-of-consciousness – jumping topics from the heist, to baseball, to school, to church, to parent problems, to cars, and girls we liked.

"Let's go streaking." Kirby said, out of nowhere.

"What? Where? When?" I asked, befuddled.

"Right now, down the road."

Kirby started pulling off his jeans and tee-shirt while he laughed at the idea of being naked in public. Never mind that the possibility of encountering any "public" at this time and place was remote at best.

With a touch of reluctance, I pulled off my clothes and left them in a pile next to Kirby's. We started down the driveway and immediately stopped and turned around. Simultaneously and independently, we'd both decided that wearing shoes on the gravel would be a really good idea.

We turned to the right out of his driveway and took off down the gravel road feeling free from the many constraints we'd endured all our young lives. We talked and laughed and recounted stories of streakers we'd heard about at major league baseball games and other public events in recent years. And though it seemed lost on us that we were alone in remote, rural Iowa in the dark, we imagined that somehow our act of naked rebellion earned us solidarity with all of those "legends" of streaking before us. After what seemed like a mile of strolling, we turned around and began the trek back to Kirby's house. We were certainly now more seasoned and worldly than when our streak had begun.

Suddenly, we heard a car coming down the gravel road. We looked behind us and saw headlights gaining on us and a cloud of dust trailing.

"SHIIITTT," we yelled in unison.

We both broke into a full run out in front of the oncoming car, which was gaining on us. At this pace, it became painfully obvious why clothes and jockstraps had been invented. It also became obvious that we weren't going to out-run the car. And though it was now close enough to be blinded by its headlights reflecting off our larva-white asses, we veered into the ditch and hid in the weeds as the car slowed, honked and drove on by.

We got back to the house with hearts thumping and adrenaline filling our veins. We laughed and recounted the micro-detail of the streaking encounter with the car till we both imagined that we would be legends, like all streakers before us.

Back inside Kirby's tiny bedroom, with his mom's left-over fried chicken in hand, we again looked over our heist strategy now complete with a timeline, drawings of the place and sketches of how alarm system wiring looked and worked. When we were satisfied with our own proficiency in such matters, we turned out the lights and stayed up most of the night talking about how we hated all the rules and moralism of our parents and the two different churches our folks attended.

We shared with each other some of our tactics for tuning out the preachers while we were at church. I shared some mindless games I'd developed for this purpose such as guessing various numbers at random and then trying to open the hymnal to those page numbers. It was sort of a lottery without any payoff. I'd also stare at the ancient clock on the wall and try to focus on watching the minute and hour hands actually move. It didn't help the time to pass any faster, but I was convinced this would help me discern the rotation of a curve ball when standing in the batter's box.

When I asked Kirby for *his* tricks, he said, "Well, mostly I just read." This was a fresh idea. I'd never really thought about actually reading – thinking he was talking about a good baseball biography or something. So I asked *what* he'd been reading and he said, "Well, the Bible of course, it's the only book they let you take in there. Duh. And lately I've been reading the book of The Revelation."

So, flashing back to our church history lesson, the Plymouth Brethren were really big on what they commonly called "end-times prophesy." Seminaries know it as Eschatology. One of the original founders of the Plymouth Brethren "movement" was a guy named John Nelson Darby (1800-1882). Darby is credited with formulating the "modern" ideas of dispensational, pre-tribulation rapture (doctrines that essentially no one believed until about 1840). Darby's dramatic teachings were sensationalized in my youth by a neo-Zionist author named Hal Lindsey in his 1969 book, *The Late, Great Planet Earth.*

There was also a little-known film from the era that gained considerable notoriety in Plymouth Brethren circles called *A Thief in the Night.* This B-grade film actually was shown in a select number of movie theaters in the early 1970s, but being Plymouth Brethren, we weren't allowed to go to the theater. The church leaders reasoned that our attendance would necessitate that "God's money" would then be used to support the "evil world of Hollywood." God certainly wouldn't be happy about that.

I remember that some "denominational" churches in Atlantic had gotten together and actually rented the tiny town theater in order to do a private showing of the film – for free. There was a spirited debate in Plymouth Brethren circles wondering if this would make it "righteous" for those of us who were "called to come out from among them and be ye separate" to go see it. After considerable, often heated debate, we were NOT allowed because of the "appearance of evil" that would be possible if someone from "the world" would see one of "the brethren" going into an "evil place." It was not until churches were able to actually rent the film and show it in their own buildings that we were allowed to view it. Of course, some of the more "exclusive" or "tight" Plymouth Brethren wouldn't allow the viewing of a film in any place, at any time, under any circumstances.

So this was the backdrop of my conversation with Kirby on this late spring night in 1975 in a farm house in rural Iowa. And as Kirby wove the stories of the book of The Revelation using the lenses given to him by the "prophesy experts" of our little world, I heard of an amazing final battle between good and evil that would surely commence any day now. An angry God would soon lead the armies of righteousness to wipe out evil of every kind through brutal violence that would result in blood running in the streets horse-bridle-deep. I was spell-bound – and frightened out of my skin.

Setting aside the eschatological perspectives of the discussion and their relative chance of accurately portraying the true heart of a redemptive God, what I heard was that there IS good and there IS evil and ultimately good wins. I was keenly aware that, based upon the thieving discussion Kirby and I just concluded an hour or two prior, I was on the wrong side of this good vs. evil battle. On the floor of my buddy's bedroom at about 4:00 in the morning, I prayed and asked God to give me the heart to do/be good and to stop doing/being evil. In some childish sense, I'm confident that there was a desire to get picked for the winning team, but it was a sincere prayer that continues to positively affect my life to this day.

The following day, Kirby was excited about our upcoming heist and initiated a new conversation about it after his mom had served one of her classically delicious country breakfasts. After a few minutes, I let him know what had happened to me before we'd gone to sleep and told him that I could no longer participate in the heist. He was pissed, and we didn't speak again for many months afterward. But though I felt like I'd lost a friend, I felt that I had gained something far more enduring – a new relationship with an eternal God who knew the future – and knew *me*.

I concluded that night, and still believe today, that good and love really do, eventually, win over evil and hate. And the choice I made that night, the faith of a child, was the second event of my childhood that radically altered the path I had been on for my first 14 years. First it was baseball and its seductive strategies; now here was Jesus and his radical, upside-down way.

LaRoyce

No one knew about post-traumatic stress disorder (PTSD) back in the 1960s; at least no one in my circles. But retrospectively I wonder if much of the struggle of my early childhood, and brief but frequent episodes during my adult life, might be explained by this phenomenon. Though I have always tested in the "very superior" intelligence level on IQ tests, I spent my kindergarten through ninth grade years of school scuffling terribly to achieve a passing grade. I under-achieved both academically and socially. I saw myself as a chubby misfit; left out of the social cliques available at the schools I attended.

How does a kid with above average intelligence barely pass elementary and junior high school classes? When I talk to intellectually accomplished friends, I find that they often remember when they learned a particular thing (multiplication tables, long division, presidential history, state capitals, discovering poetry, etc.). Not only do they remember when the tumblers clicked in their brains, they also remember the details of the event … where they were, who was in the class, the teacher's name and characteristics, and telling their parents about their conquest.

When I reflect on these formative years in *my* life, the things I remember are the struggles, the confusion, the bullying, the desire to fit in, the fear of breaking an unknown rule and suffering the consequences. I was nearly always so preoccupied with these survival tasks at the bottom of Maslow's Hierarchy of Needs, that I failed to grasp the learning opportunities being presented to me. It seemed to me that I was all alone in this struggle for survival. Much as I longed for an adult to come along side me and understand me and help me, none ever did. Though I was bullied frequently and sometimes mercilessly at school and on school buses, no teacher, playground monitor or bus driver ever once stepped in to stop the abuse. It was up to me to stand up for myself, hence my history of fighting and self-reliance.

How I longed for an adult to see things the way I saw them and to do justice.

I know people personally who struggle with PTSD as a result of war. I see what they deal with and how that trauma manifests, even decades after the war. It occurs to me that some of my own symptoms mirror what my friends with PTSD deal with. My research indicates that there may be a real and studied connection to my casual observations. Again, I'm no doctor nor have I ever talked to a professional about this, but I read one study from Harvard Medical School that showed that nearly 25% of kids who had experienced abandonment, as I did, are diagnosed with PTSD. Certainly information like this gives me pause and perhaps offers one explanation for how a bright kid could have difficulty passing grade school.

But, apparently something clicked for me at about the tenth grade. Beginning in my sophomore year of high school, I found myself routinely on the honor roll, and later on the dean's list in college. I became the first person in my adoptive family to finish high school, the first to go to college, the first to get an Associate's Degree, the first to get a Bachelor's Degree and the first to get a Master's Degree.

I chronicle these firsts only to illustrate the fact that something significant happened about the time I went into the tenth grade. My previous troubles with academics seemed to melt away and I began to live up to my potential. Why? What happened?

Well, there are the previously mentioned falling in love with baseball and my unlikely conversion to following the way of Jesus the night of the planned "big heist." Perhaps there was healing that took place in me as I gradually acclimated socially through baseball and as I got acquainted with the God who reveals love to the world and to me. I think these experiences are a huge part of my transformation.

Then there is the fact that I stopped doing illegal things, which freed me from the fear of the law, conviction and a return to institutional living. Perhaps I slipped a little bit north of the bottom tier on Maslow's Hierarchy of Needs for the first time in my life.

And then there was the fact that I changed schools (for the 7th time) to start my sophomore year of high school and I had the opportunity to start with a clean slate. The people at this new school didn't know me as a foul-mouthed, law-breaking, disrespectful, under-achieving, going-nowhere, fat kid. Armed with a hobby, faith and a fresh start, I had some powerful things pushing me toward something better in life – if I'd work for it.

And then there was a special teacher, Mrs. LaRoyce Wohlenhaus. Mrs. Wohlenhaus was a powerful force at Iowa's Cumberland & Massena High School. And it was Mrs. Wohlenhaus who became the third transformative force in my young life.

To look at her, you wouldn't have guessed that she was brilliant, savvy and influential in educational circles all over Iowa – but she was that and more. She was nearly as wide as she was tall when I met her, but there was hardly a topic that could be broached in her presence where she wasn't the most well-read person in the room. She ran in circles that I could not even imagine. I remember being fascinated as she told me that she had once met and had spoken with Helen Keller. Having been deaf and blind since early childhood, Keller had held her hand to Mrs. Wohlenhaus's face in a particular way and could, by so doing, "hear" what was being said. Mrs. Wohlenhaus described Keller as one of the most remarkable human beings in history, and I recall checking out a book from the library so that I could read her story. Remarkable indeed.

Mrs. Wohlenhaus also once told me that she dated Ronald Reagan when they were both in college. Later, when he was running for President, I asked her if she was planning on voting for him, given their past relationship. "Not on your life," she declared without a moment's hesitation – and with a wry smile on her face.

Shortly after settling into C&M High School, I got it into my head that I should talk to someone about the Contest Speech Team. I'd always had the gift of gab, and I thought perhaps I could put it to some constructive use. Lord knows it got me into enough trouble over the years; maybe this thing had a silver lining, I thought. After checking around with some kids I was getting to know, I found out that Mrs. Wohlenhaus was the Contest Speech Coach. I came to find out that she was regarded as the best in all of Iowa, but I didn't know that at the time. Retrospectively, I've come to believe that Mrs. Wohlenhaus would have been the best at nearly anything she set her mind to. She was truly a formidable woman who may have been decades ahead of her time.

I spoke with Mrs. Wohlenhaus in the hall one day and asked if we could get together sometime and talk about Contest Speech. Upon comparing schedules, we discovered that she had a free period late in the afternoon, and I had a corresponding study hall, so she wrote me a pass to get out of study hall and come to her "office" (which was just a desk in the back of a classroom) to talk with her. We talked a good while about the process of trying out for and competing on the team. My parents had never allowed me to be a part of any extra-curricular activity. But this particular activity might make me a better preacher, so permission was granted. The whole concept of participating in after-school activities was utterly foreign to me, right down to the logistics of how one got to and from the events at various schools throughout the district.

As the class period neared an end, I excused myself and stood to leave. Mrs. Wohlenhaus stopped me and invited me to take my seat again. "There's something else I want to talk to you about, Craig." She said. "You're new here at this school, and I can see that you can go down a good path here, or chose the easier but less productive way."

I had no idea where this was going, but I began to wonder if she'd heard about my inglorious past reputation at my previous schools. To say I was nervous about the direction of this monologue would be a complete understatement.

"Craig, you're a good and bright kid. You're going to do well here at this school if you make the right kind of friends. Let me give you a little head's-up on that. If you will make friends with kids like _____, and _____, and _____ you're going to do just fine. But you're also going to need to stay away from kids like _____, and _____, and _____,"

She named names. She told me WHY she was naming names. This was literally the first time in my life that ANY adult had tangibly demonstrated that they *believed* in me – shown me that they thought I had potential and could achieve something if I set my mind to it. This was a revolutionary concept to me. This was a concept of future achievement that I had literally never pondered in my life. I had never before considered anything that had a place in time outside of my present. It was so revolutionary in my life that, even now, I remember it as if I had just left her classroom. I can see the room with its rows of desks slightly askew and a chalkboard filled with sentence diagrams. I can smell the red checkered thermos of coffee on her desk and the half-eaten cream cheese sandwich on whole wheat bread lying on a baggie next to it. I can feel the yellow, hard-plastic chair I was sitting in and I can visualize the oak swivel executive chair she occupied to my right. I can hear an occasional voice in the hallway and the slamming of a locker down by Mr. Mead's history classroom. There's the faint hum of a table saw from the industrial arts area at the end of the hall.

I walked out of Mrs. Wohlenhaus's classroom just as the bell rang. My mind was abuzz in a way that could not have been more palpable than if it had been plugged into an electrical outlet. I'm pretty sure my feet never touched the ground. All I knew as I left that room and wandered into the sea of kids in the hall was that I never wanted to disappoint this woman.

I did try out for the Contest Speech Team, and I did compete all through the rest of my time at C&M. The team was really good; we won lots of contests and several of us went to State each year to compete there. I still have a half dozen or so trophies, and a bunch of tattered ribbons and medals I won during those years. This was literally the first time I had ever achieved anything in my life that was based on some indwelling ability I possessed and could hone. It was the first time that others recognized those abilities and rewarded them by seeing – really seeing – *me*.

I wasn't emotionally equipped to handle success, having never experienced it before. Initially I was insufferably proud and verbose about my achievements and quickly turned some of my teammates against me. I remember riding home in a bus after one of my first Speech Meets, having won several awards – more awards than anyone else. I was sitting behind an older girl, Sandy, whom I knew and liked from church. I droned on and on about my achievements of the day and soon she put me in my place. I don't remember exactly what she said to me, but it shut me up – which felt harsh at the time – but was something my self-importance deserved. So far as I can remember, Sandy never spoke to me again. I grieve the consequences of my arrogance to this day. Perhaps this is why the scriptures say, "Let another person praise you, not your own lips."

At the 1976 C&M awards ceremony, I was granted a letter. And though secretly I would have preferred lettering in baseball, I was nevertheless thrilled to be applauded by the whole school for my Contest Speech accomplishments. And some little part inside me began to actually believe that perhaps I was not destined to a lonely, pathetic existence. Perhaps there was something inside me that could free me from my confinement and propel me into something more than I could even imagine. There was a tiny flicker of flame developing inside me that only I could feel. But it felt like something being born in me. It felt like something more real and wild than anything I had felt before. It felt like I'd been given permission to dream – in color.

I got a second letter following my junior year, but since I'd given up my entrepreneurial thieving endeavors, I was far too poor to actually purchase a letter-jacket on which to attach these letters and all the medals I'd won, as most kids did. Mom and Dad didn't offer to buy one for me, as many parents did for their kids. And though the exploits of the Speech Team were regularly chronicled in the local newspaper, my parents didn't buy the newspaper, so I don't think they ever really knew what I was doing. In fact, they never came to any of my Speech Meets, nor plays, nor any other extra-curricular activity I was in … not even once.

I didn't really know it at the time, but my folks were poor too. Farmers who rented land weren't much more than "hired-hands" for the land owner. Dad had opportunities to buy land, but he was quite risk-averse and was never willing to put *that much* on the line. They had enough money to keep a roof over our heads and food on the table, but little else. Mom was a "housewife" who had a tasty home-cooked meal on the table every night at 5:30, and Dad was the sole "bread winner." When Dad finally tired of looking for new land to rent, he sold his farm equipment, and went to work for a local carpenter. If I recall correctly, his starting wage was something like $2.45 an hour. There wasn't much money to spare – certainly not for something as frivolous and unnecessary as a letter jacket.

After leaving Iowa permanently in 1978, I would stop in to see Mrs. Wohlenhaus from time to time when visiting from Ohio. We'd sit and talk in her home, and later in her little apartment that was about 20 degrees too warm for me. She kept after me to call her LaRoyce, but I could never do it – she'll always be Mrs. Wohlenhaus to me. She was ever a delight and an encouragement. She was always so sharp and inspirational. She didn't pull punches either. If she thought you were messing up, she'd just come right out and say it. I heard it from her a few times and have come to appreciate it more now than I did then. Mrs. Wohlenhaus died shortly after the millennium change. I didn't hear about it till well after her funeral, so I didn't get to go pay my respects. I'd have gladly driven the 700 miles to do so. She was a giant in my life.

And whenever I hear a public speaker mumbling, I can hear Mrs. Wohlenhaus shouting from the back of the room, "AMPLIFY; e-nun'-ci-āte."

Zoo

When I think about my early life, I wonder how differently I feel about it than people who grew up in their biological family units. In my own childhood I clearly have a sense of not belonging – a sense of being "other." Even today, my memories of it are something akin to an out of body experience. I know these are *my* memories of *my* life, but they seem as if I'm observing them from outside. The name I was given at birth was Craig Shepherd. As the third of the Shepherd children I felt – and sometimes still feel – like a lost Shepherd pup.

At age two, I was given over to the Annie Wittenmyer Children's Home, an orphanage whose job was to train me and help me to survive. I was kept on a short leash there, hopelessly trying to learn all the rules and stay within my enclosure. Perhaps I snapped at those who tried to feed me and care for me?

Eventually I was tamed and grew enough to be offered up to a different class of care-giver known as foster parents; and then finally taken into an adoptive family which to me felt something like a zoo – the permanent residence for interesting but orphaned and abandoned creatures.

I don't intend to sound pejorative or ungrateful here. I honestly see my life as being far, far better as a result of my adoption than it might have been had I stayed in my original family. I am eternally grateful for all that the Steffens, and everyone around them, have done to help me. But, no matter how hard they tried, and no matter how well-intentioned they were, none of these people would ever be for me what a good Alpha male and female can be for their pup. I felt cared for in the way that zookeepers care for the creatures under their charge. I was given food, water and shelter and my cage was kept clean. I can see the look in the eyes of the adults around me as if to say, "what else can he need or want?" A sincere question, I'm sure, but spoken out of bewilderment nonetheless. I was bathed and groomed and put on display as something to be wondered at, or even proud of – more of a possession than a progeny.

But I never felt understood. I wasn't fully known. I never felt the kind of connection that can be observed between parent and child linked at a mystical DNA level. It's not that anyone failed to do their duty. It's just that it *was* duty, rather than an instinctual connection with another being who had come forth out of them, and was, in a very real sense, a part of them. I was a new exhibit at the zoo, not the zookeeper's toddler.

Animals raised to adulthood within the zoo almost never survive in the wild. And as skilled and studied as the zookeepers are, they're simply not fully equipped or capable of teaching them the skills they must have to live outside the zoo. There is no way that the zookeeper can understand the animal's instincts deeply enough to reach them in their psyche. They are a different species after all. And, not understanding fully enough prevents them from discovering the inner being and timing necessary for modeling the behaviors required for fulfillment within the life and environment intended for the animal. All they can do is provide sustenance, but not understanding – compassion, but not purpose. And though these provisions are awesome and wonderful given the alternative, it isn't truly enough for the orphaned animal to be who he was created to be.

When you observe an animal in captivity, it looks nearly identical to its brothers and sisters in the wild – on the outside. But on the inside there is something missing, something wrong.

If being in a non-native family was akin to being cared for in a zoo, being so integrated into the Plymouth Brethren Assembly was something like the cage. There were lots of rules, few of which were written down and fewer still that were actually from the Bible. Along with the "big three" (sex, tobacco and alcohol) we also weren't allowed to go to movies, play cards, have "non-believing" friends, participate in organized sports, dance, wear stylish clothes or have stylish hair, listen to contemporary music, have any association with drums, work or play on Sunday, or eat food in a place that served alcohol – to name a few.

Zoo animals often pace their cages day after day living a life of pointlessness and confusion. Their reality and their instincts are completely incongruous. Sure, they are fed and protected from harm and predators; sure they are admired by visitors. But if one looks past the majestic nature of their being, one sees the pathetic nature of their circumstance.

The Steffens were really good people with a prevailing desire to do the right thing. They provided for me the only thing within their power to provide – a safe and adequate zoo. My present day girth is, perhaps, a testament to their overly ample feeding schedule. But I paced the cage until I wandered out of the zoo when I was 17, feeling every bit as lost and ill-equipped as the little two-year-old Shepherd pup who first got rescued from his abandonment in 1962. And 50 years later I find myself still longing for and searching for my pack and my place within it.

When you see me in the wild today, it's unlikely that you would ever guess that I was once in a zoo. But I confess that inside me are the emotional memories of my abandonment and the scars I acquired while grieving the loss of my pack, who I imagined were outside the fence somewhere. Did they ever wonder what had become of me? Would they recognize me if I returned?

It is true that I have more tangible accomplishments in life than nearly anyone believed possible for me, or helped me to envision. But all the while, I have known that, inside, there has been something missing, something wrong.

Fair

It is thirteen years after the disappearance.

Late in the summer of 1975, was the first time I ever met, or heard from, anyone from my original family. And it was here that the story of that family and the people in it began to take shape for me.

My sister, Theresa, had gotten pregnant in high school and had given birth to a precious little girl on February 13 of 1975. She married the baby's father, dropped out of high school, and was living with his parents, since Theresa was now a 17–year-old raising a baby. Theresa's husband, Mike, was still in high school being pressured to earn an athletic scholarship by, what seemed to me to be, an over-zealous father.

Unfortunately, Mike was not popular at my house and was often referred to by Mom or Dad as a "fornicator" and was not one of "the saved" whom we believed to be mostly made up of people from our church communities. As far as I recall, Mike and his family didn't even go to church.

In late July, Theresa called and asked if, in a few weeks, I'd like to go to the Iowa State Fair with her and Mike. I'd been to the fair with Dad and Theresa several times in previous years and always enjoyed the experience. It seemed grown-up to go without parental oversight, so I agreed. Secretly I was a fan of Mike, since he was a very good baseball player, something I aspired to be.

So in early August, Mike and Theresa came through Cumberland, picked me up and we headed east on I-80 toward Des Moines. We headed to the State Fair in their new blue 4x4 pickup truck. It was a tight squeeze, but it was an adventure.

Having just turned 15, I wasn't much of a navigator, so I didn't notice when we pulled off the highway near Ames, Iowa and headed into a small town. For all I knew, this was a short cut or we were getting close to the fairgrounds. But we ended up pulling into a trailer park in Nevāda, Iowa with Theresa explaining that she wanted to say hello to a friend who was giving her something for the baby.

She asked me to join her as we walked to the front door of a trailer so that I could help carry whatever was being donated to her cause. It seemed like a reasonable request. Theresa knocked on the door and I glanced about dumbly like the disinterested teenager I was.

A man in his early 40s opened the door. Theresa and the man exchanged knowing glances, without actually speaking. Then Theresa looked at me and said, "Craig, this is your father."

Pepper

I'd never seen anyone put that much pepper on a fried egg.

I watched Theresa making breakfast as I sat at the table in the tiny kitchen of the mobile home that my father, Alvin Shepherd, lived in. The table separated the living room/dining room from the back of the trailer where the bedrooms were. I'd slept the previous night in a sleeping bag on the living room floor, just 10 feet from where I now sat in the kitchen.

"Wow, that's a lot of pepper. Why do you make them like that?" I asked.

"That's the way Dad likes them," was her succinct answer.

It was an insignificant event in a traumatic weekend. But I've never been able to forget it because something more potent than pepper happened in that kitchen on that awkward late summer morning when Theresa and I were supposed to be at the State Fair.

I asked a question deep inside myself. It was a simple question at the time.

"I wonder if I would like pepper on my eggs too – since Dad does?"

A few days later, while making breakfast for myself back at my house, I put pepper on my own eggs – a lot of pepper ... just like Dad. And I did like it. I liked it a lot. And I've put copious amounts of pepper on every egg I've eaten in all the years since.

In the moment I discovered that I enjoyed those peppery eggs, I felt something real happen in me. I felt like I had a connection to paternity I'd never heretofore experienced. I began to wonder what other things that I do, or like, or say, or think were also like Dad? I wondered if there were things that he enjoyed, like his passion for fishing, which I would also enjoy if I just tried them. Is there some secret hidden in my DNA that could help explain who I am, what I do, and might even predict my destiny?

I spent a lot of years asking those questions each time I found something I really enjoyed. Like baseball – I wonder if Dad likes baseball? – I'd ponder. When I discovered that I have an aptitude for mechanical things, I wondered if I got this propensity from Dad?

In the late 1980s I learned from my sister that Alvin had a blood-clotting disorder that had blocked the circulation to one of his legs and resulted in a trans-tibial (below the knee) amputation. This dire health news, tragic in its own right, took my questions to a whole new place. Just how much like Dad might I really be? From that moment on, it has been in the back of my mind that I might not live a long, healthy life. And that thought has haunted and shaped me as I've made choices in business, in finance and in my relationships. We all must play the hand we've been dealt.

Disappearance

It was on this same 1975 weekend that the story of my pre-adopted life began to be told to me. There was not much emotion and not much detail, but here's what I was told.

Alvin and my mother, Beverly, married in May of 1957 several weeks before Beverly's 17th birthday. Theresa was born in October of the same year. Alvin was five years older than Beverly and got odd jobs working for farmers in rural Iowa, around the general area where he still lived. In January 1959, my brother Ricky was born, and in June of 1960 I was born. So before Beverly was out of her teens, she'd had three children.

Then two years later, just before her 22nd birthday, Beverly "stole the family car and disappeared."

The disappearance was mysterious on several levels. First, no one had any idea what had happened to her or where she might have gone. She left Alvin dumbfounded and with three kids to deal with, all under five.

But the disappearance was mysterious in other ways too. As Alvin told me about her disappearance, he never gave any indication that anyone ever looked for her. He seemed content not to know WHY she had disappeared, nor WHERE she might have gone. It didn't seem to occur to him – or anyone else apparently – that a criminal abduction might have taken place.

Right up until last year, when I was deep in the throes of my research, no one knew where this teenaged mother of three had gone when she left Iowa, or who she might have been with. And no one seemed to take the disappearance seriously enough to start asking questions. This still astounds me.

As it turns out, it wasn't the first time Beverly had absconded with a car and disappeared, and it wouldn't be the last.

A few months later, when he was unable to cope and find work, Alvin left us with a baby sitter and never returned. We ended up in the Annie Wittenmyer orphanage and he never saw us again until Theresa and I went to the Iowa State Fair in 1975.

That was about all Alvin said about the fact that we'd been orphaned thirteen years earlier. He was truly a man of few words.

Later that same weekend I met Beverly's parents at a tavern they owned in Maxwell, which was another little town about 10 miles from where Alvin was living. They told me the identical story, with some phrases such as "she stole the family car and disappeared" repeated word-for-word as if rehearsed. Another phrase her parents used to refer to Beverly was "black sheep." This seemed oddly disloyal to me coming from them.

And though everyone I met that weekend was nice enough toward me, I don't recall any warmth or emotion and I don't recall anyone expressing regret about the circumstances that eventually led to us three kids ending up in that orphanage. Does that seem as odd to you as it does to me? I'm not talking about assuming blame or guilt. I'm just thinking that biological family members who were integral to our lives at one point might say something like, "It's horrible what happened to you kids. You didn't deserve that. I'm so sorry." But no one ever uttered any such words.

My maternal grandparents also confirmed what I'd once overheard my adoptive mother tell a relative of hers – Theresa and I have a brother. His name is Ricky, and he was born on New Year's Day in 1959. But no one seemed to know where he was now.

So, all that I would know about my early life for the next 22 years fit into a few short paragraphs. However, I got some additional details in 1997, when I found and talked to my brother Ricky for the first time.

L to R Grandpa and Grandma Gardiner
Mom and Dad Steffend
Grandma and Granpa Steffen

Craig and Theresa with
"strange poopy smells"

Theresa, Craig and Kenny
at Craig's 8th Birthday

Mom and Dad Steffen

Part Two

A Journey for Mother

Gonna park in the street, gonna open the gate
Walk to the spot where you always wait
I'll be shaking my head like I usually do
'Cause the name and the dates tell me nothing about you.

But I'll sit in the shadows and let you explain
All of the sadness and all of the pain
Did it all seem so hopeless you just had to let go?
Girl of mysterious sorrow.

Marc Cohn

Wraith

It is forty-eight years after the disappearance.

I am sleeping alone in a strange, small room. I am lying on the floor, even though there is a bed to which I am lying perpendicular. There is carpet on the floor and I have awakened to discover that water is rising up through the floor, such that the edges of the carpet have now become saturated all around me. As I watch, befuddled at its source, the water creeps ever closer to where I am lying.

Silently, a young man enters the room with a small child. I know them so well that I do not get up nor do I greet them by name. I am particularly fond of the child who is about three years old. When he sees me, we both radiate mutual joy and excitement. From my prone position, I pick him up and hold him above me and call him "Munchkin." We are laughing and goofing with each other playfully and our hearts are full of a familiar, mutual love. We are known to each other.

Sitting on the floor, cross-legged and at a slight distance, is the young man. His slender build, curly full head of brown hair and period clothing all reveal him to be vintage 1970s. He silently watches my interplay with the lad with a clinical attention to detail and a slight smile.

The three year old is cherubic, full of life and exudes a frequent, infectious laugh and a never-ending smile. His friendly and personable manner exposes his love and trust of our pre-existing relationship.

After we have played and while still lying prone on the floor, I hold him up in the air again and say with energetic anticipation, "How's my little Munchkin this morning?" "What are you doing today Munchkin?"

Then Munchkin's smile drains from his face suddenly, as if life were draining from his body. With a seriousness alien to children, he looks straight into my eyes and steals my gaze. His countenance is transformed by a sage maturity beyond his years. He verbally confronts me powerfully and succinctly, "So— Craig—what do you fear?"

I awake with a deep gasp and complete intellectual acuity. I know that something profound has just happened. Something weighty has just been asked of me.

I wake my wife, Cindy, and we talk about this dream. We begin to explore its nuance and metaphor. I become acutely aware that with Munchkin's profound question I must embark upon a journey. It is my hope that the journey will take me to places where I can decipher the question. It is my hope that the journey will lead me to a series of answers that will bring healing. I suspect that Munchkin and his 1970s companion will accompany me. Perhaps they have been waiting for me all along.

Firsthand

It is thirty-one years after the disappearance.

By 1997 the Internet had become useful as a tool of research. Netscape had developed the Graphical User Interface (GUI) browser, and finding information subsequently got a lot easier. From the stories I'd been told, I knew that I had a brother named Ricky who was roughly 18 months older than me and that he was born on New Year's Day in 1959. I also knew that he had been adopted by a family in Oregon named Cronk. Using that information, I began to search. This was long before Google and search engines that make the task relatively easy today. So there was a lot of finding a name and cutting and pasting information into other documents in order to establish a list of potential contacts. I had no idea where Ricky might be. He had been in Oregon as a youth and had spent at least a few months in Iowa in the late 1970s. I was pretty sure he wasn't in either place anymore, but that was of little use. I generated a list of about 30 people named Rick, Ricky and Richard Cronk.

I took my list of contacts with me on a business trip to the Detroit area. I was staying in the Henry Ford Hotel in Dearborn and, mostly out of boredom, I mustered the courage to begin calling people from the list. I had devised a strategy to simply dial the number and, if a male answered, I'd ask him if he ever lived in Oregon or Iowa. If his answer was yes, I'd ask if his birthday was January 1, 1959.

On about the 7th or 8th call, a raspy voiced fellow answered. It seemed as if I'd woken him. I offered a quick introduction and got right to the questions. "I'm wondering if you might be the Rick Cronk who once lived in Oregon and Iowa?"

"Well, actually, yes I've lived in both those places." There was an uncomfortable silence before the man added, "Why?"

"I'm looking for my brother whom I've never met. Does your birthday happen to be January 1, 1959?"

"Is this Craig?"

A glob of adrenalin careened through my blood like a carton of cottage cheese. I suddenly realized that I had not prepared myself for the possibility that my search might actually find Ricky. My mind raced and stumbled through an ad hoc list of potential topics of conversation, none of which had any brilliance. There were long, awkward silences punctuated by what seemed like primitive, inarticulate grunts.

Eventually we settled into human conversation. We talked about our life experiences and what we're doing now. We talked about relationships, work, and the families we'd known in our lives. He shared information about my original family I'd never heard before, and he told me about two half siblings, born to our mother after she'd left Iowa, whom I'd never met. To say the whole conversation was surreal doesn't begin to describe it. In fact, the experience was on the part of the trauma scale that allows for very little retention of information – much like the time in 1975 that Theresa stood with a stranger and said, "Craig, this is your father." Now there was a new whisper in my DNA, "Craig, this is your brother."

Ricky had been living in Nashua, New Hampshire for many years and was working as a night-shift orderly in the Saint Joseph Hospital Emergency Room.

Ricky told me that he remembered being at Annie Wittenmyer Children's Home. And that he remembered when Theresa and I left him alone there. It was devastating to him. It broke my heart to imagine him there, already in a strange place away from everyone he'd ever known, and now to watch the only connections to his life drive away in a sky blue 1957 Ford Galaxie with complete strangers.

To be honest, it was the first time I'd ever considered any of the emotions and struggles my two siblings may have had at Annie Wittenmyer. I remember being quietly embarrassed at my own narcissism.

Ricky lived at Annie Wittenmyer for over two years, then he told me that it was in October of 1964 that our mother, Beverly, returned to Iowa and "got me back." Apparently she made the 2000-mile drive from Oregon with the intention of getting all three of her children back. But the legal adoption of Theresa and me had been finalized just a week or two prior to Beverly's arrival in Davenport. Somehow, however, she was able to convince the folks at Annie Wittenmyer that she had the right (and was fit) to retrieve Ricky – and she did.

Ricky returned with Beverly and her new husband to Eola Village near McMinnville, Oregon where he met his new little sister, Jacqueline Sue, for the first time. He lived with our mother and his new sister until a little brother, Steven Troy, was born in February of 1965. At that point, Beverly once again had two boys and a girl, having successfully re-casted the family she'd left in June of 1962.

Ricky was not yet six years old when he was retrieved by our mother. Though his memories of Mom were far greater than my own, which did not exist at all, they were the fuzzy recollections of a child, rather than the detailed memories of a sleuth.

In 1998 Ricky and I met each other for the first time. He traveled to my home in Ohio from his in New Hampshire and we spent a week together. We spent a LOT of time talking and picking each other's brains about our lives, childhood and memories. Most of the information was flowing from him to me, since he was the older brother and since he lived with Mom till he was seven years old.

Ricky remembered the warm, dry October day that Beverly arrived at Annie Wittenmyer and reunited with him in 1964. But on most conscious levels, he didn't remember her from before the disappearance. He hadn't seen her for two years and four months – not since he was only three-and-a-half years old; not since June of 1962. So, when she returned, she was little more than a welcome stranger showering him with familiar attention.

During his stay at Annie Wittenmyer, Ricky had been farmed out to other strangers where he lived for short periods of time in foster care. This woman visitor, though subconsciously memorable, was another in the line of would-be parental units. Ricky was a compliant little guy, averse to conflict, shy and quiet so he likely went happily away with Beverly and her new husband, Clarence. He could not have imagined what a 2000-mile trek to Oregon would feel like. But photographs of him from that time show a kid apparently fitting in to his new surroundings.

He spent some of that time with Jackie and Steven, neither of whom I'd ever met. I had barely heard of their existence, but Ricky had personal memories. In fact, after Beverly's death, Ricky and Jackie were adopted together by the Cronks, as Theresa and I had been by the Steffens two years and 2000 miles earlier.

By all accounts Jackie was a lot like her mother. She was bright, beautiful, extroverted, musical, athletic, mischievous and the-life-of-the-party. She was close and loving with her siblings and popular in her Girl Scout troop and at school, though she lacked studiousness and a vision for her future. Sadly, she apparently had Beverly's rebelliousness, sexual proclivities, and wild-child tendencies, as well. Before she reached the age of 14, Jackie was pregnant, engaged to be married, and "wild" according to those who knew her. She told her adoptive sister, Sharon, that she "expected to die young."

On August 14, 1977, two weeks after they became engaged, and a few weeks before her 14th birthday, she and her fiancé, Phillip Curtis Bixler, took a late-night drive along country roads southwest of Amity, Oregon. Jackie pestered her 21-year-old boyfriend into letting her drive his car. Though only 13, tiny and without any training on how to operate a motor vehicle, she took the wheel at about 10:30 p.m.. By 10:50 p.m., she'd lost control of the car on Bethel Road; it flipped and she was thrown from it. She was pronounced dead at the scene, just after midnight. Her boyfriend walked away with a few cuts and bruises.

As Ricky and I talked, and he shared this information with me, it was clear to me how much he loved his sister. His voice cracked, his words were slow and interrupted with emotion and pools of water collected in his dark brown eyes. There is no doubt that Jackie's accident, which occurred shortly after Ricky had left Oregon to live in Iowa with his biological maternal grandparents, profoundly affected Ricky. Soon after, he moved to New Hampshire, sold his car, allowed his own driver's license to expire and never drove again.

Ricky also told me how he'd reconnected with Steven years after Jackie and Ricky had been separated from him. Steven had been adopted by a member of his father's family and, like Ricky and Jackie, his last name was changed. Steven had actually lived with Ricky for a time in New Hampshire before Steven got sick. In Steven's final months, he lived with another paternal relative in Idaho. In 1996, after a debilitating illness, Steven died at age 31.

After Ricky's visit to my home in Ohio, my curiosity piqued and I began seeking more information about the circumstances that led to Theresa, Ricky and me being abandoned, adopted and separated. I contacted the Iowa Department of Human Services. After a fair amount of getting transferred around, I finally got hold of someone able and willing to assist.

After months of calls, forms, fees and waiting, I received a few pages of redacted paperwork from our intake and stay at the Annie Wittenmyer Home. The quote below was the first thing I read upon opening the envelope.

The County Child Welfare Officer signed a petition alleging the three Shepherd children to be dependent on 9-5-62 when it appeared to her that the children had been abandoned. Beverly Shepherd, the children's mother, deserted the family in the middle of June 1962, taking the family car with her. Her present whereabouts are unknown.

I can't really explain why, but seeing this statement on a form from the State of Iowa somehow cemented the reality of my past into greater certainty and permanence than any of the verbal accounts I'd heretofore received.

Abandoned. Deserted. Those powerful words were right there on page one.

So it was really true. It happened. Here it is written down all official-like. I'm an orphan — and not by accident — by parental choice.

*An **orphan** (from the Greek ὀρφανός) is a child permanently bereaved of or abandoned by his or her parents.* — Concise Oxford Dictionary 6th edition

Alternative Definitions Commonly Used:

1. "Minor child whose parents have died, have relinquished their parental rights, or whose parental rights have been terminated by a court of jurisdiction."
2. "A child who has lost the love of its natural parents due to death, abandonment, abuse, or neglect."

Clipping

Ricky and I never grew particularly close. We loved each other in a distant, unfamiliar way. I saw him only twice more after his week at my house in Ohio. Once, when Cindy and I were in New England, we stopped to see him and take him to lunch. And then, a few months before his death, I traveled to Oregon to see him one last time. He'd fallen several years prior and suffered a severe back injury. Two unsuccessful surgeries left him first in a wheelchair, and later bed-ridden. He returned to Oregon to live with his adoptive sister, Sharon, who cared for him till his death in October of 2009.

In the 14 years we were in contact, we saw each other three times and chatted on the phone on a few dozen occasions. But Ricky and I never really seemed to strike on anything that we shared in common.

Just two years after Ricky's passing, and in the wake of Dad Steffen's death in 2011, I was assaulted with a blur of stresses from many sources. There was an estate to settle, bills to pay, a company to run, a wife to love, three properties to care for and unwarranted betrayal from two siblings to try to understand. For the first time in decades I didn't play baseball in the summer, and I cast aside even trying to keep that baseball body in shape. Sports and fitness both seemed like temporal childish pursuits in the face of the permanence of death and loss. I was, and maybe still am, depressed.

At the end of the year, I wrapped up the tiny estate left over after the medical system had, in 18 months, picked clean the carcass of all that my father had worked for and saved during his 90 years. The process required just as much time, detail, paperwork and redundancy as if there were hundreds of thousands in assets to liquidate and distribute, instead of a few thousand. There was the work – but there was not the legacy.

By December I was able to wrap it all up, having divided the spoils and said goodbye to my father, his life, my hometown and the only siblings I had ever known who had abandoned me during the estate settlement process. My older brother, Kenny, had accused me of taking money from Dad … never mind that there *was* no money to take. Dad had been on Medicaid for over a year, which necessitated that his total assets be less than $2000. Dad asked me to take over his finances a year before his death. Beginning on day one, I fastidiously recorded every financial transaction in my computer financial software package. After Dad's death, all the records were audited and certified by an estate attorney, and all the records, along with the attorney's written opinion were sent to both of my siblings. Despite all this, Kenny's opinion has, apparently, never changed as we have not spoken to one another since his initial accusation. My sister, Theresa's, silence toward me since my brother's false accusations demonstrated her seeming solidarity with Kenny, despite the reams of evidence to the contrary. Frankly, it was a loss that blind-sided me, and broke my heart.

Just after Christmas I was alone in my office, distractedly puttering through piles of papers, drawers of documents and folders of correspondence trying to put some semblance of order to the flotsam that had collected during my year of exile in executor hell.

I didn't know it at the time, but at the bottom of one of those drawers of papers was a single scrap of yellowed memorabilia that I had no memory of possessing. That faded newspaper clipping started me on a new journey of discovery.

The clipping was a 1992 obituary of my maternal grandfather. Here's where the story starts to get complicated. This clipping was about the death of the father of my biological mother, Beverly Shepherd-Hiner?-Goodenough.

As I read the obituary of my Grandfather Robbie I was struck by the great chasm fixed between me and this "original family," as I have come to refer to them. As I pondered my own lack of knowledge, relationship and connection to these people who contributed to my own DNA, I was flooded with a slurry of emotion.

This same kind of emotional fog filled me like a zeppelin as I sat and stared at my Grandpa Robbie's obituary. Names, locations, prior deceased, survivors, services, interment – all things I should have known, had relationships with, and attended. But there, in my office, nearly 20 years after the fact, I might as well have been reading about the demise of grandfatherly Captain Kangaroo – someone familiar, but with whom I had no real-world connection.

It was as if the abandonment that had happened in 1962, happened all over again each time the thought of my original family crept into my mind.

As I sat in my office in virtual paralysis, mentally departed from my current circumstances while traveling back in time, it occurred to me that during the few times I had ever spoken to people familiar with the events of 1962, each narrator portrayed the abandonment as solely accomplished by my mother, who "had stolen the family car, and disappeared." I could never tell whether it was the stealing of the family car, or the abandonment of children that was deemed the more egregious offense.

But here in 2011, it became clear to me, perhaps for the first time, that the abandonment was accomplished not just by Beverly, but by literally everyone I had ever known in those first two years of my life.

None of the Shepherd family had stepped up to take us kids in. None of my mom's family had done so either. Beverly and Alvin apparently had no friends or siblings or cousins or neighbors or babysitters interested in caring for three, cute little kids (and we WERE cute). All of these had abandoned us then and continued to abandon us now — hence the lack of connection with anyone or any place mentioned within the obit. And it was this realization that created a veritable "perpetual emotion machine" within me.

Looking at my mother's name on this obituary, "preceded in death by one daughter, Beverly ..." Death. Daughter. Beverly. Death. Beverly. Death. It's all so final. I think, there's really no hope of ever getting answers. I wonder if any of these other people remain alive? A lot of years have passed since Grandpa Robbie's death. Is Grandma Robbie still alive? What about my mother's three sisters listed here? Theresa had once told me that the youngest sister was considerably younger than our mother. I wonder if she is young enough to be on Facebook?

I take this question and the obituary down the hall into the family room and conduct a private show-and-tell session with Cindy. I wonder aloud about Facebook. In her practical wisdom, she simply states, "There's only one way to find out." I take this as some sort of approval and wonder why I need it. I retreat to my office and fire up my computer. After 5 minutes of booting, the machine whirrs to life and I click on "bookmarks" in the browser and select "Facebook." Navigating to the search window, I pause to decide what I should type in — maiden name or married name? I decide to start with both. Copying exactly from the obituary held in my left hand, I hunt-and-peck and hit enter. There is only one match for this very specific search criteria. I click on it and wonder if this is Aunt Sherri — whom I've never met, nor even seen an adult picture of. Her profile doesn't list where she's from, so I click on "photos." Scanning through her photos I see a thumbnail that looks like something from the 70s so I select it to enlarge. There is a picture of Sherri's parents, my maternal grandparents. This MUST be the right person I conclude – an aunt from a past world I'd only seen in my imagination.

I walk back down the hall, laptop in hand like a "blankie," to show Cindy this easily acquired discovery. "What are you going to do?" she asks. Timid as a two-year-old, I answer, "I don't know. I honestly don't know."

It took me the rest of the day to craft a private Facebook message to Sherri that read:

———*Conversation started December 28, 2011*———-

Hello Aunt Sherri. I don't believe you and I have ever met, but I'm the youngest son of your sister Beverly and Alvin Shepherd. I'm pretty sure you've met my sister Theresa, and probably my brother Ricky.

I was cleaning out a drawer today and ran across the newspaper clipping from your father's death and decided to see if you might be on Facebook – and here you are. Is your mother still living? My wife and I visited them sometime in the late 80s, but I lost touch with them after your father passed.

I don't know if you heard, but Ricky died October 31, 2009 (cancer). I visited him in Oregon a few months before he passed. I found him via the internet and we re-connected in the late 90s for the first time since our childhood.

Theresa is still in Griswold, IA and doing well. My wife and I are in the Dayton, Ohio area and doing well also.

I wonder if you might be interested in having a conversation by mail, email or phone? I've long been curious about some things of the past and with the passing of my adoptive parents (Mom in 2003 and Dad earlier this year) I'm thinking it may be time to ask those questions. If you consider this request intrusive, I'll certainly understand, but I'm hoping we can talk. Thank you for your consideration.

Craig Allen Steffen (Shepherd)

I checked my Facebook page every few minutes the rest of the night, and began again the next morning as if hovering over the proverbial "watched pot."

I never got a reply. I waited impatiently for a response, visiting Sherri's page daily to monitor other activity. Maybe she was traveling over the holiday and hadn't yet seen my message? But secretly I felt that she was probably uninterested in communicating with this ghost from her past. I imagined her thinking, "What does HE want anyway?"

I don't know where it comes from, but I've always been a tenacious little shit. While "stalking" Sherri on Facebook, I noticed that she is a realtor and thought she might also be on LinkedIn. So I went to that site and started searching for her there. As I suspected, she was there as well. So on December 30, two days after my Facebook message, I ventured a second risk and I sent this note via LinkedIn:

On December 30, 2011 9:22 AM, Craig A. Steffen wrote:

———————

Hello Sherri:

I'm your sister Beverly's son, Craig. I sent you a message on Facebook a few days ago — don't know how often you check it. I'd love to chat if you're willing. Maybe connecting here & learning a bit about each other would make it less awkward.

- Craig A. Steffen

The following day I received a cryptic response:

Sherri Realtor

To: Craig A. Steffen

Date: December 31, 2011

Craig,
Thank you for sending me the request. Yes, I did recognize your name.

Sherri

So what did this response mean? Was she merely thanking me for the request to connect on LinkedIn? Or was she referring to my request to talk? Was she saying, "Hey yeah, I recognize you my long lost nephew?" Or was she saying, "Stop bothering me, I recognized your name the first time I saw it and that's why you haven't heard back from me – you orphaned little troll."

Of course, I don't know Sherri from a load of coal, so I have zero prior information on which to decide between these two equal and opposite meanings. I need the wisdom of Solomon to discern her meaning. Sigh. New confusion and subsequent paralysis sets in.

2012 starts and I get thrust into meaningful work on behalf of my clients. Before I notice, six weeks have passed and I've still not made first phone contact. So on Tuesday, the day before Valentine's Day, when I saw her as "logged on" to Facebook, I muster the courage to try one more time – hoping against hope that there is a kinder, gentler aunt out there than the cold and selfish one who is clearly possible. The following is our actual "chat" dialog that day:

On February 13, 2012 4:55 PM, Craig A. Steffen wrote:

Craig A. Steffen
Hello Sherri. Would you mind if I gave you a call sometime?

-

- *4:56pm*
- *Sherri*
- *That would be fine. Weekends are generally best.*

4:57pm
Craig A. Steffen
Ok, thank you. I'll try to find some time this coming weekend. Have a wonderful Valentine's Day.

-

- *4:58pm*
- *Sherri*
Sounds good. I generally answer my cell unless I am with clients. Leave me a message and I will call you back when I am able.

-

- *5:01pm*
- *Craig A. Steffen*
- *Will do. I'll be calling from area code 937 when you see the caller ID.*

Immediately after I finish this exchange with Sherri, I start experiencing pain in my jaw. With all the stress in my life, I'm wondering if this isn't a symptom of a heart attack. Just my luck, I think. "You're closer than ever to getting some answers about your original family and you're going to drop dead before the scheduled call; perfect." But once I get hungry I realize that it's not a heart attack but a tooth ache. Over the next few days it gets worse and worse and I end up with an "emergency" visit to the dentist who drills through a 12 year old crown and drains some nastiness out of a molar. Lovely. My dentist scribbles a couple of prescriptions and I head off to the pharmacy to get them filled.

Is this going to be a metaphor for my re-introduction into the original family? "Like pulling teeth … just what I need," I think.

Each year since our honeymoon in 1984, Cindy and I have endeavored to watch as many of the Oscar nominated films as possible. That year, 1984, the Academy Awards show was in April, but lately it has been much earlier. This year it's on February 26. In addition to trying to spend time together for Valentine's Day, we're in full blown movie going mode. This week we finished up with *Albert Nobbs*, a film for which Glenn Close and Janet McTeer are both nominated for an Oscar. I sat through the film in agony, with a cold can of pop pressed to my jaw to help with the pain.

All the movie going has been a nice distraction to help pass the time as I await the weekend to call Sherri. I'm really nervous.

On Sunday, February 19, Cindy returned home from our farm in southern Ohio and I called Sherri in the afternoon. The first shot at it got me her voice mail and I left a message. She called me back about an hour later and, initially, I found myself shaky and thick-tongued trying to communicate with her. Anyone who knows me realizes what a rare condition this would be for me. This is an excerpt from my journal about that initial conversation:

We had a 45 minute chat. She was warm, friendly and open. She is 58, 14 years younger than my biological Mom, her sister Beverly. She says she only remembers meeting Beverly twice, so she doesn't have much memory of her. Sherri would have been only two years old when Beverly got married at age 16 and moved out. Sherri was only seven when Beverly left Iowa (and her first three kids) forever.

Sherri told me that her parents are both dead now, her dad in 1992 and her mom in 2008. Robbie died of lung cancer and Dorothy of Alzheimer's. Sherri's older sisters, Barb, (a year older than Beverly) and Rosi (7 years younger than Beverly and 7 years older than Sherri) are both still living. Rosi lives in the area near Sherri and Barb lives in Missouri.

We talked about us kids and we filled in some blanks for each other. She said she met Theresa in 1976 and Ricky sometime in the late 70's when he lived with her folks a while. Grandpa Robbie got Ricky a job and a car and then Grandpa believed Ricky stole from them and they kicked him out. That broke their hearts according to Sherri.

We talked about my suspicions that Alvin Shepherd is not my biological dad. That seemed surprising to her. But she quickly understood when I explained my reasons. She's going to talk with Barb about it since Beverly and Barb were the closest relationally and in age.

Sherri and I seem to hit it off pretty well given it is the first time we've talked to one another in 50 years. In some ways we are alike, outgoing and talkative. She's the first person I've talked to from my original family who isn't extremely introverted. That is refreshing. She promises to send some photos and claims to want to talk again soon. That would be nice, but I have to say I'm really guarding against expecting too much.

Cindy and I talk at length after my call with Sherri. Cindy's great at helping me process the information and my emotions. I feel numb and exhausted and my brain feels like it's plugged into an electrical outlet.

Have I introduced a rift into the time-space continuum?

Murder 1

Since my telephone call with Aunt Sherri, tidbits of information about my original family have become like sugar cubes laced with LSD for me. Each time I take one of these nuggets in, it sets my mind ablaze with questions and psychedelic imagination. Once these questions set root in my mind, I simply MUST get to work to find new morsels to repeat the high.

On an August afternoon, I came home from work early, being too distracted by curiosity to be productive on behalf of my client. Cindy was out running errands, so I had solitary time available to dig for information. I'd discovered a newspaper archive website and I wanted desperately to explore it, mining for clues to the mystery of my life. I typed in a flurry of keywords and came up empty time after time. I felt like a junkie must feel ransacking dresser drawers looking for a long forgotten fix. But finally I had a hit on my mother's married name, "Goodenough," that had a date and location stamp that looked promising. I clicked, wondering what might lie at the base of this link. Here's what I found:

THE SHERIDAN SUN

Willamina Tavern Killing Nets First Degree Murder Count Against Area Man

A 55-year old McMinnville man remained in Yamhill County Jail Yesterday morning on a charge of first degree murder.

Clarence Goodenough, manager of Eola Village, was charged with the murder of his wife, Beverly, 25, in a Willamina tavern late Saturday night.

Goodenough was arraigned in Yamhill County District Court Monday morning before Judge Carl G. Stanley, Linn County, acting in the absence of Judge Kurt Rossman.

According to Sheriff's officers, Mrs. Goodenough was in the Willamina tavern visiting a friend who worked there as a bar maid.

Goodenough came in and they talked 10 or 15 minutes and he then left. According to witnesses at the scene, Goodenough returned a short time later, talked to his wife for a few seconds, and then shot her with a .25 caliber pistol.

The witnesses told Sheriff's officers that there were two shots. The first hit Mrs. Goodenough and the second, believed to have been fired accidentally, went wild.

Officers said the tavern was nearly full at the time of the shooting.

The officers reported that Goodenough then apparently fled from the tavern and drove at high speed to McMinnville where he walked into the Sheriff's office and handed the gun to Deputy James McBride.

The shooting is believed to have occurred about 11:15 p.m. Saturday. Goodenough arrived at the Sheriff's office about 11:30 p.m.

No exact reason was given for the shooting. The Goodenoughs were not living together at the time. Mrs. Goodenough had filed a divorce action.

Goodenough was living at Eola Village at the time of the shooting and Mrs. Goodenough was living in a trailer near Amity.

The couple had two children and Goodenough had six children by a former wife.

Five of the children are married and not living at home. One, a 15-month old boy, was living in Amity with Mrs. Goodenough. A 3-year old girl was with relatives in Silverton and an 18-year old girl, a daughter by another marriage, was living with Goodenough at Eola Village.

This single article, a veritable speck in the digital universe of the Internet, hidden in plain sight, contained more information about the murder of my mother, than I had been able to collect in a lifetime from those who knew her.

Sitting in my office staring at the computer screen and reading the words over and over again, seeking comprehension, my hands trembled, my eyes filled with tears and I was overcome with a sense of loneliness unlike any I'd ever experienced. How could this act of senseless rage be allowed to happen? Who was this person Beverly had gone to the tavern to meet? Were they male or female? If the bar was full, why couldn't someone have stopped this person bent on violence? What drove Beverly to estrangement in the first place? What pain was she feeling even before this man arrived at the tavern door and before he returned with a pistol in his hand and evil on his mind? How could the cold, nameless, faceless Internet know more about my mother's murder than her son did?

So many questions. So many miles and years between me and the answers. I wondered if any of the witnesses in the "tavern [that] was nearly full at the time of the shooting" were still alive? If they were alive, would their memories of the event be intact and accurate? If intact, how would I find these folks to inquire? The Internet is ever so useful for endeavors such as these, but even the Internet can't help you find someone who has married and changed her name. I was guessing several of these folks fit that description.

Moms

I'm not really given to vivid dreams. It's a pretty rare event when I actually remember my dreams for more than a few fleeting moments after I awake. So the fact that I'm about to share another dream with you is more remarkable than it probably seems.

I went to bed the night of that first-ever phone call with Sherri and awoke the next morning with a startlingly vivid dream memory. This is how I recalled it in my journal later that same day:

I had an interesting dream last night. I dreamt Mom – Flora Steffen – was sitting in a chair and I was sitting on the floor in front of her. We were having a normal conversation – but without any notable emotions. At the end of the dream, I moved toward her to kiss her, but there was something invisible that hindered me from getting to her for what seemed like a long time. Finally, I got to her and kissed her on the cheek and the dream ended.

Cindy and I talked about the dream and what it might mean. Certainly all this recent talk and angst about "mom" (meaning biological Mom Beverly) had likely triggered this dream. But since Flora is the only mother figure I have any memories of, it is understandable that it is her image that I saw in my dream. Certainly there are obvious explanations for the invisible force that kept (or is keeping) me from emotional attachment to my mother – regardless of whether that mother is Flora or Beverly. With my original mother, the fact that I have no memory of her and the fact that she has been dead for over 45 years would certainly explain the "invisible force." With Flora, we had difficulty connecting emotionally. She simply wasn't an overtly warm person. She was kind and responsible and cared for my needs, but warmth, depth and connection were not part of the relationship in either direction. In fact, I don't recall her ever telling me that she loved me. And I don't recall her ever initiating a hug. Conversely, I don't think I ever told her that I loved her either. But we did, and we both knew it – at least in our heads.

Like Dad Steffen, Mom Steffen went through the Great Depression as a young girl. Mom was born in 1916 in Larkhall, Scotland and immigrated to South Central Iowa with her parents and five siblings in the early 1920's – Mom was six years old at the time. Mom's father and her older brothers worked in the coal mines near Chariton, Iowa and when the depression hit, it was devastating to these little "black-collar" towns. All the kids got jobs doing something – regardless of their age. All the money made was brought home and put in a communal till. Every Saturday they would go to the store and purchase a bit of meat, and it was the only protein they'd have all week. It was a desperate existence.

Mom once told me about the time that the family dog got pregnant and was having puppies. Clearly there was no money to care for a litter of puppies – they were simply seen as consumers of vital resources. So my mother and her mother sat with the dog during the birthing process and caught each little life as it birthed into the world and immediately drowned it in a bucket of water.

Little wonder that soft, warm maternal emotions were in short supply with Mom Steffen.

So the dream could certainly have been about Mom Steffen, but given all the proximal emotion surrounding reconnecting with my original family, it seems reasonable to assume that it was at least as much about Beverly as Flora.

Though I've collected a few photographs over the years of my pre-adoption life, I don't have a single photo of Beverly and me together.

As a result of that void, I wonder how warm she actually was toward me. Why did she leave after I was born? Did she feel trapped? Were there marital problems? Post-partum depression? Was she overwhelmed with being a teenager with three kids all under three years old at the time of my birth? Who wouldn't be?

I really don't know, tangibly, how either of my mothers regarded me. Intellectually, but not emotionally, I know that Mom Steffen loved me. But I don't know, and probably never will know, what Beverly may have felt about me. Perhaps it is this lack of emotional bridge that is the invisible force that keeps me from being able to approach my mother figures in the dream?

But equally important in this dream, I think, is that I was trying to *kiss* my mother figure. Something I never did in their lifetimes. Something they may not have done with me either. Deep within me there is a desire to have this kind of emotional connection to my mothers. Deep within me lays a primal need to get out of my head and into my heart with regard to the two moms in my life. And, as you'll learn, deep within me is the desire to have this same metamorphosis with respect to all my family relationships.

Searching

In September of last year I decided to drive to Iowa and do some research; there is just so much I don't know about Beverly, her upbringing, maturation, marriage and early adulthood. Perhaps there are clues to be found in libraries, historical societies, newspaper offices and by finding and talking with her friends and family.

And then there is this nagging suspicion that Alvin Shepherd may not be my biological father. I really had nothing on which to base this suspicion other than empirical observations and a gut-level hunch. But even though my sister hadn't talked to me since my adoptive father's death, I thought it was time to try to persuade her to provide a DNA sample to answer this question once and for all.

After a 10-hour drive, my first stop was at the courthouse in Marshalltown, the mid-sized Iowa town where I was born in June of 1960. It has a population of only 27,000, but for Iowa that makes it the 17th largest town in the state. By comparison, the 17th largest city in Ohio has a population about double that of Marshalltown.

I ascended the ancient stone staircase in search of birth records for me and my siblings. I knew there was little chance that I'd be able to find them, since these records were sealed at the time of our adoption, but I was compelled to at least inquire. I bounced around the building and finally found the records office. The young woman I spoke to was quite helpful and led me to a room full of racks, and the racks were full of oversized books that were best handled by two people at a time. We searched these books together for each of Beverly's Iowa-born children's birthdates. There was nothing for

Theresa – she had always told me she was born in Des Moines, so I didn't expect to find her here. Then there was Ricky's birthdate – we found the spot where he should have been on January 1, 1959 – but in that spot was a piece of paper taped over the original entry with the word "SEALED" and a legal instruction not to remove the piece of paper under penalty of law. It seemed so odd that a thin piece of paper separated me from the truth of his birth – as if a mere piece of paper was intended to hide the reality of his birth from the outside world forever. It was as if what happened in this county on the first day of 1959 had retroactively been deemed NOT to have happened. We found the same paper, tape and legalese in the place of my birth record as well.

It seemed to me like such a scam. Truth lay just on the other side of that yellowed paper mask. If one held the page up to the light, the truth could, no doubt, still be read. Maybe the precise reason the books were so large was to prevent curious folks like me from doing just that. Standing there with my hand on the page, I was living, breathing, three-dimensional proof that life had come into the world on June 26, 1960. But so far as Marshall County and the State of Iowa were concerned, no such event could be confirmed. Were these secrets so dark or so dangerous? Could the hubris of the government be so great as to think that simple paper and tape could become an animated sentry by merely placing a few magic words upon it? How is it that this imaginary sentry had power to obliterate past truth for all these fifty years?

Everything in me wanted to just tear the paper patch from the book and let the light of day illuminate the truth written beneath. By doing so, I felt at that moment that I would become more legitimate by the action. Perhaps, like Pinocchio, I thought then I would become a "real boy." But, with deep sorrow, I admit that I conformed to the social norm of law abidance. I left the mask in place upon the book and perhaps condemned myself to wear one too; maybe forever.

116

Before leaving the courthouse, I asked for directions to the library. I was hoping to find yearbooks from the Clemons School. I was able to find out that the last class to graduate from Clemons was the class of 1962. After that year, the school had been absorbed by the West Marshall school system. But the library had no yearbooks. They suggested that I try the historical society and the school office to see if yearbooks might exist there.

An hour flipping through dozens of books about regional history, founding families and their still resident progeny revealed nothing of personal interest about my own family. Whatever my biological families may have been like, they didn't appear to have figured prominently in the development or history of the region.

The historical society also pointed me to West Marshall Schools, as well as a quaint little library, both located in State Center.

I didn't have any trouble finding the little town of State Center which has a population of less than 1500 folks. Even though the school is away from the commercial center of the town, I found it without difficulty. By this time it was late in the afternoon, and classes had been dismissed for the day. I parked and walked into the school's main entrance and wandered down the halls with none of the students or adults paying any attention to my presence. I learned that it was Homecoming weekend which explained what seemed like unusual hustle and bustle for this late in the day.

My relative "invisibility" made me keenly aware of how most of Iowa can be a throw-back to a simpler time, conjecturing that I could never have gotten into a school in Ohio without encountering security, or at least scrutiny. I wondered what film might be showing at the local theatre, if there was one. A first run of *American Graffiti* or *Rocky* or *Star Wars* seemed entirely plausible.

The office person didn't know anything about yearbooks older than the age of the school's campus itself which, according to the cornerstone to the right of the entrance, was built in 1968. That certainly precluded the ones I was looking for from the mid to late 1950s featuring Beverly and her future class of 1958. The office person gave me the name and phone number of the person who used to take care of archives at the School.

"She might be hard to get hold of, and she might not know anything but you can give her a call." She offered.

"Hmm, sounds promising," I thought, as my sarcasm filter failed.

I took the scrap of paper with the name and number of the closest thing the school had to an archive expert and headed off to the Gutekunst library. Maybe they'd have something helpful.

Gutekunst was located in a 1920s vintage historic house in a residential part of State Center. The library, named for its original owners who bequeathed it to the city in their will, has a quaint collection of items of regional interest.

Eight or ten pairs of eyes turned to me as I entered the foyer and scanned for visual cues as to protocol and location of the type of items I sought. By the expressions on their faces, everyone was immediately aware that I was "not from around here."

Upon making eye contact with the person most likely to be working here, I presented my question.

"Hi, my mother grew up in this area and went to high school in Clemons before that school closed. She was in the class of 1958. I'm looking for information from Clemons High School from that era; yearbooks, school newspapers, photographs, whatever you might have."

The woman listened intently, quickly answering my question with her facial expressions even before she spoke a word. "I really don't think we have anything from those years, but I'm happy to take you upstairs and show you where we have a partial collection of yearbooks from schools that are now a part of the West Marshall system."

With that, she turned and proceeded behind the counter and up the stairs, past a bathroom with antique fixtures and into a small room on the second floor. It was likely once a bedroom for one of the Gutekunst family, and was now outfitted with a long, folding school table and a few chairs with book shelves along the walls. There were a couple of dozen school yearbooks organized together by year on two shelves knee-high. A quick look didn't reveal anything from Clemons. I thought it was possible that Beverly may have attended more than one school over the years, but having no idea what schools those might be, I pulled yearbooks from 1950 to 1955 to see if she might be in yearbooks from any of the surrounding towns.

I hoped to discover one of two things from this exercise. First, I wanted to learn the names of students in her class in hopes of locating some of them in the region. If I could find some of them, I could arrange to meet those who were interested in talking and perhaps learn more about Beverly's life in her formative years. I thought this might be insightful as I tried to piece together the fragments I was learning of her later life.

Second, I wondered if I might find a picture of one of Beverly's male classmates (or teachers) who might look surprisingly like me. This kind of discovery would provide some clues about my own paternity, not to mention illuminate Beverly's lifestyle.

But after a couple of hours flipping through book after book, I found nothing particularly relevant. So I put the books back in their places and reversed course back through the stares of patrons gawking at me, as if I had floppy-ears and a tail.

I left the library and headed to Ames to check into a hotel for the night. I had arranged to meet Beverly's sister Sherri and her husband Steve for dinner at a local BBQ place, Hickory Park, that Sherri said was popular for locals and travelers alike. I arrived early and was surprised by the crowd of folks awaiting a table. I went in and got on the waiting list and went outside to check email on my phone and await meeting Beverly's sister for the first time since I was about two years old. I know that I had met her previously because Sherri had sent me a copy of a photo that showed Theresa, Ricky, Sherri and me all together. Given my age in the photo, the shot must have been taken just weeks before Beverly "stole the family car and disappeared." When Sherri and Steve arrived, we recognized each other from the photos we'd exchanged earlier in the year and from the resemblance to Beverly that we both share. Our first encounter was warm and enthusiastic with hugs, smiles and explorations of our full-faced, high-cheeked, cherubic countenances that so reminded us both of the sister and mom we'd known only from old pictures.

Sherri was only two when Beverly married Alvin in 1957. Beverly never lived at home again after that. When Beverly left Iowa without us kids in 1962, Sherri would not yet have turned eight years old. At that age, I'm guessing that Beverly seemed to Sherri more like a friend of the family or an aunt, than a big sister. In all of our phone conversations, Sherri had repeatedly mentioned that she had very few personal memories of Beverly, having "only seen her a few

times in my life."

With Sherri's folks both having passed away by this time, the real keeper of my maternal, biological family history was Sherri's oldest sister, Barbara. She was only 14 months older than Beverly and apparently the two of them had been extremely close as they grew up. There is even one photograph of the two of them dressed alike, as if they were twins.

Throughout my several phone calls and emails with Sherri during the year since we'd made first contact, most of my questions were left unanswered with an explanation like, "I'm really sorry, I just don't know. I was so young when Beverly left I just don't have many memories," Sherri would say. And then she'd follow that statement with the declaration, "But Barb would know."

Unfortunately, Barb was hesitant to open lines of communication with me. Sherri explained that "Barb and Bev were so close that Beverly leaving and her eventual death were just devastating to her. She's just not sure she can re-open that painful chapter of her life."

And though I'm longing for answers to my own past, I have made every attempt not to allow my desire for information to bring pain to anyone else, so I respect Barb's desire not to talk.

There is another sister, Rosi, who also lives in central Iowa. She is seven years younger than Barb and seven years older than Sherri. But apparently she keeps to herself and has very little contact with her siblings, even though Sherri tells me that she and Barb both desire a closer relationship with her.

So, whatever I will learn about the maternal, biological side of my own past will have to come through Sherri.

As I sat in Hickory Park with Sherri and Steve, I was overwhelmed with gratitude that they were so open to me and willing to answer whatever questions they could. Secretly I was also grateful that we seemed to have some things in common – not the least of which were being extroverted and having a sense of humor.

We arrived at Hickory Park around 5:30 in hopes of beating the crowd – which we failed to do. But we avoided the crowds when we departed since we closed down the joint. In between were a whole lot of words as we snapped topics of conversation before one another as if slapping cards on a black jack table. It was a wonderful evening of discovery of past events and present personalities; of a painful history and a grateful now.

When the night was over, Aunt Sherri gave me an envelope full of dozens of old pictures. Most were of Beverly growing up and her relatives. I had brought a high-speed scanner with me from Ohio, so I took the pictures back to my hotel room and scanned them into my computer. Many of the pictures had writing on the back, so I scanned both sides of each picture to capture whatever identifying remarks might exist.

There was a beautiful 8x10 Portrait of Beverly all dressed up sporting a pearl necklace. As I turned the picture over to place it in the scanner, I noticed a faint, faded stamp on the back. It was from a photography studio – in Amarillo, Texas.

Bingo. So when Beverly left Iowa, she had gone to Texas. I had no idea why she'd have gone to Texas, but here was proof that she'd been there. Something tells me her presence there has something to do with whomever she might have been with.

Ignored

By the summer of 1962 Beverly had become restless. Or perhaps she'd been restless for a long time and found this particular summer night in June to be opportune enough to act. It seems that she had met a guy named Jack Cox Hiner. How or where I do not yet know. Jack was four years older than Beverly, who was not quite 22 at the time. Those who knew Jack describe him as "a drunk," and "couldn't keep a job," and "irresponsible." Not exactly the traits one ought to look for in a partner, but there it is.

At the time Beverly met Jack, she was still very much married to Alvin. I've not been able to piece together Alvin's employment record in those early years of their marriage, but it doesn't appear to have been particularly stable either. He seemed to be able to get jobs fairly readily, but keeping them appears to have been quite another thing. They lived in Story County, Iowa when they met in the town of Collins and married. But a few months later they were near Des Moines when Theresa was born. By the time Ricky was born they were in Marshall County. When I was conceived they were living near Renwick, Iowa, but by the time I was born they were back in Marshall County. And when Beverly and Jack "stole the family car and disappeared," Beverly and Alvin were back near Des Moines. That's a lot of moving around in five years.

It's a mystery to me why Beverly and Alvin's families were so passive at this time. Beverly had broken the law by lying about her age on her Marriage License and as a result was literally never legally married. Yet there's no record that Beverly's folks ever tried to bring these legal facts before the courts. They just let it happen.

Five years later, Beverly and Jack steal a car and disappear. Yet, again, there's no record that anyone ever called the police to report a missing person or a stolen car. How did anyone know that she hadn't been abducted or murdered – or probed by aliens for that matter? Whatever was going on – and they all claim to have had no idea what – both families seemed content to just let it happen. I find that VERY odd and disturbing.

Notable Irish/English Quaker and Parliamentarian Edmund Burke famously said, "All that is necessary for evil to prosper is for good men to do nothing." So it is.

Broken

❦

Many years ago, in the late 1980s, my wife Cindy and I had stopped in to see my maternal grandparents in Marshalltown, Iowa. Cindy had never met them and I had met them only that one time back in 1975. It was a brief visit of an hour or so at their home, as we were on our way to the southwestern part of the state to visit my adoptive parents.

I recall sitting in their modest ranch home in a tiny housing development. They were telling me their version of the story about my mother's "wild side." They explained why they had not taken in their daughter's three children when she left the state abruptly in 1962 just prior to her 22nd birthday – leaving behind all three of those small children, each of whom was under 5 years of age. It involved something about an illness Grandma Robbie had in that timeframe, having two of their own children still at home and being "too-old" to raise little kids again. It was a blur of information spoken so matter-of-factly that it seemed to refer to some other family and some other kid – not my family and me.

The whole awkward scene was punctuated by Grandma Robbie slipping into another room and returning with a box of photographs of me and my sister Theresa and brother Ricky. Here were two virtual strangers, nice as they were trying to be, who possessed photographs of me which I had never before seen. It felt as though I'd been caught by an interstate spy ring that was showing me clandestine photographic proof of some mysterious investigated offense.

The next week, after Cindy and I returned home to Ohio, I had a vivid, shout-in-my-sleep nightmare that woke Cindy with a start. Later, she informed me that I had been loudly screaming, "It's broken. It's broken. OH, NO it's broken" When she asked me, with great concern while I still slept, "What's broken?" I sat up on one elbow, looked at her with eyes open, and answered, "The family. It's all BROKEN." A few minutes after this sleep-talking dialog I woke up. Cindy and I sat in bed for a long time and we alternately talked and wept about my broken life.

Faultline

Early in our marriage, Cindy and I had a dog, named Timber, who ran off with a mutt from up the street. The neighbor's dog came back, but our beautiful Shepherd pup never did. We anguished over this loss for months, filled with sleepless nights. We put up signs, went door to door, and drove the roads evenings after dinner. We never found a trace of Timber, nor found a person who had a clue what had happened to her. Did she get hit by a car? Did she step in a hunter's leg-trap? Had she been shot while hassling a neighbor's cattle?

The pain of that loss still reaches me today as I write about it. I've concluded over the years that it wasn't so much the losing of a beloved pet (probably the smartest dog that ever lived) that tortured our minds so much – it was not knowing *what* happened.

In all of my investigation, research and interviews I've never found anyone who can tell me what happened in my original family. For all of the big questions, I have no answers. And it's the not knowing that is the ever present torment.

I've literally never told anyone this, but even now, I have to confess to feeling like my mother's disappearance was my fault.

Of course, I have no memories of her at all, much less her disappearance – I wasn't even two when it happened. But she gave birth to Theresa in 1957, and she didn't leave. She gave birth to Ricky in 1959, and she didn't leave. She gave birth to Jackie in 1963, and she didn't leave. Then she gave birth to her last child, Steven in 1965

127

— and when she did leave her husband almost exactly a year after this last birth, she took her children with her.

But she gave birth to me in June, 1960, and just four days before my second birthday she disappeared. And when she did leave, she left her children behind and vanished for over two years. No one had a clue where she'd gone. All the paperwork from that time states that her "whereabouts are unknown." She never saw me or Theresa again after that June day in 1962, when "she stole the family car and disappeared."

Eventually Beverly came back to Iowa, but it wasn't for me. The official adoption documents from the State of Iowa indicate that Beverly and her folks were notified in September of 1964 that Theresa and I were to be officially adopted by the Steffens later that month — IF she did not appear to protest that decision. She did not. Her parents did not. But a month *after* the adoption, already pregnant with her last child, she did return — to get Ricky.

Was it simply a matter of slow communications back in the day that prevented her from arriving in time? Or did she wait until I had been removed from the scene before she stepped in to rescue Ricky?

I wish there was a diary that Beverly left behind that explained the trouble in her life and declared her love for us kids. But there isn't. I wish that one of her sisters could remember a phone call that filled in the blanks and made sense of her actions. But they don't. I wish there was a long forgotten letter in a box retrieved from an attic that provided the missing puzzle pieces. But there is no attic, no box, no letter.

I'm left to the anguish of not knowing.

Of all the photos I've been able to find from about a dozen of her family and friends over the years, there is not a single photo of

Beverly with me. There are photos of her with every one of her four other children – but none with me. Is this simply the bad luck-of-the-draw? Is this an unfortunate coincidence, all such photographs having been ill-fatedly destroyed?

Or perhaps there never were any photos of Beverly and me. Maybe I was the final bar in the prison that was being constructed around her. Maybe I was a problem child who would never let her rest. Maybe with my birth came an acute case of post-partum depression. Or maybe she could never look at my blond hair and blue eyes without feeling I did not belong. Was there shame for a forbidden act that created me? Perhaps she saw in my face the image of the man with whom she had an affair – if that is what it was. Maybe she was raped, and could never speak of the atrocity of that kind of humiliation; my life an ever present reminder? Maybe her pregnancy was the consequence of poverty – paying a bill with the only "currency" she had that an immoral creditor might want?

Or worse, maybe all the photos were destroyed on purpose because of what they represented?

In all these scenarios, I am the causal centerpiece for her departure. And as the causal centerpiece, it is I that has set into motion the decisions and events that would soon lead to her disappearance.

In my heart of hearts, I have never stopped wondering if I am responsible for my mother's pain and disappearance. And if that is true then, indirectly, I'm also responsible for the pain, suffering of my entire biological family.

It's the not knowing that creates the torture.

And the more I dig for information, the more manic I become that there are no answers to be found. In that vacuum, my self-ascribed guilt grows in its probability.

For decades I have done pastoral counseling in churches I've been a part of. In my pastoral role, if someone were to share with me this story and the kind of self-ascribed guilt I've confessed to you, I'd assure them that it's not their fault. I might even queue up that classic film clip from *Good Will Hunting* where Robin Williams tells Matt Damon over and over again, "It's not your fault. Look at me son; it's not your fault. It's not your fault. It's not your fault. It's not your fault. It's not your fault. It's not your fault. It's not your fault. It's not your fault. It's NOT your fault." And in making these repetitive assertions, I'd be absolutely convinced that I was correct – "It's not your fault." I'd be compassionate and resolute in my desire for the truth of my declaratives to sink in and be a healing balm to that person's broken and mistaken heart.

My head fully understands. But as crazy as it sounds, that a not-yet-two-year-old could be responsible in any way for the demise of a whole family, my heart has not yet been able to receive the balm of truth that Robin Williams offered in that epic movie scene.

Instead, I feel much more like the orphaned Dakota Fanning character in *The Secret Life of Bees* when, toward the end of the film, she finally confesses to Queen Latifah that she killed her own mother. And in that moment the inconsolable Fanning makes the heart-wrenching profession, choking it out through her sobs, "I'm unlovable."

I cannot watch that scene without tears streaming down my face and my heart literally aching inside of me. And I can't think of better words to offer her than the ones that Queen Latifah whispers while stroking Fanning's hair. "You listen to me now; that's a terrible, terrible thing for you to live with. But you're not unlovable, child. There's love all around you."

And, on a good day, I can say that there is for me too.

Cataclysm

The apartment above the Maxwell, Iowa tavern is bustling on Mother's Day Sunday, 1966. Sherri and her dad are busily brushing teeth and getting dressed for a lunch out, in honor of Dorothy, a mom four times over. Sherri is the only one of the girls still at home. Two of her sisters, Barb and Beverly, more than 14 years older, are no doubt celebrating with their own children miles and states away, respectively. Sherri's other sister, Rosi, is 19, married and newly pregnant, starting her own life just down the road.

"Sherri, go get your shoes on, we need to get going." Her dad instructs. "They're over by the door where you left them."

Twelve-year-old Sherri is excited. Being part of a family that owns a tavern doesn't leave much time for fun or going out. Usually their only day off, Sunday, is filled with cleaning the tavern downstairs and maybe sharing a pizza together in a dimly lit booth at the back. Sherri is thrilled to get a reprieve from emptying and wiping dozens of "icky" ashtrays.

Sherri can hear her parents talking in the back bedroom as she sits on the floor in her Easter dress, putting on her shoes. Her attention piques when she is sure she hears something from downstairs. Someone is knocking – loudly.

"It's Sunday, moooron; we're cloooosed." Sherri shouts.

But the pounding on the door continues, and now she can hear that each burst of knocking is followed by a loud voice that she cannot decipher.

"DAAAAD, someone's knocking downstairs," Sherri projects to the back of the apartment.

"I'm getting dressed, Pudge, can you go see what they want?"

Sherri pulls on her other shiny black shoe and buckles the strap across her almost white stocking. She pops to her feet and scampers down the stairs at the back of the tavern as she's done a thousand times before. She sees a man looking dapper, dressed in a dark gray suit, complete with a tie and topped with a bowler hat, standing at the pane of glass in the battered, green wooden door. He does not see her, and the knocking continues.

It's a small town. Sherri recognizes this man as the county sheriff. He's been in the tavern before. Several months ago, he stopped in when the town drunk was getting too rowdy and his ex-wife called the sheriff from the pay phone at the back of the tavern – just to piss him off.

Sherri's cute, chubby-cheek smile appears in the glass as she unlocks the front door and lets the sheriff in. "Hi, Mr. Sheriff."

"Isyourdadaround?"

"He's upstairs getting dressed. We're taking Mom out for lunch at OJ's for Mother's Day. Then we're going shopping at Woolworth's with my friend Deb, we're in a go-go together."

"I need you to go get him."

Sherri waits for an explanation that does not come.

"Right now," the sheriff says.

"Ok. Wait here. I'll be right back."

Sherri skips back up the stairs to the apartment.

A few minutes later Sherri and her dad clump noisily down the bare wooden risers.

"Don't run in your good shoes, Sherri."

Sherri hits the stairs at twice the rate of her 47-year-old father.

Entering the dark entry at the bottom of the stairs, Sherri's dad finds the light switch to add illumination. The effect is barely noticeable.

"Can I get you a beer, sheriff?"

Robbie always felt that not offering a person a beer was about as rude as one human being could be to another – regardless of the day, hour or audience.

"No thank you, Robbie. I need to talk to you about something … well … something important."

"Alright. It must be pretty important to get you out of bed on a Sunday morning, and in your Sunday-go-to-meetin' clothes. What is it?"

"Umm, well, it might be better if we talk alone." The sheriff glances sideways at Sherri.

"Ok, Sherri, go on back upstairs and help your mother. We'll be ready to go in a few minutes."

Sherri sulks, turns, and heads back toward the stairs in slow motion. Sherri mumbles, "I never get to be around for the excitement."

The stairwell is awkwardly silent as the two men wait for Sherri to complete her assent up the stairs, where she hides silently to listen. There is a cool, spring breeze slipping through the crack in the door, which did not fully latch behind the sheriff. The uncharacteristic circulation orchestrates an unpleasant harmony of grease, beer spills, cigarette ash, and body odor from the tavern.

The footsteps on the stairs end and the gaze of the two men again meet.

"Sir, do you have a daughter named Beverly Kay who lives in Oregon?"

"Yeah ... she's the black sheep of the family. She disappeared four years ago. She stole the family car, left her husband and kids, and I don't know where she is. Why, what has she done this time?"

"Well, sir, I got a call this morning from the sheriff in McMinnville, Oregon. He says that Beverly was ... he said that Beverly ... got shot last night."

"I'm sorry, sir, but she's dead."

The blood drains from Robbie's face. His eyes grow glassy and stare off to nothing in particular. His bottom lip trembles, as if plugged into AC current. The hum of the beer coolers, on the other side of the wall, seems to grow louder and push cogent thought from his head.

The two men stand stalk still with mouths agape, paralyzed – the father as a result of this devastating news, the sheriff, as if in freeze-frame, waiting for his reaction.

The pregnant silence is broken by the sound of a child's sobs from atop the stairs. Sherri and Beverly were not close as some sisters are. Beverly had married when Sherri was just two. She had left the state permanently when Sherri was eight. But at this moment, the news penetrates her eavesdropping soul like an errant tomahawk throw.

There is no invention capable of calculating time in moments like these. Minutes, days, or alternate lifetimes are equally plausible. At some point, Robbie's murky brain forms words again. Questions are asked, assurances sought, answers and information given. None of it remembered.

The sheriff turns and leaves, the door clicks shut and echoes thru the hollow stairwell. Robbie does not now remember why he is alone. Where did the sheriff go? Were they done talking?

As if by teleportation, Sherri's dad finds himself upstairs. Sherri sits on the kitchen floor by the stairs cross-legged like the wooden Indian at the Woolworth's in Marshalltown. She is afraid to make eye contact with the man she does not now recognize. He shuffles past her, though his legs do not seem to move.

Sherri's mother appears in the bedroom doorway, pretty and primped for her special day. Her eyes are locked onto the face of the man she has been with for over 30 years. She has never seen him like this ever before.

"What is it, Robbie? Who was that downstairs? What did they want?" Dorothy probes. "Robbie? … What has happened?"

Slowly Robbie's eyes retract from their distant gaze and focus aperture onto his wife's worried green eyes.

"They said … that she's … it was the sheriff. They said that she's … dead … that she got shot … last night … they got a call from Oregon this morning … Beverly … she got murdered last night."

For a few seconds Dorothy freezes. The only movement in her body comes from eyes desperately searching the faces of her husband and little Sherri, still motionless in her pretty little dress, hair done-up so nice. She finds in those faces no consolation. She finds nothing but confirmation that these cryptic words are true and irreversible.

Like a soulless body, she turns and retreats to the bedroom from whence she has come. She collapses on the bed as if she herself has been shot. The screams and sobs that erupt from deep within her reveal years of pent up love, anguish and longing for her second-born daughter. The pillows into which she screams are utterly inadequate to contain her heartache.

The grief-stricken mother, the disbelieving father and the terrified sister remain encapsulated in this cloud of audible anguish, feeling in their burning chests the unbearable weight of the awful news. It is a kind of hell.

A moment or an eternity passes.

Robbie enters the bedroom and sits on the end of the bed, mute and numb.

Dorothy unfolds from her contorted position and faces him. "How can you be so DAMNED cold and quiet? This is YOUR fault – you unforgiving bastard. All that girl EVER wanted was her father's love. She just wanted you to SEE her, to LOVE her for who she is. But she was NEVER good enough for you. She wasn't the SON you wanted, so you wouldn't let her be your DAUGHTER either. And now she's DEAD!"

"She came here last year and got Ricky. I met her husband. He's older than YOU. He's an old broken-down man with a heart condition. Don't you SEE it? She just wants a FATHER in her life. She's been looking for someone to replace the father who disowned her; the father who couldn't forgive her; the father that wouldn't even take her collect phone calls." Dorothy accused.

"She came to see you, you know. She walked right into the tavern last year with Sherri and bought a six-pack. You didn't even say hello. You didn't act like you even knew her. You just held onto that

136

damned proud grudge like YOUR shit don't stink, took her money and watched her walk right outta here. You broke her heart … again. She cried when she told me you didn't recognize her. But I knew better. A man recognizes his own daughter – you KNEW it was her, but you were just too damned cold and stubborn to even let her know you saw her. I hate you. I hate you for killing her. I HATE you!"

Robbie never turns his head to look at her. He stares forward into the baseboard like a man receiving the pronouncement of his own death sentence.

Sherri rises in one motion from her sitting position as a balloon suddenly untethered. She floats down the staircase, enters the tavern without a sound and robotically moves from table to table – dutifully emptying and wiping each ashtray.

Outrage

A typical workday finds me leaving my home office and traveling to a client location to work from there at an office the client provides. I usually make time to slip out and go somewhere for lunch; it gives me a chance to disengage for a few minutes, and I like to read the news and sports of the day to clear my head. On Wednesday February 13, my niece Kerri's birthday, I found myself awaiting a Cobb Salad at Bob Evans when I noticed on my iPhone a notification that I had an email. Upon checking, I found an email from the Polk County, Oregon Records office – with an attachment.

Since I began this research, I've been looking for the Sheriff's report of their investigation of my mother's murder. Dozens of inquiries back and forth to a variety of destinations in Oregon has gotten me exactly nothing. To date, no one has been able to find these records – even though I'm told that Oregon law requires these records to be retained for at least 75 years.

I wasn't really expecting anything from Polk County, at least not yet. I'd already corresponded with them several times and they had assured me that a thorough check of their records had revealed nothing regarding my mother's murder. They were confident that the records, if they exist at all, reside in Yamhill County. Conversely, the Yamhill County Records office still thinks that the records would be in Polk County. It's been a true run-around. All of my own research indicates that everything about Beverly's case took place in Yamhill County – that's why I initiated my search with them.

But during my last conversation with Melissa and Echo at Polk County, they told me that they had contacted the Oregon Department of Corrections, in hopes that these folks would have a copy of the Sheriff's records from the murderer's incarceration. They also told me not to get my hopes up, since records dating back nearly 50 years are notoriously missing, hard to find or vague. They expected it might take a month or two to hear back from them.

Just a week or so since my last conversation with Melissa, I find myself staring at an email from Echo.

Her email says:

I don't want to get your hopes up too much, but we could not let this request go. We contacted the Department of Corrections and they have a "very fat" file on Mr. Goodenough. We are hoping it will contain a copy of the original case file or other pertinent information to your request. We will be back in touch as soon as we get the records from DOC.

I have attached some of the information we were sent from DOC. I hope it will help you some, please contact us if you need anything else.

Have a great day,

With an elevated heart rate and shaky hands, I opened the attachment and began to read. My mind raced with questions. Would this contain clues to what was going on in Beverly's life in 1966? Would there be things written here that will penetrate my dispassionate armor and wound me? Would I be like Adam in the Garden of Eden, partaking of the Tree of Knowledge of Good and Evil, forever altering the course of my life? Scary as all these questions were, it never occurred to me not to read on.

The first page was mostly a form with names, dates, check marks and notations to "see attached."

Page two was much more informative. As I read it, I found that it fanned the spark of interest inside me into a raging fire of righteous indignation:

Re: Clarence Goodenough, No. 31465

Facts-history of the crime:

The defendant, a 55-year old man, was married to the decedent, a 26-year old female. The decedent, Beverly Goodenough, had begun divorce proceedings against the defendant and was living separate from him. On Thursday, May 5, the defendant purchased a pistol from a local sporting goods store. On Friday, May 6, the first hearing in divorce proceedings between the decedent and the defendant was set. However, the defendant's attorney was ill with the mumps and there was merely a default order entered involving temporary custody of the children. On Saturday evening the decedent went to a tavern in Willamina, apparently to meet a man with whom she had been going. The defendant came into the tavern shortly thereafter and engaged in an argument with the decedent. He thereafter left the tavern, went outside, returned a few minutes later and shot the decedent. One shot was fired into the decedent's heart; the gun apparently jammed, defendant then worked the mechanism by hand, firing another shot which went wild. Defendant thereafter left the tavern, drove toward McMinnville, being pursued by police at various times at speeds in excess of 100 miles an hour, avoided the police when he came into McMinnville, but then went to the sheriff's department and turned himself in.

In this moment, sitting alone in a crowded restaurant, ignoring a perfectly good Cobb Salad, I am no longer the dispassionate detective. I am the enraged son of a murdered mother.

So Beverly had left this guy and was apparently seeing someone new. Whatever their differences, they were substantial enough to file divorce proceedings. There is no record that Beverly ever divorced her first husband, so this is something new, more serious or more mature than what happened when she left Iowa at age 21. There is a conspicuous absence of detail about what her motivation in leaving her eventual killer may have been, or when that leaving actually took place. It certainly seems like this man's rage was fresh, either because she had left him recently, had gotten a new boyfriend recently, or because the court proceedings had made the whole ordeal more real or more final than it had seemed before.

The initial charge against the killer had been First Degree Murder, but it had later been pleaded down to Murder II. Yet right here in black and white is undeniable evidence that there was, in fact, premeditation. Two days in advance of the murder, he made a decision to go to a sporting goods store to purchase a gun. He wasn't there to buy a baseball glove so he could play catch with his children. There was no intention to purchase fishing gear so he could get out in the fresh Oregon air. He bought a gun two days before using it to commit a murder. How is this not premeditation?

It seems that he was stalking Beverly. How else could he arrive at the exact place that Beverly was, "shortly thereafter?" This tavern was at least 10 miles from where he was living at the time. So it was not likely a coincidence. How many times had he stalked her? Was she aware? Did she feel like a lover pursued, or was she afraid? And in this stalking endeavor, he had planned ahead so as to have the newly purchased gun with him.

The estranged couple argued publicly in front of a room full of people at the Willamina Tavern, so he had cast off all pretense of civility. I suspect he imagined that he could order her to leave with him, ruling over her as if she were his property or child. She was, after all, younger than some of his own children. He likely never truly saw her as the young, independent, adult woman that she was. Failing to control her in the way in which he'd become accustomed, he was enraged even further and stormed out to his car where he retrieved his premeditated tool of domination.

Given the time frame described, it appears he did not take a deep breath. It appears he did not stop to think, to reason, to ask himself even the most obvious of questions. He did not ponder the consequences of his primal intent nor contemplate a timeframe even five seconds into his future. He acted as an inhumane creature not accustomed to being told "NO." It was the height of narcissism with utter disregard for anyone, or anything but self. He sought to control with an iron fist and defiance of all authority but that of his own small, dictatorial, soulless frame.

There is no mention of further conversation between murderer and victim. He fired a shot from his cheap, malfunctioning gun, intended for this single usage. Before Beverly had a chance to move or defend herself, the bullet exploded in her heart. Though these documents don't say either way, I suspect he fired the shot from behind her, coward that he was, and that she never saw it coming.

But this was not a mere crime of passion. Not content with the first fatal shot, "he worked the mechanism" of his jammed gun in hopes of firing it again. These seem to me like the actions of a psychopathic monster, not of a jilted lover. Had there been other murders in his past for which he'd never been brought to justice?

At that moment, five children lost their mother. Two parents lost their daughter. Three siblings lost their sister. And all those who loved her lost access to what was really going on in the heart and mind of my 25-year-old mom.

For me, there is no room for compassion here. There is no room for doubt as to the coward's premeditation. There is no doubt that his thoughts had been murderous for at least three days, and likely since the day Beverly decided not to return to this demanding creature's home. Who could blame her?

But the "ol' boy's network" was clearly in full function, its members "reasoning" with their penis-shaped brains. "She probably deserved it," they no doubt thought – and probably said. "She got what was coming to her," seems to have been their mindset. A cadre of objectifying, white misogynists connived successfully to blame the victim.

```
Parole:

    Despite the circumstances which indicated that there might be
elements of premeditation in this crime, it was felt by this office
that due to the age of the defendant and to the reputation and history
of the decedent that it would be advisable to accept a plea to a
second degree murder charge in this case. Because of these facts
and because of the relatively light sentence given under the cir-
cumstances, it is recommended that the defendant not be considered
for parole until 1976.
```

Even though the legal and law enforcement authorities clearly had a long history of contempt for this ex-convict and now murderer, "it was felt" that, as a male, he should get more respect than a woman – especially a woman with a "reputation and history."

Further information concerning this person, etc.

This defendant was executive director of the Yamhill Housing Authority, which required him to be the manager of Eola Village. This village is housing which is furnished mainly for itinerant farm workers in this county. As such this is a source of much of the crime and trouble within this county. The defendant was an ex-convict in that he had been convicted of a burglary in 1928, and fornication with a previously chaste female in 1936. I do not know if this past record of his was the reason for his attitude, but in any event he wholly failed to cooperate with the authorities during his management of Eola Village. At the time his case was under consideration both attorneys that had previously held the office of district attorney were contacted relative to defending this person. They both felt that they could not do so conscientiously inasmuch as they had both had considerable trouble with Mr. Goodenough because of the way he operated Eola Village during his tenure of office.

Because Beverly was not alive to tell her side of the story, the authorities chose to believe only the murderer's account of the situation. There is no indication they sought to dig deeper than the events that occurred at the tavern. No doubt the murderer's account painted himself in the best possible light. Yet my investigation would eventually reveal that the same belligerence that caused him to "wholly fail to cooperate with the authorities," also caused him to create a toxic home environment of fear, abuse and misogyny.

And where were the voices of friends who were willing to rise up and paint a more complete picture of Beverly? Who would reveal her as the extroverted, funny, hard-working mom that she was? Where were the champions of impartiality? Who demanded that there be other voices to, at least attempt, to balance the scales of justice? Apparently there was no one on Beverly's side.

It was far easier to use the absence of conflicting testimony from the dead victim as an opportunity to do a little case-load management and keep things moving in the "justice" system. So the murder took place on May 7, and by May 26 the whole matter was settled and the murderer was off to serve a "relatively light sentence." It was less than three weeks from start to finish – how efficient.

It took longer than that to get Beverly's body transported back to Iowa and to have a funeral for her there. Her body had not yet been buried when the "authorities" in Oregon had ceased talking about her premeditated murder and had "slapped each other on the back" and the gavel on the bench.

I can't help but wonder what the circumstances might have been, but for the bout of mumps endured by the defense attorney. On May 5 the murderer purchased a gun in anticipation of seeing his estranged wife at the hearing on May 6. Had he planned to take his .25 caliber pistol to the courtroom the day following its purchase? Was his original plan to kill her in the courtroom along with anyone else who got in his way? Did he intend to not only kill Beverly, but to kill the attorneys who would soon decline to defend him and the law enforcement personnel who had encountered his lawless belligerence multiple times previously when he "wholly failed to cooperate with the authorities?"

Had the murderer been afforded the opportunity to carry out what may have been his original plan, do you think it likely a plea bargain would have been offered? If no plea would have been offered, then his sentence had more to do with WHO he murdered, than THAT he murdered. Sure, I'm biased – I get that. But it seems to me that there is no semblance of justice to the actions of "the authorities" in this case.

Two years later, another person too familiar with injustice would also be gunned down in public. I'm not trying to say that there is any simpatico between him and Beverly – there isn't, but *his* now famous words resonate with me here as I tell you this disturbing story:

"In the end, we will remember not the words of our enemies, but the silence of our friends."
- Martin Luther King Jr.

Birthdays

Even today I can remember how exciting birthdays were when I was a kid growing up in rural Iowa. We were so unplugged from the world around us that we probably couldn't have defined "consumerism" much less become involved with it. But birthdays were a glimpse through our little keyhole into the great big world that was out there.

For a kid, the arrival of the mailman down our dusty gravel road was of no consequence – except when birthdays were near. For me that was June, when summers were hot, school vacation was in full swing and the sense of being marooned on a remote island was at its height. But by the third and fourth weeks of June there would be the faint hint of a voice calling from the beyond. A birthday card would arrive in the afternoon mail, and my name would be on it. I was somebody. I did exist. Others in the world were thinking about me, even when I wasn't with them. And all these people could reach out to me through the magic of the U.S. Postal Service and acknowledge me and the special day when I was born. I loved birthdays.

I'd open these cards ever so carefully, as I'd been taught to do, so that we could repurpose the envelope later. I'd look at the cartoon image on the front of the card and barely read the outside copy, quickly opening the card in order to see the punch-line – and discover if there was something special inside. In the 1960s the tradition was to tape coins to the inside of the card – often a variety of different coins. A quarter, dime and nickel combination was a particular treat – an amount that far exceeded the standard tip left for a waitress after a meal. This was *serious* money.

I could feel the presence of money in these envelopes because of the weight of the coins. But in 1968 something changed. I got a birthday card from my Uncle Ken and Aunt Helen from Washington State. I was disappointed when Mom handed it to me because I didn't feel the characteristic mass. Perhaps they deemed me "too old" to be getting coins taped inside my birthday cards. I was, after all, about to go into the *third* grade. But after going through the opening and reading ritual, I opened the card to find a crisp, new dollar bill inside. This had never happened before. A whole paper dollar was *grown-up* money. And this experience changed my level of expectation for all birthday card senders henceforth. Paper money was clearly the superior method of sending those special birthday greetings. After all, the senders weren't tipping their hands by adding all those heavy coins. It was more clandestine and preserved the mystery for the birthday boy. Definitely superior; for sure.

So in recent months I've been calling, emailing and providing signed, written requests for information mostly in Iowa, Texas and Oregon. And then I wait for the slow cogs of government bureaucracy to grind out a result. I'm discovering that when 50 years separate the request from the creation of these desired documents, there isn't much of a spirit of urgency. I gather that the lack of expediency is due to two things. One is that people seem to think that if you've waited 50 years to ask for this thing, a few weeks more won't matter much. And two, 50 years of exposure to the layman's understanding of the second law of thermodynamics (the idea, in unsophisticated terms, that things move from order toward disorder) often means that the documents can't be found at all – at least not with ordinary effort. And I've found that many people aren't up for *extra*ordinary effort.

But with all these requests sent out into the world, my days feel a little like the 1960s again as I anxiously anticipate the arrival of the mailman. As the envelopes trickle in one at a time over the course of months, I peel each one open, recklessly now, to discover the secrets within.

There is so much I do not know from those early years in Iowa, from my mother's flight to Texas, from the final years in Oregon. Each envelope contains tiny little gifts of information unsuspectedly attached throughout. Sometimes what I find inside is a "penny" or a "nickel," only a slight glimpse of something heretofore unknown. Occasionally I find a crisp, new "dollar bill" hiding inside awaiting gratifying discovery.

Last week I got a packet of information from the Yamhill County, Oregon District Attorney's office as a response to my request for records pertaining to the murder of Beverly Kay Goodenough. Inside were 11 pages of 8.5 x 11 white copy-paper with no added notations or descriptions. Some of the pages contained such a slight amount of toner that I could not read the content. Most of the pages were forms that had been filled in here and there with specifics related to this case, but were otherwise generic to all cases.

The death of any person is cataclysmic. Philosophers, theologians and mathematicians have pondered these profundities since the beginning of time. The ripple effects of that death spread out through untold numbers of people across generations and millennia of time. The commissions and omissions of any one life are incalculable. The acts of Adam and Eve continue to touch us universally thousands of years later. The life and teachings of Jesus retain their profound effect throughout the planet, though he may never have been more than 100 miles from Bethlehem. Beverly wasn't famous or widely known but her life touched so many others, directly or indirectly, for good or for ill. And, if you can grasp my meaning, the absence of her life has left a sucking black hole in people whom she would have touched, with whom she would have been in relationship, whom she would have loved or loathed in all the years since her disappearance.

But all that was Beverly's life, and the selfish act that ended it, got summed up by the District Attorney at the bottom of the page entitled "Information of District Attorney on Waiver of Indictment," with this statement:

That said Clarence Goodenough on the 7th day of May, 1966, in the said County of Yamhill and State of Oregon, then and there being, did then and there unlawfully, feloniously, purposely and maliciously, kill one Beverly Goodenough by shooting her with a pistol.

And though this act created an instant rift in the time-space continuum from the perspective of all who knew Beverly, knew of her, or would have known her or known of her, one matter-of-fact sentence on an obscure legal document in a remote Oregon county is all that is required from the perspective of the law. Shocking.

In that same packet of eleven pages were two hand-written requests from the murderer addressed to the county clerk in McMinnville, Oregon. The first was written in June of 1968, the second almost exactly one year later. Both letters "request a copy of the court record of my trial or hearing of May 23rd, 1966." Reading these letters reveals that the convicted murderer is seemingly frustrated, having not been able to get a copy of the court record. His increasing irritation is seen within his selected words, punctuation and the deterioration of his hand-writing.

It occurs to me that, for the past several months, I've been writing similar letters to similar office holders in the same places as was the murderer. I've had no more success in acquiring these records than he did 45 years earlier.

Perhaps the karma of this angry man, and the irritation he created in those forced to read his self-centered and condescending remarks, caused someone to make these records disappear? Perhaps the stark deterioration of his handwriting between 1968 and 1969 indicates that he was severely distressed by this lack of response. Or perhaps his distress came from either his internal guilt or from external retribution he suffered at the hands of those provoked by his ignorant arrogance.

Mom Steffen often repeated the words of Jesus, "a man reaps what he sows." Though there is a part of me that is not proud of saying this, seeing the illustration of this timeless truth in the hand-writing of this murderer is to me like the dimes taped inside the birthday cards Beverly and I would have been receiving in June, the month that both letters were written.

Coffeehouse

My Aunt Sherri sent me a copy of the birth announcement that Beverly had mailed to her sister, Barbara, the day after I was born in Marshall County, Iowa in June of 1960. There are several things within that announcement that are curious and/or informative. But one is Beverly's mention of a person named Katey who was in the room next to her at the hospital. I presumed this was at least an acquaintance of Beverly and set out to find Katey via Internet research. Perhaps she would possess a piece of the puzzle that is Beverly's too-short life.

I was able to find Katey living in the same area of Iowa as she'd been in 1960. I got her phone number and arranged to meet her for a cup of coffee at the Remarkable Rose in State Center, Iowa.

Katey was a pleasant, helpful person who didn't know Beverly well, but certainly remembered her from childhood, though they didn't attend the same school. Katey had indeed been in the hospital at the same time as Beverly and had given birth to her first child on the same day that Beverly had given birth to me (Beverly's third). Katey shared her memories of Beverly and worked hard to help connect me with others still living in the region who would have known Beverly.

I met several people that day who each shared distant and sparse memories of their personal contacts with Beverly as children. It was fun to get a glimpse into the life and experiences of Beverly while she was still untouched by teen pregnancy and a succession of increasingly bad choices. Friendly, athletic, musical, fun, happy, mischievous, outgoing, adventurous and bright were words that recurred as I spoke with her old friends.

Katey also told me that the owner of the Remarkable Rose, where we sipped good coffee, enjoyed a homemade cinnamon roll and were surrounded by the sweet aroma of flowers, was the son of one of Beverly's classmates. In talking with Jeffrey, I learned that both his mother and his uncle had been in Beverly's class of 1958 in Clemons – a small world.

Unfortunately, Jeffrey's mom, who still lives in State Center, was away in Florida and wouldn't be available to talk. His uncle lives in Fort Dodge, Iowa which I learned was about 90 minutes northwest of State Center. Jeffrey didn't have his Uncle Richard's phone number, so I decided to make the drive on this beautiful autumn day and see if I might find him home and available for a walk down memory lane.

Fort Dodge

When I met and spoke to Beverly's former classmate, Jeffrey's Uncle Richard, he invited me into his pleasant home and I met his friendly wife.

The three of us took seats around the kitchen table and began to talk about his memories of Beverly. Richard's wife had never known Beverly and didn't know Richard until after his first wife had died from diabetes in the 1980s. Nevertheless she was engaged in the conversation, asked great questions and seemed quite interested in the stories we told.

Richard told me that he and his family had lived just outside of Clemons, just up a gravel road, an easy walk from the little town. He remembers the kids who lived in town used to like to come out to their farm and play around in the barnyard. From my computer, I showed Richard some photos of Beverly as a child and a few more from her young adulthood.

As I clicked through the pictures, I went past a black and white shot of Beverly posing in a dress with a farm building, gas barrel and tractor in the background.

Richard stopped me and said, "Wait, go back to that last one." As I did, he examined the picture more closely and said, "I'm pretty sure that picture was taken at our farm in Clemons."

"Really? Oh wow, that's so interesting that you recognized that and that she was there at your place."

It was a bit surreal to be sitting with Richard, a man who had known my mother well, and to be looking together at a picture of her from a place where he used to live. For a moment, I felt like Beverly was real, and more than just a dispassionate collection of photos shining out from my computer screen. I liked the feeling, and I think Richard felt it too.

"Oh, I don't remember a lot about Beverly," Richard said. "I suppose we went to school together down at Clemons for, I don't know, six or seven years. We were young, you know, probably eight or ten at first, till we were about fourteen, fifteen. I think she and her folks moved away after the tenth grade, or something like that. Then my parents moved away to Fort Dodge when we were in eleventh grade, so I kind of lost track of her after that.

"The only thing I can tell you for sure is that one time, after we lived in Fort Dodge, Beverly was married to somebody who worked for a farmer up by Renwick, Iowa; its north of here about 30 or 40 miles. And she had one of her kids in the hospital here. That would have been in the, um, 50s; late 50s. So how old are you?"

"I'm 52. I was born in 1960; June of 1960."

"Well anyway, she was here and she knew us from Clemons. It's a small town, everybody knew everybody, you know, 150 population. And my mother invited her over for dinner. And that's probably about the last time I ever saw her. Then I heard later, from somebody in Clemons, that she had left her husband and went out of state somewhere – I wanna say something like California or Colorado, I don't remember. But then I didn't hear any more about it till I heard she'd been killed."

We talked about things he remembered from school and many of them corresponded with the memories I'd heard from others. He asked about Beverly's sister, Barbara, and wondered if she'd been able to tell me significant details of their lives growing up together.

"No," I explained, "Barbara and Beverly were really close growing up. There was only a little more than a year separating them; I can't remember now if Beverly or Barbara was older."

Richard interrupted and said, "Barb was older. I think she was two years ahead of us in school."

"When Beverly left Iowa in 1962 and left everyone behind, it was really hard for Barb. I'm told they were almost like twins growing up. I even have a picture of them as young girls dressed in identical outfits. So when I first got in touch with Beverly's younger sister, Sherri, several months ago, Sherri called Barb to tell her that I'd like to talk. Sherri was so friendly, but she was only two when Beverly got married and moved out, so she has almost no memories of her."

"Yeah, I don't remember Sherri. I remember that Barb and Beverly had another sister who was quite a bit younger, but she wouldn't have been that young."

"Yes, they had a sister who was seven years younger – her name is Rosi. She still lives in Maxwell, where her folks owned a tavern in the 1960s and 70s."

"So, Barb told Sherri she didn't want to talk to me or about Beverly. It was just too painful for her. I certainly hope that Barb eventually changes her mind, but as of today I've never spoken to Barb. Every time I ask a question of Sherri or one of Beverly's old friends, they usually say 'I can't remember, but Barb would know.' It's a little frustrating to know that the answers are out there and I can't access them, but I certainly understand Barb's reluctance to reopen a painful chapter of her life, and I want to respect her wishes not to talk about it."

"I heard about Beverly's murder sometime after it happened. I don't remember exactly when. Some people from Clemons told me about it." Richard offered. "And did you ever hear about the TV show they did on her murder?"

"TV show? NO. What TV show would that be?"

"It was one of those, "true crime" kinda shows. I don't remember what it was called. I think this would have been in the late 1960s or early 70s. I never actually saw it, but I heard that it was an episode about Beverly and how she was killed." Richard said. "Yeah, I'm pretty sure I'm right about that. That kind of thing doesn't happen to people from Clemons very often, so it was the talk of the town for a good while."

I'd never heard this factoid before, and made a note to research this later. But, to date, I've never found anyone else who had heard of Beverly's story being told in this way. But I continue to look.

We would go down one rabbit trail after another, as I attempted to tell as much of Beverly's story as I knew and ask questions as I went. Throughout the process, we kept circling back to the evening when Beverly had come to Fort Dodge and had dinner with Richard and his folks. I asked questions about that night, hoping that the frightened teenage girl might have shared some of her heart with her old childhood friend, perhaps giving me a glimpse into her troubled life. But, as one would expect, Richard remembered few details of that 50-something-year-old conversation.

But I did notice that each time I would bring the conversation back to Beverly's visit to their home; Richard's face would become noticeably red. I got the distinct impression that he knew something more about that visit than he was telling me – or perhaps something more than he himself could recall consciously.

Richard's wife stopped me at one point to clarify aspects of the story I'd told so far. "So Beverly had three children with her first husband, Alvin, before she left Iowa?" she asked.

"Well, yes, she did have three children in Iowa. And so far as anyone knew at the time, they had all been fathered by Alvin, her husband at the time. But I have suspicions that Alvin is not my father."

"So then who do you think is your father?" she followed up.

"I don't actually know." I said. "I'm hoping that as I learn more and more about Beverly and her story, I might discover other candidates for who my biological father might be. I thumbed through several old yearbooks at libraries yesterday to see if anyone looked like me."

"So when were you born?" Richard asked.

"I was born in June, 1960" I said. "Theresa was born in October of 1957, and Ricky was born in January of 1959. He was only a few months old when he would have been in the hospital here in Fort Dodge."

"Do you have any memory about what time of year it would have been when Beverly was here?" I asked.

"Well, I had just gotten back from the Army, and I was living back with my parents while I was looking for work and a place to live. But I don't remember what time of year that was exactly."

I had a nice chat with this childhood friend of Beverly. When I left, Richard and his wife wished me well in my quest to learn more about my mother. As I drove away, back to meet up with my Aunt Sherri again, I felt really good that my mother had a friend who recalled her so fondly.

Hospital

Two days after my trip to Fort Dodge, I drove to Missouri and talked to Beverly's sister Barbara for eight hours. It was the first time I'd met her. After I got back to Nevada, Iowa from visiting Richard in Fort Dodge, Aunt Sherri told me that her sister Barb had called and had now agreed to talk with me. In Sherri's realty office, we called Barb and we talked for about half an hour. As Aunt Sherri's phone battery began to die, I offered to drive to Aunt Barb's house to meet with her and her husband Dale the next day. It would be a 400-mile trip well worth taking.

A year older than Beverly, Aunt Barb had so much more information about my mother than anyone I had talked to so far. During those eight hours of conversation, Aunt Barb told me of her childhood with Beverly, their love for one another and their sibling rivalries. She told me of Beverly's out-going personality and her need for fun and excitement. She talked of Beverly's early years of marriage and how difficult they were for her. She recalled the time when Ricky was sick and how Beverly had to rush him to the hospital in Fort Dodge and she told me of the troubling details of Ricky's illness. She mentioned a time, a few weeks after that Fort Dodge journey, when Beverly alluded to "something that happened in Fort Dodge," and a mysterious phrase that Beverly had used to describe her time in that strange city that haunted Aunt Barb all these years – "I think he still likes me," Beverly had said. Aunt Barb wasn't sure what it might mean, but she was pretty sure Beverly meant something significant by it.

I have since obtained copies of the medical records from Ricky's stay in the hospital. As I combine that information with what Aunt Barb told me about Beverly's personality, her countless personal memories of Beverly's life, and the hospitalization of my older brother, the following narrative formed in my imagination.

Ricky won't stop crying. It isn't the typical cry of a baby with a need for food or a diaper change. It is a cry of desperation and anger. It is a cry that often results in such fury that he turns blue, stops breathing and convulses. Beverly tries to ignore it.

These fits of rage from this tiny baby, only 8 months old, become more and more frequent. They start to happen outside of the secrecy of Beverly's tiny home and the townspeople notice the unusual nature of the screams. Their disapproving glances have a more convicting effect on Beverly than the cries themselves.

Finally, after being cut through with shame and the judgmental stares of little old ladies throughout the tiny north central Iowa community, the teenaged Beverly resolves to take this kid to a doctor and see if she can get pills that will sedate these embarrassing outbursts.

She takes the family car and drives into the nearby community of Eagle Grove, to Dr. Harding's office. Ricky has another episode while at the doctor's office. Dr. Harding is concerned and overmatched in his little country clinic. He refers Beverly to a specialist at the Trinity Lutheran Hospital in Fort Dodge, Iowa. Harding's colleague, Dr. F.G. Dannenbring, has been honing a reputation for innovative approaches to childhood diseases. Perhaps he can help understand these disturbing episodes that are increasingly frequent in Ricky.

Beverly drives the fifteen miles north back to her little home. She talks to Anna, her husband's employer, and asks if she'd take care of two-year-old Theresa while Beverly takes Ricky to the hospital in Fort Dodge. Anna agrees. Beverly rushes off to Fort Dodge with a diaper bag, but does not think to pack a bag for herself.

It takes over an hour to drive the narrow roads southwest to "the city." She gets lost several times and has to stop to ask for directions. She has a seductive way of getting the men at the filling stations to help her. They are eager to fill her tank and provide navigational assistance – for free – even as Ricky screams unabated in the car.

Beverly has likely never been to Fort Dodge before, and to someone from towns like Clemons and Collins, Fort Dodge seems like a metropolis by comparison.

Eventually she finds the hospital and gathers Ricky into a bundle of clothes from the back seat to shelter him from the warm rain that followed her here from home. Dr. Harding has called ahead, so they are expecting her arrival. Beverly answers a flurry of questions from the intake nurse as she hastily records the information for the doctor. Beverly answers all the questions dutifully, aloof to the bawling baby boy in the crook of her left arm.

All the nurses and Dr. Dannenbring are far more concerned about Ricky's condition than Beverly exhibits. There is a spirit of urgency in their manner. They take Ricky from her and unwind the mishmash of clothing tangled around him to reveal the loaded and leaking diaper, putrid and sagging from his chubby legs. They quickly discard it and carry him away, leaving Beverly behind and bewildered.

Beverly feels the anxiety of being alone in such a big, unfamiliar and strange place. She wonders if there is anyone in the city that she knows. The reality of being alone here is already unbearable. Suddenly she has an epiphany. She had a crush on a boy named

Richard in high school back in Clemons. He had moved to Fort Dodge during his junior year, a year after Beverly's family had moved to Collins. She hadn't seen him since, but his sister, Connie, had come back to State Center after graduation last year and had married her high school sweetheart.

Beverly wanders the hospital halls that reek with a disturbing mixture of chemicals, medicine and sickness. At a nursing station, she asks to see a local phone book. She looks up her former heartthrob but does not find him. She has a vague recollection that he may have joined the army or something. But in the looking, she discovers his parents' listing. She writes the number down on a scrap of paper and traces her steps back to the waiting area.

It is starting to get dark outside. A cooler breeze begins to blow through the open window next to the leather-seated metal chairs that force her to sit up straight. It had been so warm and humid earlier that she feels sticky all over. Finally a door opens and Dr. Dannenbring steps in staring down at a clipboard.

"Your son is a very sick little guy, Mrs. Shepherd. We've taken a chest x-ray and we've determined he has pneumonia. That would explain his labored and raspy breathing. He's probably very uncomfortable and the more he cries the more uncomfortable he gets. I'm sure you can imagine how that would be."

Beverly has difficulty concentrating on the details, but notices how handsome and confident this young doctor is.

"We're going to have to admit Ricky. He's going to be here for a few days while we run some more tests. We need to figure out what is causing these episodes of convulsion and abated breathing. When he turns blue and passes out, it's an indication that he's not getting sufficient oxygen to his brain. This is really bad for his development and could cause permanent developmental damage if it continues to occur as often as its happening. Do you understand?"

Beverly is thinking about the fact that she hasn't planned on staying here. She thought she'd drive down here, see the specialist, pick up some pills and then be home in time for supper. "How long will I have to be here?"

"At this point I'd think at least three or four days. Do you have a place to stay? Do you have family or friends here in town?"

"Not really. I've never been to Fort Dodge before. I don't think I know anyone here, except maybe some people who used to live near me in Clemons. I think they still live here."

"Well, most moms just stay in the waiting area up near the pediatric rooms. It's not very comfortable, but moms wouldn't dream of being farther from their children than that. I'll show you where that is."

Beverly follows Dr. Dannenbring, makes note of the waiting area's sparse décor and watches as the doctor disappears through a set of double doors.

Before his footsteps fade, she retreats to the nurses' station, and asks if she can use the phone.

Beverly is not accustomed to phones, nor the convenience of indoor plumbing for that matter. She did not have access to these at the many houses she lived in growing up and certainly not at the little farmhand house she'd left a few hours ago. She tries to dial the number, but isn't able to get it to connect. The hospital employee assists her, showing her how to access an outside line – a concept Beverly accepts, but does not understand.

Helen, Richard's mother, answers the phone. Beverly explains her situation in the dramatic manner of a teenager experiencing life for the first time. Helen is kind and hospitable in the way that was, and is, common in rural Iowa. Beverly explains that she'll be in the city for several days and doesn't know what to do with herself while tests are done on Ricky's condition.

"Why don't you come to our place for dinner tomorrow night? We live only several blocks from the hospital. Richard is just home from the Army and I'm sure he'd be happy to see you. We usually eat around 6:00."

"I'd love to. It'll be just like when I used to walk up the gravel road to visit back in Clemons."

Beverly sleeps at the hospital that first night and tries to be a mom to Ricky. Fortunately he is sedated and a lot less trouble than the screaming child she walked in with. But she doesn't get much sleep. The chairs are uncomfortable and the interruptions numerous as hospital staff make their regular rounds. She goes outside to get some fresh air, but it is still raining. So she retreats to wander the hospital hallways and take in their disconcerting odors. She is bored.

The next day is filled with tests and lots and lots of waiting around for things promised, but never delivered. By 5:00 p.m. Beverly is pacing the room like a caged animal. Ricky is crying again from all the moving, poking, prodding, transferring and testing. Beverly is sleep-deprived from her uncomfortable night – Ricky is too from his unusually active day. Despite the resumption of Ricky's cries and obvious discomfort, it is time to go to dinner. Beverly leaves the hospital right on time.

On foot, Beverly has trouble finding the apartment building Helen had described on the phone – but eventually she stumbles upon the place. She is self-conscious of her frumpy style, wrinkled dress and bad breath. She hadn't packed a bag for herself and didn't bring even a toothbrush. When she'd left her little farmhand house 30 hours ago, she didn't anticipate what might happen in her future.

Helen is matriarchal in her welcoming of Beverly to their apartment. The warmth and familiarity exchanged is perhaps a surprise to Beverly. For a few surreal moments, it is as if Beverly and Helen have serendipitously met while vacationing – perhaps on Beal Street in Memphis, with Elvis in accompaniment.

They haven't seen one another for almost four years, when Beverly was still just fifteen, single and a high school freshman. In those four years Beverly has gotten pregnant, married, moved several times, gotten pregnant again and now finds herself in the city hospital with the drama of a mysteriously ill child. She is trapped and yet feels the strange independence of anonymity, unlike anything that she's encountered in the scrutiny of the tiny rural communities where she has always lived.

Helen's husband, Merle, returns home from work about 30 minutes after Beverly arrived. He seems especially glad to see Beverly in his home again, as she had often been back in Clemons; yet he is awkwardly quiet.

Beverly's old schoolmate, Richard, arrives shortly after the three have begun eating the wholesome meal Helen has prepared for the occasion. Beverly and Richard exchange shy, mischievous glances reminiscent of former childish crushes.

The evening goes by quickly, and it is getting dark earlier now. The four talk in spurts with Beverly and Richard bouncing back and forth from their new adult roles of married mom and enlisted man, to the more familiar role of teenaged classmates.

New School

Clemons is a tiny blip on the map in central Iowa, about halfway between Ames and Marshalltown. Like most little towns in Iowa, it has declined substantially since Beverly lived there with her family in the early 1950s. Her class of 1958 had approximately 15 students. There was a church across the street from her home and a tavern about a block away. A walk up the hill took her into the country, where she could visit her classmates, Richard and Connie, whose folks rented a farm there.

There were about 200 people living in Clemons in 1950. World War II had ended only a few short years earlier. Television was a novelty item for the rich, with formal programming beginning two years prior in 1948. It's pretty safe to assume that few, if anyone, in Clemons, Iowa owned a TV while Beverly lived there. Without the church and its youth choir and the tavern and its rowdy evening hustle and bustle to bookend each redundant week, not much would have happened in Clemons, or in the lives of those who lived there.

Beverly liked music and sang both at school and in the church youth choir. She and her friend, Sharon, once responded to a school contest to see who could write the best song for the Christmas program. Beverly wrote the words and Sharon wrote the music. Their entry into the contest turned out to be the winner, and the two performed the song at the Christmas program, with Beverly singing the words she'd penned and Sharon accompanying on the piano. It was a wonderful triumph for these inhabitants of sleepy town Clemons.

I've talked to Beverly's friend Sharon at some length and we've become pals as she shares her memories of Beverly with me. One of these memories involves sneaking out the back door of the church when they were supposed to be at choir practice and roaming the streets instead. What scandal for the day.

But, on at least one occasion, this dynamic duo stepped into a brand of mischief that just might have planted a seed in Beverly that grew to maturity many years later – they stole a car together.

As Sharon recounted the story to me, the two mid-teen girls were walking around the streets of Clemons looking for a bit of 1950s rural adventure. As they neared the tavern on a warm summer evening, they began to hear the raucous sounds from within. For young girls of the time, just being close enough to a tavern to hear voices was sufficient to stir the buzz of danger. Giggles mixed with the fear of getting caught. And then they saw it, a brand new car parked in front of the tavern like a shiny new toy on Christmas morning.

Beverly froze in her tracks and with excitement began to persuade Sharon with the skill of a defense attorney. "Hey, let's take it for a drive."

"We can't do that. It doesn't belong to us," protested Sharon.

"But the keys are in it. Think of how much fun it would be."

"We don't even know how to drive," Sharon wisely pointed out.

"I don't care. It will be fun. I'm going to do it whether you do or not."

"But you can't even see over the steering wheel, Bev. How are you going to do that? You'll wreck it and get hurt or even KILLED."

"Well then, you drive and save my life."

And so with logic like that ringing in their ears, the two hopped in, with Sharon behind the wheel, and launched off like Thelma and Louise. They drove around country roads with windows down and hair blowing in the wind. They were freer than either had ever been before. They were experiencing an adventure that exceeded anything they'd ever read in a comic book, heard in a radio program or dreamt of from a Nancy Drew Mystery. On that sultry summer night, they created a shared memory that has lasted a lifetime.

As the sun began to set, they drove the car slowly back into town, not knowing if they'd been discovered. But as was usually true in these stereotypical small towns, nothing had happened. No one had discovered their caper. There were no police, no punishments, no shame. In fact, the parking space was still empty so the girls quietly parked the car, got out, closed the doors carefully and slowly walked to the end of the block feigning innocence with the skill of Hollywood actors. When they reached the end of the block, they spontaneously broke into a combination of sprints, shrieks and mischievous laughter and distanced themselves from the scene of the crime. They'd shown they could do it and get away with it. The seed of freedom and adventure had been forever planted, and for Beverly, that experience might have been like a first hit of crack cocaine. She was instantly addicted to all the unknown possibilities freedom might bring.

In talking with Beverly's sisters, I often hear things like, "She was just different," or "I don't know how we could all grow up in the same house and turn out so differently."

Beverly's "difference" was apparently off-putting and frustrating to her parents and especially to her dad. The documents I have retrieved from the Annie Wittenmyer Home indicate that her parents considered her "the black sheep of the family." Interviews with friends and acquaintances from her school years point to a child who was wholly out of sync with the culture, norms and expectations of her family, time in history and rural mores.

Though her parents were both physically present in her life, they lived on the edge of poverty. The family moved and changed jobs several times in Beverly's early years and she attended several different schools. Beverly dropped out of school after her sophomore year due to her pregnancy. And, by all accounts, alcohol was an all-day, every-day part of Beverly's father's life. I'm told that if you visited Grandpa Robbie at any time of any day, the first thing he'd do is offer you a beer. One person close to Beverly's father recounted that he couldn't remember ever seeing Robbie without a beer within ready reach.

There are many ways to be absent as a father. I feel as if I can speak to some of these nuances from personal experience. Mr. Shepherd never once reached out to me. All my contacts with him from 1975 until his death in 2002 were initiated by me or my sister. Proactivity was absent. My adoptive father was a faithful husband, father and provider, but did not know how to reveal himself nor discover who his children were inside. Emotional connectivity was absent. And my biological father has not stepped up to identify himself at all. He was and is absent in every literal and figurative sense of the word.

I believe that Beverly felt her father's absence and disapproval in a profound way. I believe she longed to be seen, understood, accepted, wanted and loved unconditionally. Each of the men for whom she bore children was older than she. Alvin was five years her senior. Jack was four years older. Clarence was 30 years older than Beverly and nine years older than her own father. There's no way to know the age of the man who sired me – but, based on the pattern, there's a good bet he was a father-figure to Beverly.

Perhaps on the same day that Beverly sensed she had been disowned by her dad, she subconsciously began in earnest seeking a replacement.

School's Out

Beverly had a hard time fitting in at her new school in Collins, Iowa. There were troubles at home. Her mom just had another baby, and now Beverly had lots of baby-sitting and diaper-changing responsibility. She was 14. All she wanted to do was have fun with her friends, go roller skating, see movies and get asked out to school dances.

Then she met someone. Someone older, who had a car and a job and a little money to spend on her. Alvin was tall, dark and, she thought, handsome. Best of all, he liked her. He didn't talk much, but that was ok, since Beverly could talk enough for both of them.

By Valentine's Day of the first year in the new school, Beverly discovered she was pregnant with Alvin's child. Her parents were furious. They didn't like this older guy she was with and now their worst fears were realized. They disowned her for her unrepentant, rebellious behaviors and attitudes. By the time she was 16, she was on her own.

Beverly and Alvin decided to get married. Alvin was 21, but at 16, Beverly would need parental consent, despite her condition. That consent was never going to happen. Once her father had judged something or someone, it stayed judged. There was no changing his mind. He was like that, and everyone knew it.

So she lied. On the marriage license all she had to do was tell the justice of the peace at the courthouse that she was born in 1938, instead of 1940. Simple. And then she'd have to get some witnesses to vouch for them.

Apparently, back in the day, the witnesses had more clout when vouching for marriage candidates than pesky things like birth certificates. Vouching for Alvin was his sister Patricia. Vouching for Beverly was her older friend from Clemons, Sharon Funke. A friend of Sharon's (and her future husband, as it turned out), Duane Zobel, also served as a witness. All three signatures are on the marriage license. And just like that, 16 year old Beverly was "legal" to marry 21 year old Alvin May 3, 1957.

There wasn't much time to just be young and in love. There was morning sickness, bloating, ankle swelling and just plain not feeling very pretty. Five-and-a-half months later, beautiful little Theresa was born, and responsibility was pressing in on Beverly from all sides.

In October of 1956, Beverly had been starting her junior year at Collins High School amongst a sea of new faces, hoping to make a few friends and get a date for homecoming. One year later, she was pregnant, married, and living 50 miles from her friends and the family who had disowned her. And now there was a baby with needs 24 hours a day, seven days a week. There was no escaping the utter lack of fun. Fun that most 17-year-olds crave – and Beverly craved fun more than most.

Theresa tells me that she is terrified of confined spaces and having anything over her face. When, many years ago, she told Alvin of this phobia, he told her a story about her early childhood that sent chills up her spine.

STATE OF IOWA, Story County, ss.

No. 15613

In the District Court of said County.

In the Matter of Application for License

For _Alvin Shepherd_ to Marry _Beverly Robertson_

I, _Patricia Shepherd_ being duly sworn, say that I am acquainted with the above named _Alvin Shepherd_ a resident of _Colo_ who is at least _31_ years of age, and said _Beverly Robertson_ a resident of _Collins_ who is at least _18_ years of age; that they are both unmarried and capable of entering into any civil contract; that there is no legal disability to the marriage of said parties; and that their marriage is to be solemnized in _Story_ County; that my residence is _Colo_

Subscribed in my presence by said _Patricia Shepherd_ × _Patricia Shepherd_ and by him sworn to before me this _29_ day of _April_ 19_57_

Betty Laugh- Deputy
Clerk of the District Court

License No. _15613_ issued _29_ day of _April_ 19_57_, for marriage of above named parties.

RETURN OF MARRIAGE

GROOM	BRIDE
Full Name (Print) _Alvin Lorain Shepherd_	Full Name (Print) _Beverly Kay Robertson_
Usual Residence: _Colo_ City, _Iowa_ State	Usual Residence: _Collins_ City, _Iowa_ State
Street Address, or Rural Route Number	Box 215, Street Address, or Rural Route Number
Place of Birth: _Murray, Iowa_	Place of Birth: _State Center, Iowa_
Date of Birth: _8_ Mo. _11_ Day _1935_ Yr. Age Last Birthday _21_ Yrs.	Date of Birth: _6_ Mo. _29_ Day _1938_ Yr. Age Last Birthday _18_ Yrs.
Color-Race: White ☒ Negro ☐ Other (specify)	Color-Race: White ☒ Negro ☐ Other (specify)
Number of times previously married _0_	Number of times previously married _0_
Number of previous marriages ended by: Annulment ☐ Divorce ☐ Death ☐ No. of Times Each	Number of previous marriages ended by: Annulment ☐ Divorce ☐ Death ☐ No. of Times Each
How was previous marriage terminated?	How was previous marriage terminated?
Usual Occupation _Farming_	Usual Occupation _Waitress_
Business or Industry	Business or Industry
Religious Denomination _Methodist_	Religious Denomination _Lutheran_
Father's Name _Alvin Roscoe Shepherd_	Father's Name _Lowell Dale Robertson_
Mother's Maiden Name _Doris Draper_	Mother's Maiden Name _Dorothy Wengert_

We hereby certify that the information given above is correct to the best of our knowledge and belief.

Signature of Groom: _Alvin Shepherd_ Signature of Bride: _Beverly Robertson_

Signature of Witnesses: (1) _Duane A Zobel_ (2) _Sharon Funke_

I hereby certify that the above is a correct return of the marriage solemnized by me at _Nevada_ City or Town County of Story, Iowa, on _May_ month _3_ day _1957_ year.

Signature of Officiant _Howard Mills_

Title and Church or Office _Justice of Peace_

Address of Officiant _Nevada, Iowa_

179

Apparently there were times when Beverly was so fed up with the confinement of her own life and the constant responsibility and needs of her first-born child, that she would hold a pillow over Theresa's face, smothering her, until the crying stopped. Alvin walked in on Beverly doing this on more than one occasion and, he believed, saved Theresa's life.

Beverly, on the other hand, told Alvin that she believed this to be a clever and effective new technique for getting some peace and quiet. She was convinced that if mothers everywhere weren't already practicing this technique – they should be. And she continued to practice it with her subsequent children.

I have no personal memories of this disturbed behavior from Beverly. But when I consider the most terrifying situations I could find myself in, I think of a foreign film, *The Vanishing*, I saw more than a decade ago that still haunts me to this day (I literally had a chill go up my spine just now, writing about it). Without wishing to spoil the film for you, let's just say it involves waking up alone in a dark, silent, inescapable place.

But even after having seen that movie, I have always said that the most terrifying thing I can imagine is floating alone in an ocean at night. Both scenarios involve being abandoned, cold and surrounded by black, hopeless fear. Perhaps these phobias are ubiquitous. Or perhaps they are a remnant of the kind of early childhood that Theresa, Ricky and I endured, and Alvin described.

And perhaps those early childhood experiences have left a malevolent presence inside me.

Darkness

There is something dark and angry inside me. Very few people have ever seen it, but I feel its presence snarling in a corner most every day. Whenever I think I may have overcome its pull on me, it makes itself known in startling ways; lest it be ignored.

This darkness jerks on its chain at a variety of stimuli. Sometimes the stimulus is "noble" such as an injustice done in the world. I wish I could say that the injustices that trigger the darkness were always universally unrighteous like tyranny, human trafficking or ethnic "cleansing" – and often they are. But too frequently they are petty, personal injustices like someone cutting me off in traffic, the perception of a condescending tone in a conversation or an obvious hypocrisy.

The stick of stimulus is poked into the face of the darkness and an accelerant ignites a fire within me. The darkness lunges into my chest at a lizard-brain level. Nano-seconds prior, it had been imperceptible; then suddenly, it is so present that my own rational self is displaced, seemingly pushed outside my corporeal home. I watch from above as the rage boils inside the body I had occupied just a few moments before.

The squatter inside my body reacts with violent words and destructive actions, without rationality or fear of consequence. Screaming, raging, profanity-laced tirades are the most common manifestation when the darkness snaps its chain. But, over the years, there have also been plenty of fists through walls, bullies laid out bleeding or unconscious and aggressive drivers confronted and cowering in the street.

In my youth and teens, the darkness overthrew rationality multiple times per month. As I've aged, and hopefully matured, the frequency of episodes has diminished to a few times per year — still far too many.

But it happened again this week.

I was driving to an appointment to get my hair cut. It was the evening rush hour. I had an audio-book playing on the car radio, and I was coming down off a busy day of work.

I pulled up to a four-way stop, deliberately assessing the timing of each arriving car at each of the other three corners, so as to take my turn at the right time. When my turn came, I proceeded into the intersection as an SUV arrived at the corner to my right. It slowed, but did not stop, and turned right, cutting me off and causing me to slam on the brakes and swerve to avoid a broad-side collision.

I honked my horn.

The driver of the SUV flipped me the "bird" as it sped away in front of me. My darkness snapped its chain.

I caught up to the SUV and when it was forced to stop at a red light. I put my car in park and got out to confront the driver of the SUV. The driver was shocked at my aggression, clearly fearful of what I may be capable of. But the driver failed to show contrition and when the light turned green and the SUV lurched forward, I punched the shiny new vehicle hard, leaving a noticeable dent.

I returned to my own car and continued to follow the SUV for several more miles, till finally I turned off, back toward my appointment.

My soul returned to my body bringing rationality with it. What kind of crazy person does such a thing? What if the driver had a gun? What if all those cars around us were video-taping me? What if on-lookers recognized me? Was there a police car in the traffic? Had I even bothered to check?

But more importantly, where does this darkness originate? How can it have lived within me for so long? From whence was it birthed? Is it a remnant from childhood abuse and abandonment? What does it feed upon? Will I ever have the will and the means to starve it to death?

Death

Today my friend Richard Twiss, Taoyate Obnajin "He Stands with his People" died. Richard and I had become friendly over the past six years as we met up at Christian Festivals like Cornerstone and Wild Goose. The last time we talked it was over pizza and beer at Wild Goose in Shakori Hills, North Carolina. There were some amazing similarities between his early years with Katherine and mine with Cindy. The four of us told stories and laughed and grieved together over the state of Jesus' church in our lifetimes. Richard was only 58.

Shortly after I learned of my mother's death, Billy Joel introduced the lyric, "Only the good die young." And it always seems so to me. So many friends and family have left this earth far too soon. And each time it happens, like today, I find myself grieving all those who died too young before them. And then I find myself examining my own mortality and wondering how and when my own demise will come. I wonder if my life has changed the trajectory of the planet for good because I have been authentically a part of it? I wonder if there are individuals who are better off because I have been their friend? I wonder if anything that I have contributed, while riding around on this blue-space-marble, will endure beyond my own years here? And I wonder how one balances these eternal desires with the mundane need to earn money and pay bills?

I've experienced a lot of death in my life. At least it seems that way to me. Growing up in a household where my adoptive parents were older than my original family's grandparents was a key contributor to this morbid fate. Many of my parents' friends and family were quite old, so funerals were a seemingly regular occurrence. Mom and Dad

Steffen always took us kids to these funerals, as if they were equivalent to going to visit a friend or a store. It always seemed odd to me and I never quite knew how to behave. To this day the smell of roses in the house will instantly remind me of death and funerals.

When I was seven, my adoptive maternal grandma Gardiner died a few months after suffering a heart attack at our house where she'd been living for several months. I grew quite fond of her and her native Scottish brogue and cultural witticisms that she regaled upon me during her stay with us. She laughed easily and seemed delighted to be with all of us and, of course, I imagined that I was her favorite. Even though she was delightful, she struck me as lonely, even when surrounded by her family. Later I would learn that her husband, my grandfather, had died 10 years earlier, six years before I was adopted. A heart attack took him as well.

I was already asleep the night Grandma suffered the heart attack and got whisked away to the hospital – but I awoke at the commotion and looked out the second story window of my bedroom to see the flashing lights of the ambulance in the graveled barn yard. That snapshot is still vivid in my memory. I also remember sneaking downstairs and standing stalk-still and unnoticed in the shadows as my father helped the ambulance driver awkwardly wrestle the gurney, with my strapped-on Grandma aboard, through the front doorway and down the steps while Doc Johnson issued urgent commands.

I wasn't allowed to visit her in the hospital. In those days children weren't allowed into the patient rooms. I don't know if it was an extension of the "children are made to be seen and not heard" policy common in the rural culture; or if they simply assumed that kids were little bags of germs. But in either case, I was left to wonder about Grandma's condition. And I let my morose imagination run wild.

When she was eventually transferred to a nursing facility, I was excited to get to visit her there. My sister, Theresa, and I would dote over Grandma a while and then wander the halls while Mom and Dad talked with her alone. There was an elderly World War I veteran on the same wing as Grandma, but on the opposite side of the hall. He had lost all his limbs in the war and his torso lay in his bed utterly helpless. Theresa and I would sit next to his bed and talk with him sheepishly. He seemed so appreciative to see us each time we'd visit Grandma. He would always have us light a cigarette for him and place it in his lips. The first time we assisted him with this, he moved the cigarette to one side of his mouth with his tongue and said mischievously, "Look kids, no hands." Having just assisted someone in the act of smoking, which we were certain was sin, I don't think we knew how to respond to his jovial statement, so we just sat there in awkward silence. But we made it a point to talk with this fellow during every visit. Truth be told, I was always as interested in lighting his cigarettes as I was in seeing his face light up when we entered the room.

Then there was the night when my mother took a phone call on the party line informing her that Grandma had taken a turn, and that we should rush to be with her.

The funeral was in Williamson, Iowa about 100 miles from where we lived in Grant. I was a veteran funeral-goer, so I behaved admirably and composed myself, as if I were a miniature adult. I folded my hands on my lap, sat still in my little blue suit, complete with clip-on tie – and shed no tears.

After loading the white 1965 Ford Galaxie station wagon with flowers, we drove the two and a half hours back home in the dark and in silence. I fell asleep in the back with the pots of odiferous flowers surrounding me and lay there as if in my own grave.

We arrived home late at night, and I was groggy from my slumber. At the edge of the barn yard where we parked was a long sidewalk that we accessed through a silver chain-link gate. The sidewalk ran parallel to the clothes line on the right, past the well pump on the other side where we'd take a left turn around the rear corner of the house to the back door. There were two steps up to the door, where we entered into the back porch that housed a huge chest freezer, hog-smelly coveralls and muddy boots. Through that room another door opened into the kitchen.

My dad and I made this trip back and forth from the car to the kitchen and from the kitchen to the car until everything had been schlepped from the Ford. I shadowed my dad as we exited the porch for the final trip. Eyes straight ahead intent on the task at hand, my dad stepped down heavily and crushed a kitten under his size 12 foot. I can still hear the terrified but truncated squeal of the kitten, followed by the muffled sound of bones snapping and entrails squishing. I froze above the step looking down at the sudden and stark site of death and watched a pool of blood appear from under the dying kitten's still kicking body. I sobbed instantly and bitterly and could not be consoled.

I have found this same inconsolable response to many deaths since. On October 31, 2009, my brother, Ricky, died of cancer in Oregon. He was just 50 years old. Two months later Tim, a dear friend from San Diego, died of a brain tumor. He was just 38. After I had just grieved the loss of Ricky, Tim's death hit me particularly hard. He and I had bonded in a brotherly way. We were kindred spirits. Tim died on Ricky's birthday, and in some mystical way, it linked him as brother in my soul. I can't stop wondering about Tim's children and how they will fare in this world without their wonderful and loving dad.

Bev and Jackie

This week I made a phone call to Ricky's and Jackie's adoptive sister, Sharon, in Oregon. I knew from my conversations with Ricky, that Sharon and Jackie were close. Though we had never met, I'd spoken to Sharon a couple of times when Ricky was sick, and once after his death. I called several times and didn't reach her. It didn't seem to matter what time of the day I called, whoever answered the phone always sounded like I'd woken him up. Finally I got another phone number from the groggy dude on the phone and I eventually reached her.

I explained who I was and that I was calling to try to understand my biological family better and build a family tree at Ancestry.com. Sharon remembered me from our previous phone conversations and seemed glad that I called. Sharon said that she had been doing some genealogy work for the Cronk family as well. She was excited that I was doing some family history research too.

To be honest, while talking with Sharon, I had strange emotions I still can't identify. I'm not sure there are words in the English language for these emotions. They were some odd hybrid of excitement, embarrassment, neediness, shame, and anticipation. I felt like a troubled, slow, bothersome child. It was as if I were devolving and regressing to an earlier state of being. It is truly surreal to talk with a person, whom you've never met, who knows more about your family than you do. It is as if it violates some law of nature, and the emotional scramble is the result of having to walk through a rift in the time/space continuum to mine for answers on the other side of normal.

Sharon confirmed that Jackie's biological father was a guy named Jack Hiner. Sharon talked about Jackie in a warm sibling manner, as one would expect from a loving older sister. She talked of Jackie following her around wherever she went, being the pesky little sister who's unaware of the great chasm a few years can bring to a youthful relationship. Sharon described Jackie as a bright, beautiful, outgoing child – until she was about 12 years old. Then something shifted; changed irrevocably. Jackie became selfish, wild and obsessed with boys.

It is nearly impossible for me to think of Jackie without also thinking of Beverly. Both of their lives were so similar – though Jackie's only half as long. According to the accounts of those who knew them, they were each sweet, bright, pretty, energetic young women suddenly immersing themselves into destructive behavior just as they reached their teens. I can't help but ask the question, WHY? Was it simply the onset of adolescence that drove them to caustic conduct in a flood of hormonal prodding? Or is there something more – something darker?

I'm certainly no psychiatrist, but I can't help seeing the pattern here. When I compare this pattern with the patterns of girls who have suffered sexual, physical or emotional abuse, it's hard not to see the similarities.

One of Beverly's friends told me a disturbing story that may provide a glimpse into what happened in Beverly's young life. I'll call the friend Margaret, since she'd be uncomfortable if I used her real name.

Margaret told me about a party that took place at Beverly's house while her parents were away. The party wouldn't have been allowed, had her parents known about it – but that's what made it exciting and fun. Beverly's older sister was there, as were several of their friends from the small town where they lived.

Margaret recalls that Beverly would have been eight or ten years old and the other girls would have been twelve or thirteen. At some point during the party, Beverly emerged from a back room with a pornographic magazine and began showing it around to all the girls. Margaret described the magazine timidly, but said it was "more than just women without clothes. It was sexual. It was shocking. None of us had ever seen anything like it before."

One important detail of this party that Margaret mentioned was how comfortable and informed Beverly seemed to be "about all the sexual stuff." As she remembers it, Beverly was teasing the older girls about how little they seemed to know and how uncomfortable they were with these explicit pictures.

Was this just an act put on by the younger Beverly in an attempt to impress the older girls? Or had Beverly been exposed to the realities of the sexual behavior depicted in this pornography? Where did she get a magazine like this? Was it something that had been given to her by someone, or had she found it somewhere? Did Jackie have similar experiences in her thirteen years?

I make no accusations here, only observations. It is unlikely that I'll ever know the answer to this curiosity, since both Beverly and Jackie likely took those answers to their graves. But I wonder if these young girls arrived at their careless teenage promiscuity at the hands of some evil person in their proximity. I wonder if their sexual circuits got activated at a time and in a manner that no child should ever experience. And I wonder if the consequences of that evil led to Beverly's and Jackie's early deaths, and have rippled through my family's history ever since?

Grave Voice

Tonight I got a phone call from the daughter of the man who murdered my mother.

Cindy and I were down at our farm on Friday, March 12. We'd been working all day outdoors preparing the barn for a new brood of chickens. By 6:30 we were back inside and relaxing for the evening. The farm is a quiet place where we have intentionally avoided adding the distraction of television. The pace of the place is much more attuned to the rhythms of nature than our home near Dayton. So when darkness is coming on outdoors, rest and inactivity seeps into the cedar home, and into our very bones, indoors.

The cell phone reception in this part of rural Ohio is very poor. So when my iPhone rang on this particular evening we were startled by the intrusion and surprised at working technology. The caller ID indicated the call originated in Idaho. I immediately recognized the town's name as the place where Beverly's last child, my brother Steven, had died.

For more than a year I'd been trying to track down the Goodenough children. I had Steven's obituary from a 1996 edition of an Idaho newspaper which listed the names of all his surviving brothers and sisters. Several of them were half-siblings from his biological father's (Beverly's murderer) first family. A few were siblings from the progeny of his adoptive parents.

But Steven had been dead for over 18 years, so there was no telling if any of these folks were still living. And if they were alive, where on earth might they be? I had done countless Internet searches, had sent scores of Facebook and LinkedIn messages and made dozens of phone calls, all to no avail. I wasn't any closer to finding these folks than I'd been before I started. I was about to give up the hunt.

But, a week prior, I took a day off of work and did more research on ancestry.com. While on the site, I found Clarence Goodenough and the six children he'd sired with a woman named Jane Harriet West. From the family tree it appeared that four of these children could still be living.

So I sent a note to the person who had established the family tree and asked if he knew these people, or if they were simply unknown, auto-populated names on a tree? The next day I had a note back from him indicating that he did know this family and that four of the kids were still living. I explained that I'd like very much to have a conversation with these folks, but also indicated that, given the fact that their father had murdered my mother, they might be quite reluctant to make contact with me. I assured him that I didn't want to make trouble, but was simply looking for information about my mother. I provided my phone number to him and asked him to pass it along to anyone who might be willing to talk with me.

Awkward as a conversation with the Goodenough family would likely be, these were the people who had known my mother at the time of her murder. And these were the people who would likely be able to fill in the blanks for me from those years since Beverly had left Iowa.

And now there was a woman on the other end of the phone named Judy, who was willing to talk.

Clarence's daughter, Judy, was soft-spoken and dutiful in her willingness to share information about her memories of those terminal days in 1966. It was quickly clear that Judy's memory was keen and that she was not a tangential figure in the story. At the same time there was a measured reticence in her manner.

Having not been prepared for this call at this time, I stumbled into the conversation haltingly. "Wow, so Judy, first let me just say thank you for making this call, I really appreciate it. I understand that this conversation may be awkward given the circumstances of the past."

Judy responded with a noticeable slow sadness in her voice. "It won't be awkward for me. You have a right to know what happened and I'm willing to answer any questions that you have."

"Well, I guess I'll start with some background – you're the daughter of Clarence and Jane West, right?"

"Yes, Clarence was my daddy and Jane was my mother."

"I have read that there were six children from this union. Where do you fall in the birth order?"

"My brother Clarence Jr. is the first born. He was born in 1941. I'm the second born and was born in 1943."

I felt a bit like I was questioning someone on the witness stand. Judy would quickly answer my questions, but it became clear that she wasn't inclined to share information I wasn't asking for directly. I felt certain that there were things she was holding back, or at least not volunteering.

"So I know that Beverly married Clarence just a few days after she gave birth to her daughter Jackie Sue – what can you tell me about that timing? Do you know how Clarence and Beverly met?"

"When I met Beverly for the first time, it was in 1963. She was pregnant with Jackie Sue then. Jackie was fathered by a guy named Jack Hiner. Jack had left Beverly for another woman and Beverly had no place to live. As I understood it, Beverly was really holding out hope that Jack would come back to her, so she went to Jack's sister's house hoping to be around whenever he returned. Jack's sister's name was Frances. Frances was married to a guy named Larsen — I can't remember his first name — but she had left her husband and had moved into a small apartment. That's where Beverly was living. And though Frances wasn't divorced, she was dating my father. So Daddy would go over to the apartment to see Frances and Beverly would be there. That's how they met initially."

Judy continued, "Eventually Frances decided to go back to her husband, so she gave up the apartment and moved back in with him. That left Beverly without a place to live and Daddy without a girlfriend. I think that Daddy felt sorry for Beverly and her situation and wanted to help her. They didn't live together till they were married, so I don't really know where Beverly was living between when Frances went back to her husband and when Daddy and Beverly married on September 11, 1963."

I broke into the information to ask some clarifying questions. "What do you know about Jack Hiner? Do you know how and where Beverly met him?"

"I don't really know much about him. I think he was a drunk and I don't think this was the first time they'd split up. I think they had a pretty tumultuous relationship. I think Jack had been a truck driver, but I think his drinking kept him from working much of the time. I heard that Jack and Beverly had spent much of their time virtually homeless, living out of their car as they moved around the country."

"Do you know if they met in Iowa?"

"I think they did, but I don't know how or why Jack would have been in Iowa. Seems like the Hiner family had some kind of tie to the Midwest, but I also know that Jack had family living out here in

Oregon, and I think that's how he and Beverly eventually ended up here."

"I've received some pictures of Beverly over the years from my brother Ricky and Beverly's family. On the back of one of those pictures, taken after Beverly left Iowa, there is a photography stamp from Amarillo, Texas. Do you know why she, and presumably Jack, would have gone to Texas?"

"No, I don't know if they went to Texas. And I don't know what might have drawn them there. I'm sorry. I don't really know much about Jack really. I only knew of him for a short time and then he left and I don't think he ever came back. After Daddy and Beverly were married and they started having trouble, Beverly started saying that Jack had come to see Jackie Sue and wanted her back. I don't think this was really true, but she said it several times. It's a small community around here. No one else could ever verify that Jack had been around. I think she just said that out of wishful thinking or to make Daddy jealous."

"You mention that Clarence and Beverly started having trouble. What can you tell me about that?"

"Beverly was on birth control after she and Daddy got married. She was having some kind of female health problem and went to the doctor. This would have been sometime in the middle of 1964. After the exam, the doctor told her to stop taking the birth control pills because she was pregnant. When she came home to tell Daddy this, I think he was skeptical. He got out a calendar and told her that if this baby was born before February 15, there was going to be trouble."

Beverly's fifth and final child, Steven Troy, was born on February 15, 1965. But trouble was not averted.

"Shortly after Steven was born, Beverly started cheating on Daddy with other men. I know this to be true because one of the men she was sleeping with was my first husband."

There was a silence on the phone and it was clear that this topic was still emotional for Judy even after nearly 50 years. Her words broke and a lump rose in her throat as she struggled to continue.

"After Beverly and Daddy were married, I moved into a house across the street. I was about 20 then and had been the woman of Daddy's house for a long time. It was my house and my kitchen and I didn't think it was right for me to stick around with a new woman in the house. If they were going to have a chance to make this marriage work, I thought it would be more likely if I was out of the house.

"So after Steven was born, Beverly started messing around with my husband. Apparently everyone in town knew what was going on, except me. Something changed in her; she was just different. Beverly and I had been friendly up till then. She seemed amazed at how naïve I was and wanted to show me the ways of the world. The first time I ever had too much to drink, I was with Beverly. But now she seemed to be doing things to prove that she was wiser in the ways of the world than I was. She seemed to want to prove to me that she could take anything I had, and she was going to start with my husband. It was very hurtful.

"Beverly used to show up at my husband's place of work and try to entice him there. Even after he changed jobs, she found out where he was working and kept showing up. Eventually we moved to California and took new jobs there, trying to get away from this pain and to try to give our own marriage a chance to work. I don't even know what Beverly saw in him. He was a drunk like Jack. He was nothing special. It seemed to me that she just wanted to teach me a lesson that she could take anything I had."

"Earlier you mentioned that Beverly cheated with other men – plural – were there others besides your husband?"

"Yes, there were, but I don't remember anyone else's name. I know she was with another man the night ... the night ... she died." Judy's words trailed off as if realizing these were difficult and not entirely descriptive words she had settled on.

"So what exactly happened leading up to that night? What was going on?"

"Well, Beverly had left Daddy and had filed for divorce a few months earlier. She took her three kids and was living with Vean and Wanda Cronk. Daddy was devastated by this, especially because he was so proud of little Steven. He tried to make a deal with her. He told her that she could leave and that he'd give her the car and some money if she'd just leave Steven with him. But Beverly didn't want anything to do with that deal. She told him that she'd take his money and the car and that she'd have Steven too."

"So what was going on the days before the murder? It seems like there was some kind of escalation of emotion for it to end in a shooting?"

"Daddy had been seeing a woman whom he'd known for many years. She was living in California at the time, and he decided to drive down to see her. He drove straight through, but when he got there, she wasn't available. So he turned right around and drove back to Oregon. He had to go to Portland for something – to see my brother, I think – and then back home. He'd been driving a long time. He hadn't slept in maybe a day or two. When he got back home after dark that Saturday night, he found a note from Beverly in the house. She'd been there. The note said she wanted to talk. So instead of just going to bed and arranging to talk later, he went to look for her. I don't know if he knew where she'd be or just happened to find her, but he found her at the tavern in Willamina."

"He went into the tavern and Beverly was there at a table with some friends. Daddy told me that he went up to her and told her that he'd found the note and that he was here to talk as she'd requested. Beverly was upset that he was interrupting her fun. She told him to go wait in the car and that when she was done with her friends she'd come out and talk to him. He went to the car, got increasingly angry as he waited, found the gun and went back into the tavern and ... and it happened." Judy said in a manner that indicated she'd told this story many times before.

Judy quickly wanted to clarify something. "I don't tell you that to make an excuse for what Daddy did. It was wrong what he did, there's no excuse for it. I tell you as more of an explanation, that's all."

I asked Judy about the gun and the report I'd read that said it had been purchased at a sporting goods store just a few days before the murder.

"I don't believe that is true," she said. "Daddy always had guns, I'm pretty sure this was a gun that he had all along. But the police confiscated the gun and they wouldn't give it back to us even though we requested it several times. But I don't think he had recently bought it."

"When you kill someone, you kill yourself too." Judy added unsolicited. "That's what happened to Daddy – he was never the same after that. He was so devastated by what happened. He could never understand why he had done that. He was just empty afterward, right up till when he died."

I find it interesting that Judy never mentioned the M-word at any point in our conversation, though I referred to "Murder" in my questions to her. She seemed interested in painting her "daddy" in the best possible light, even in the face of the known and undisputed fact that he had murdered the mother of his beloved son – his own wife – my mother. I suppose that this is normal behavior on Judy's part, wanting to speak well of one's family. And I suppose it is true that she defines her father using a much broader set of information, history and personal experiences than I ever could. And because I can never have the breadth of that information, to me he is a murderer, nothing more. That is my only point of reference for him.

I found her attempts to humanize him to be both utterly incongruous with my own mental picture and admirably loyal at the same time. I began to wonder if perhaps I'd misjudged the situation. Maybe there was less "monster" here and more jilted lover. Maybe this *was* a case of an otherwise decent person being goaded into actions heretofore completely foreign?

But then there was the report from the Department of Corrections that had portrayed him as a convict with a record of burglary, statutory rape, and numerous counts of defiance of the legal authorities – so much so that the attorneys in the area refused to defend him in court. And there was his desperate attempt to clear the jam in his cheap, dime-store weapon so that he could fire another shot into the body of the woman he claimed to have loved, even while she lay at his feet writhing in a gathering pool of her own blood.

And then I had another phone conversation, this one with the granddaughter of the murderer and the adoptive sister of my half-brother, Steven. Holly remembers having met her grandfather only a few times. She recalls that her mother, Yolanda, was frightened of him and would never allow him to come into their home. She would permit him to see his son, Steven, but never unsupervised and never indoors.

In 1960, Yolanda had married the murderer's son and namesake and the two had adopted Steven after the murderer had been sent to prison. But Yolanda and Jr. later divorced, and Yolanda gained custody of both Steven and Holly.

According to prison records, the murderer had been allowed a few instances of furlough while still serving time. During these brief furloughs, Clarence would come to Yolanda's house to see his eldest son who was now serving as both uncle and adoptive father to Sr's. youngest son, my brother Steven. And when he made these rare visits, Holly recalls them gathering under a tree in the yard to have short discussions. He was called Grandpa, not Dad, during these visits. One of Yolanda's fears seems to have been that Sr. would be inclined to tell Steven that he was not really grandpa, but father – a fact Steven finally discovered at age 14, after Sr. was already dead.

Yolanda and Clarence Jr. divorced while Sr. was still incarcerated, and a review of his prison record shows that she was almost immediately crossed off Sr's list of authorized visitors.

Though Judy tells me that all her father really cared about was getting custody of Steven, it appears that he actually only saw Steven a handful of times after the murder.

Judy told me, and the Department of Corrections papers confirmed, that my mother's murderer was released from prison in March of 1972, after serving less than six years of the 15 year sentence that itself had been described by the court as "relatively light." I will resist the temptation to go on a tirade about the injustice of this. But, make no mistake, this IS outrageous injustice.

As I was rehearsing the phone conversation with Judy in my mind a couple of days later, I realized that I had no idea when or how Clarence Goodenough Sr. died. I sent an email to his daughter, Judy, to see if she was willing to share this information with me. Today I got her reply.

My dad died of acute pneumonia in 1976. He was on dialysis for a year or two. Was on his way home from a session and lost control of his car. He died after a day in the hospital, though not from injuries.

Judy

Judge

One of the newspaper articles I have found describes the trial of Beverly's murderer and names the judge who passed sentence on him in the case. That Judge was Darrell Williams, a long-time judge in Oregon. With some effort I was able to locate a bio of Judge Williams on an Oregon historical website and the article accompanying the bio indicated that he had retired decades ago and had moved to a city in California. Continuing the search with that information, I located a man there who was approximately the right age, early 90's, and seemed to still be living. I found a phone number and called him. To my great surprise, he answered the phone and was quite lucid.

"Good afternoon. Am I speaking with the Darrell Williams who was once a judge in Oregon?"

"Yes, that's me. I retired in 1986 and moved here to California."

"My name is Craig Steffen. I live in the Dayton, Ohio Area. My mother was murdered in Willamina, Oregon in May of 1966, and you were the judge who sentenced the murderer. I've been unsuccessful in finding any of the records of the case in Oregon, and I'm hoping that you might have some personal records or might at least recall some of the details of the case."

"Well, I don't know if I'll be able to help you, but I certainly will if I can. I do have some records that I keep in the basement, and I'm happy to look through them to see if I have anything about the case you're interested in. What was your mother's name?"

"Her name was Beverly Kay Goodenough. She was murdered by her estranged husband, Clarence Arthur Goodenough, on May 7, 1966. The murder was a shooting that took place in a tavern in Willamina. According to the newspaper articles from the time, the sentencing took place in your courtroom on or about May 25, 1966. Does any of that sound familiar to you?"

"Well, no, I can't say it does."

"I just thought this case might be unique enough that you would remember it. I was thinking that there probably weren't that many murders in rural Oregon back in the 1960s."

"Well, you'd be surprised. We had more than our share. But no, I can't say I remember any of this, but I'll be happy to take the information you've given me and look in my records."

"I'm also happy to send you some of the newspaper articles I have that may serve to spark your memory."

"Well thank you; that may help."

"And thank you for taking the time to talk with a complete stranger about something that happened so many years ago. I'll put that information in the mail to you in a few days."

A couple of weeks later, I received a thoughtful and informative note from Judge Williams, who had gone out of his way to try to help me. Unfortunately, he didn't have the information I sought.

DJ Williams

From: "DJ Williams"
Date: Tuesday, March 19, 2013 12:00 PM
To: "Craig Steffen"
Subject: Response from Judge Williams

Hi Craig: I have been trying to send you this note e-mail, but have not been sucessful. But I do want to respond to the memo's you sent me recently, so I hope this information will be somewhat helpful to you.

I am indeed sorry that the additional info you sent me did not spark my memory on the situation. But I did want to mention a few things to you, first of all I am terribly sorry that I have no memory of the situation. But I wanted to tell you that the court appointed attorney for Mr. Goodenough was Francis March, who was a well respected defense attorney and received many court appointments in the County and the District Attorney for Yamhill County was Don Blensly and he also was very well respected attorney. Don was later appointed as Circuit Judge for Yamhill County and a few years ago he died. I have been trying to think who might have interviewed the defendant and made notes, and possibly a Lt. with the Sheriff's office , but I dought that the notes are still available 45 years later.

Craig I also want to tell you that when the crime was reduced from Murder 1 to Murder 2, the District Attorney has complete discretion to to so and he must have had good reason to do so in this case and likely believed that he could not prove to a jury that the defendant acted with premeditation as would be necessary for a conviction of 1st agree Murder.

Now on the sentence. I do not believe that the 15 year sentence was" a relatively light sentence", and I don't recall this particular sentence, but the term would probably not have imposed without the consent of both lawyers.

Well Craig that is about all I can say, except that I am sincerely sorry that I could not be of more help and the best to you and your family.
Sincerely Darrell Williams

But in his note to me he mentioned Attorney Francis March, so I decided to see if Mr. March was still living; another lead to follow.

Cross-checking with documents for Oregon Corrections, I discovered that Judge Williams had misspelled the attorney's name. The last name of the attorney representing the murderer was actually Marsh, not March. I was able to locate a Malcolm Francis Marsh who is currently a judge in the US District Court in Salem Oregon. I sent Judge Marsh a letter mentioning my correspondence with Judge Williams, asking him for any records he might have regarding the case.

March 17, 2013

Honorable Judge Malcolm F. Marsh
U.S. District Court Oregon
1507 United States Courthouse
1000 Southwest Third Avenue
Salem, Oregon 97204-2945

Re: The Murder Case of Clarence A. Goodenough, May 1966

According to newspaper articles from the time, you were appointed as counsel to Clarence Arthur Goodenough following his murder of his estranged wife Beverly Kay Goodenough on May 7, 1966 in a tavern in Willamina, Oregon. Beverly Kay was my mother.

I have been doing considerable research regarding my biological family during the past year and that research has led me to you. I've been attempting to acquire the Sheriff's investigation and report from this case but the Yamhill County Sheriff's office states that they are unable to locate any file regarding the case. Likewise, the District Attorney's office in Yamhill County has been unable to find a file.

Last week I contacted Judge Darrell Williams in California, who was the judge on the case, and he too was unable to find any personal files from that case. Judge Williams suggested that I contact you. BTW, Judge Williams is still quite sharp for a person in his 90's and we had a pleasant conversation. Unfortunately he does not recall the case from memory either.

I have two questions. First, do you have any memory of or files from the case that you could share or send to me? Second, is there anything you can do to encourage a more thorough records search in the Yamhill County Sheriff's office that might result in the discovery of their records regarding this case?

I have included a bit of information about the case with this letter in hopes that it will either spark your memory, or assist you in locating files that exist somewhere in the beautiful State of Oregon.

Thank you so much for your assistance in this matter.

Regards,

Craig A. Steffen

In less than two weeks, I had this reply from Judge Marsh's office:

United States District Court
DISTRICT OF OREGON
1507 United States Courthouse
1000 S.W. Third Avenue
Portland, Oregon 97204-2902

Chambers of
MALCOLM F. MARSH
United States District Judge

March 21, 2013

Craig A. Steffen
2330 Schnebly Road
Spring Valley, Ohio 45370

Dear Mr Steffen,

I received your letter with enclosures, but I am unable to help you. The Francis Marsh referred to in the judgment order, was my father. He passed away in 1995. While I was in practice at the time of the case, I have no memory of working with my father on the Goodenough case. I was in a different office in Salem while his office was in McMinnville. I have no idea where any files would be located. The firm that my father practiced in is now called Haugeberg, Rueter and Cowen, located at 620 N.E. 5th St. P.O. box 480, McMinnville, Oregon 97128. Ph. 503-472-5141 Dave Haugeberg of that firm would be your best chance for a meaningful contact.

Very Truly Yours,

Malcolm F. Marsh

Malcolm F. Marsh
United States District Court Judge

MFM

Once again, I'd come up empty. I can't tell if the absence of these records is an incredible unhappy coincidence, the result of a proactive intent to suppress them, incompetence in clerks to either file or retrieve them properly, or merely an example of the layman's notion of the second law of thermodynamics illustrating that, over the course of nearly 50 years, things really do go from a state of order to a state of disorder.

But also, once again, I had a new lead to follow. So I contacted Dave Haugeberg, as Judge Marsh suggested.

I had a cordial conversation with Mr. Haugeberg, and he agreed to search his firm's archives to see if any residual files from the 1960s might still exist. He also warned me not to hold out much hope.

About a week later, I spoke again to Mr. Haugeberg who informed me that his office was not able to find the records I sought, but provided me with the name of a former employee of the firm who had given them years of valuable research service. This person had recently retired and he felt she might be willing to assist me on a fee-for-service basis. The trail of breadcrumbs continued.

So I contacted Sandy Parr, at Mr. Haugeberg's suggestion, and I shared my need for assistance with her. After agreeing to help me for a reasonable fee, I emailed her documents spelling out the back-story. She went to work looking for the missing files; but this time I had someone on my team who could do some searching face-to-face. And this time the person who would be contacting all the same people I'd been talking to for months, would have a personal relationship with the folks who sat in those offices. I was again hopeful.

Several weeks went by, and I got a call from Sandy while I was traveling in Iowa doing research of my own. Unfortunately Sandy hadn't been able to locate the desired files I was looking for either. Sandy was feeling guilty that her retirement activities were preventing her from doing as thorough a job as she'd intended. She explained that the project had become more difficult than she'd originally anticipated, and she simply didn't have the necessary time to commit to it. She was so good to work with, and my hopefulness dissolved into discouragement.

But Sandy had someone else for me to talk to, Carol Reid. Sandy thought that this person could help me better than she, because Carol is a private investigator.

When I called Carol, we followed the same protocols as with others. I sent her the same background information I'd sent to everyone else. Since I was no longer hopeful that Carol would be able to find the missing files I really longed for, I added several new questions for which, I hoped, she might be able to find answers.

As expected, Carol was no more effective at finding the files than anyone else had been. Maybe these records truly don't exist anymore. I had so hoped that they were misfiled in some obscure box, in some obscure room, of some obscure warehouse, in some obscure little town in rural Oregon. Maybe these files do exist somewhere, but I've struck out about 15 times in a row here, so I'm not holding out much hope.

Hiner

One of the other questions on my list to Carol Reid was to see if she could help me find Frances Hiner Larsen. According to Judy, the murderer's daughter, Frances was the woman with whom Beverly had been living just prior to the birth of my sister, Jackie Sue Hiner. And Frances was the sister of Jack Hiner, Jackie Sue's father. Since I have no idea who my father might be, and since Jackie and I look so much alike, I needed to track this down to see if Beverly and Jack had met about three years before they may have run away together in 1962. It's as good a lead as any I had at that point.

But, I'd been searching for Frances for months without success. If she were alive after all these years, (and I'd found no record of her death) she was eluding me.

After several weeks and a number of phone calls, Carol was able to find a current address and phone number for a Frances Larsen who seemed to be the right person. On the day before my birthday, I called the number.

"Hello."

"Hello, is this Frances?"

"Yes it is."

"Hello Frances, my name is Craig Steffen and I believe that you knew my mother back in the early 1960s. My mother's name was Beverly Shepherd. Do you remember her?"

"Noooo, no, I didn't know no Beverly Shepherd."

"So let me make sure I'm talking to the right Frances. Do you have a brother named Jack Cox Hiner?"

"Yeeess"

"Ok. So, Beverly and Jack were, uh, I guess, friends and lovers, back in the early sixties. And Beverly actually gave birth to one of Jack's children."

"Yeeess"

"Beverly gave birth to a little girl named Jackie Sue."

"That was, that was the one that was killed over in McMinnville?"

"That's right, in 1977."

"Yes, I know about that, yes."

"But you don't remember Beverly?"

"Well, yes, I kinda do. She only stayed with me about a month. And, uh, me and my husband had the farm out by Newberg. And she stayed with us a while and then she went to live with Clarence Goodenough. I don't know where Jack and her was together – in Texas someplace I think."

"Yeah, so do you remember how Jack and Beverly met?"

"No, I don't know. I mean, nobody ever told me. I don't even know if they were legally married."

"No, I don't think they ever got legally married, at least I haven't found any evidence of that."

"So, Jack, uh, died in, uh, 2008. And I'm the only one left outta that bunch."

"I spoke with Clarence Goodenough's daughter, Judy, and she told me that Beverly had lived with you for a little bit, while Beverly was pregnant with Jackie Sue."

"Yeah, uh, but I, uh, never did see Beverly after that. She had the baby and, uh, after the baby was a little bit older she, uh, Clarence took her back east to get her other children and then they came back and she let him take care of the kids and the baby and she started runnin' around and, uh, he caught her in a bar in McMinnville and shot her."

"Yeah, well that's pretty much the story I've heard too."

"Well, I know it's the truth because I went over to see her, uh, where she was at and, uh, he was comin' outta the funeral home in handcuffs with two cops. That's the only information I can give you."

"So after Beverly left her first three children behind, I'm the third child, she left us kids behind in Iowa and somehow went through Texas and ended up in Oregon."

"Well, did you come out to Oregon with Clarence and her when they come back to get the kids?"

"No, I was in an orphanage with my sister Theresa and my brother Ricky. And my sister Theresa and I got adopted and Ricky didn't."

"Oh."

"So when she went back to Iowa, she was able to get Ricky, but Theresa and I had already been adopted. So she wasn't able to get us."

"Oh, I see.

"As far as I know, I don't know where the little boy is now but he was with a good family, uh, after she got, uh, shot Clarence gave the kids to these people, uh, I've forgot their names; I'm getting old too. But, uh, anyway, I know that he was in good hands and, uh, so was Jackie. But, uh, Jackie got kinda wild and loose and she was comin' back with a boyfriend of hers from Amity and hit a deer – swerved to miss a deer and the car wrecked and that's what killed her."

"Ohh, so I had not heard the part about the deer. I knew that it was an accident but…"

"Yeah, she was drivin'; she was old enough to have her driver's license and she swerved to miss the deer and hit the ditch and the car turned over and, uh, it killed both of 'em – the boyfriend and her. I don't know his name. But I know that the people who was takin' care of 'em had adopted 'em and they talked to me about it because I was related to Jackie, and they thought I might want to git her, and I said no, I have, uh, five kids of my own and I don't need another one. And I didn't know her very well; she knew of me, but she never contacted me, or anything, and, I just went over to see Beverly at the, uh, funeral home and paid my respects and that's all. And I seen Clarence – didn't speak to him – but I seen him in handcuffs. He was comin' out of the funeral parlor."

"Well, thanks for paying your respects. I know that she sort of had a dark side and wasn't always the best person, but I think she had a good side too."

"She had a good side; yes she did. She was just all mixed up because, uh, she couldn't, I mean, she didn't know what else to do. Jack left her at my place. Just plain left her. She didn't know where to go, she didn't have a job and she stayed with me for about a month. And we enjoyed her company. And then when she left us and went over to

Goodenough's, I didn't see her anymore. But Clarence really loved her, I mean he took good care of her and, uh, for some reason and another she left him and went to that bar, and he went in there, and she was sett'n on a bar stool next to a man, and he had his arm around her and he jist, you know he was older than she was, and he jist couldn't take it, I guess, and he jist up and shot her."

"Do you have any idea who she was with?"

"I have no idea. I really don't. And I don't think it was in the paper. Uh, I can't remember the people's names that, uh, that Jackie lived with. They would know more about that than I do, but I don't remember. They lived in that Eola Village in McMinnville."

"Yes, their names were Wanda and Vean Cronk."

"Cronk"

"And they've both passed now.

"Well, one thing you can really be sure of is that the Cronks were really good parents to those kids. They loved 'em. See, they didn't have a child early. They had ther, that gal that they had, when they was in ther, well, they were fairly old, cuz she woulda been about the same age as I was."

"Oh, I see. So their daughter, Sharon, was a natural child?"

"Yes."

"I thought she may have been adopted too."

"Well, I hope you get some satisfaction outta it. It was a sad thing. Because – I don't know that anybody coulda played a part in it that coulda helped her. Because she was doin' what she wanted to do. But why her and Jack, my brother, ever separated, I don't know. Jack just left. He came and brought her there, and told me to take care of her and I said, well, whataya mean? And he said well, she's gunna have a baby. And I said, well alright. So I did, until she decided that she was leavin'. She didn't have the baby at my house, in fact I never seen the baby, but she went over and was livin' with the Goodenoughs. He had three kids, but they were teenagers. Judy was one of them. Did Judy tell you that, uh, her dad shot Beverly?"

"Yes, she did. And I had found newspaper articles on the Internet, and so I knew that my mother had been murdered, but I didn't know anyone who had known her at the time."

"Well not – I don't know if it was murder or if it was jist an accident; I'm not sure, because he was a nice man. I knew him and my husband knew him a long time before, uh, Beverly was there. We thought highly of him. He raised those kids by himself, and they were all nice kids. So, I don't know; I wouldn't call it murder. I jist said shot. But she brought it on herself, honest to God, I'm jist bein truthful with ya."

"Well, that's what I'm looking for is truthfulness."

"Well, that's all I know and, uh, I'm sorry to have to tell you that but, uh, you're a grown man and you actually shouldn't have, uh, hatred for Clarence because I think she mistreated eem pretty badly. He spent a lot of money on her and bought her a car and was good to her. He took her in when she needed to be – have a place. He helped her with her kids. Went to – well tried to get the babies out there in Iowa. And, uh, she jist turned on eem and, uh, and it was more than he could handle."

"It was a little more than a year after Steven was born that she left him. I've often wondered if she may have had what they now call Post Partum Depression?"

"As far as I know, she didn't have any health problems. She wasn't a hyper type of person or anything. She didn't drink all that much, I mean, she jist, she wudn't satisfied at home with Clarence and then she jist, uh, she jist left. I don't think she'd done it before... When she was at my place, she never done anything. She smoked cigarettes but, ya know, that wasn't anything. She was a good worker; she was a good cook, and I had a lotta respect for her but, uh, my brother and her jist didn't git along, uh, cuz he was a drunk. He was an alcoholic."

"Did he treat her well?"

"I don't know. He didn't live with her when I was around. He just left her. He brought her there in his car and he left. Since then, he lived in Grants Pass and, uh, we buried him in 2008."

"Do you know why he was in Texas?"

"Well, he had a brother that was in Texas and we all lived in Texas; my mother's buried in Texas. But we weren't there at the time. We were in Oregon and the rest of his family was in Kansas and Missouri. And, uh, he was in the Army. And after he went in the Army, I don't know where all he went. But anyway, when he came back to my place, out at Newberg, he had a car and, uh, he unloaded her and her suitcases and wanted to know if I'd take care of her because she was havin' his baby."

"Did he leave for another woman, do you think?"

"No. No, he didn't have another woman at that time. They had Texas license on their car. He hadn't been here long enough to change his tags."

"Well, the story I've heard is that she really liked Jack and that she was devastated when he left. And even after she married Clarence, she always talked about that maybe Jack would come back."

"I don't think so. I don't think so. Because when she was at my place, uh, she never said anything to me about, uh, I'm not sure that her and Jack was ever married?"

"Yeah, I don't think they were."

"I think she left him, err, he left her because he didn't want the responsibility of the baby because he wanted his freedom. He was a musician and a drunk and that's all he wanted to do. And she didn't – with her bein' pregnant and everything – he wanted her to have a place to stay. And so, uh, he never did remarry anybody after that. He never seen the baby, Jackie. He never went over and seen her or anything. We told eem where she was at and, uh, he acted like he really didn't think the baby was his."

"Interesting."

"It was interesting. But I, uh, she told me she was – the baby was Jack's, so I don't know. But we, we, we liked her. We had a lotta respect for her. She was, like I say, she was right in there to help when we was doin' anything in the kitchen or when, when we was workin'. And my husband he thought she was good – really a nice lady. I don't know what else to tell you. Anyway, I hope you find some peace in knowing what you've found out. And, uh, if you're ever out this way, why, you're welcome to stop."

"Do you have any pictures of Jack?"

"Well, my daughters have all my pictures."

"If I were to send you a self-addressed, stamped envelope, would you be willing to have one of them put a picture of Jack in the mail for me?"

"Well, I'll do one better than that; I'll give you my daughter's phone number, and you can call her, if you can catch her home."

"Well, Frances, you've been so nice and so helpful. I really appreciate your kindness toward this stranger who called you outta the blue."

"Well, I hope you find some peace in that and, uh, know that your mother was well liked by a lotta people from around here."

"Thank you so much. If I find myself in Oregon, I'll stop in and see ya."

"You do that. I'd like to see ya."

"Thank you so much, Frances. God bless you."

People remember what they remember. No one's memory is iron-clad – especially not when they are in their 90s. But Frances' memories were very helpful to me in piecing together who my mother was, what she was doing in those mystery years since the disappearance.

For the record, Jack Cox Hiner died in 2005, not 2008 as Frances had recalled. And Jackie's boyfriend, Phillip Curtis Bixler, was not killed in the car accident that took Jackie's life – in fact he was barely injured. Bixler was in and out of prison and died in 2009, before my search began. I wish I could have spoken to him to learn a bit more about my sister.

It is also interesting that Frances never admitted to having her own affair with Clarence Goodenough, as Clarence's daughter had described. I was, of course, curious about this fact but didn't think it particularly relevant to my story, so I refrained from asking.

The part of the conversation with Frances that I found most troubling was how she could, essentially, deny that what happened to my mother was murder. None of the newspaper articles at the time had called it anything but murder yet, as a friend (and perhaps former lover) of Clarence, she couldn't bring herself to call it what it was.

Murder. He was found guilty of murder in the second degree. That's still murder. In my biased opinion, it was really murder in the first degree, premeditated, but it was murder either way.

Frances' words, "she brought it on herself," and "she mistreated him badly," ring in my ears and heart as a way of tragically missing the point of what happened. Which is worse: "mistreatment," leaving one's spouse and going to a tavern with someone else or shooting someone in the heart (and then struggling to shoot again – being prevented in the second shot only by a cheap malfunctioning weapon)?

"He was really a nice man," she said. I've endured some injustice in my time. I've felt the sting of jealousy, abandonment and betrayal – differently than the murderer for sure – but felt them deeply nonetheless. Yet, I cannot bring myself to see his reaction, blasting a 25 caliber hole into the heart of a defenseless 25-year-old woman, as "nice."

It seems he had a penchant for bamboozling younger women:

- The "previously chaste minor" he raped in Wisconsin
- The woman who bore him six children, but whom he never married
- Frances herself, the married woman with five children
- Beverly, 30 years his junior

All these were younger women. All were taken in by his gifts and masks. All were willing to stick up for him, despite his despicable actions toward them and those around him. But the legal record for this man paints an entirely different picture – Robber, Rapist, Murderer and Thug.

As Frances recommends, I don't "have hatred for Clarence." But neither will I ever be deceived into seeing him as "a nice man."

Migration

In some sense, I am like a Monarch butterfly.

Ever since this longing-to-know settled into me like a virus rewriting my DNA, I have been drawn to Oregon. It wasn't intellectual attraction. It wasn't emotional desire. It was something that had gotten programmed into me at a cellular level. It wasn't optional, it was something I MUST do – like a migratory instinct.

A few years ago my wife, Cindy, wrote a short-story called *Monarch*. In her amazing story, she tells of the Monarch butterfly that migrates to a place in Michoacán, Mexico – even though the generation of butterfly that migrates has *never* been there. In fact, the generation of monarch has never been within a thousand miles of Mexico – but its mother has. It's astounding how these tiny, fragile creatures are drawn instinctively to a very specific place thousands of miles from where they originated, metamorphed and matured.

So 48 years – to the day – after Beverly lost her life in a remote, Oregon, logging-town, my sister, Theresa, and I migrated over 2000 miles to witness the scene of the crime.

Last autumn, I worked with Marguerite, the editor of the *Sheridan Sun Newspaper*, to do a follow-up story about the murder. *The Sun* had covered the murder extensively in 1966, so I called to see if they would be interested in doing a retrospective. Marguerite was intrigued with the idea and agreed. It was my hope that bringing the topic back to the fore might help me to find some folks who had known Beverly back in '66, or who had been in Benny's Tavern on the fateful night.

After the new *Sheridan Sun* article ran, I got a phone call from the current owner of the establishment, which is now called Dillon's Bar and Grill. Carolyn said she was moved by the story in the newspaper and that she wanted to talk with me to see if there was anything she could do to help me find the people and the answers I was looking for. She also said that she wanted to honor Beverly's life by having "Beverly Day," every May 7 – the date of her death – from this time forward.

I was amazed by her sweet spirit and her willingness to assist in my journey for mother. For someone who had never known Beverly, Carolyn was certainly going beyond the call of duty to initiate an event to honor and celebrate a life violently cut short.

Over the following months, I sent Carolyn additional articles and photographs to help facilitate "Beverly Day." Eventually, Theresa and I began to make plans to be there for the inaugural event. The stars had aligned to signal the timing for our migratory journey.

On the morning of "Beverly Day," Theresa and I drove out to Amity, Oregon; about 15 miles from McMinnville, where we were staying. From September, 1963 till February of 1966, Beverly and her husband had been living at a migrant workers village near Amity, where her husband was the village manager. Theresa and I wondered what might be left of Eola Village, so we stopped at the post office to inquire. The helpful folks at the post office gave us what seemed to be sketchy directions, and we were told that everything about Eola was now gone.

We drove to the area and slowly turned down Eola Village Road, marked by a badly leaning street sign. We meandered down the old gravel paths in our rental car and eventually saw a large barn that looked like it might be old enough to have been there in the 1960s. There was a pick-up truck in the driveway with its driver's side door open, so we pulled up in front of it to take in the scene and conjecture about the age of the building. After several minutes without seeing any human life, we began backing out toward the main graveled path. Just then, a man appeared on the side of the truck with an expression on his face that seemed to say, "who in hell are you?"

I pulled back in, and introduced Theresa and myself, telling him about our mother's history with this place.

"Hi, I'm Gary and I know that story. So you're the children of the woman who got killed?"

"Yes. We were very young and didn't live with her at the time, so we have no memories of her or the murder, but today is the 48th anniversary of our mom's death, so we're here to learn more about her from that time in her life."

"I bought this place 22 years ago and we've learned a lot about the history of the place since. We were told that the Eola manager was quite a bit older than your mom and that he didn't treat her very well – making fun of her because of her weight and belittling her in public; stuff like that. And then she lost a bunch of weight and he got insanely jealous – always thinking that other, younger guys were looking at her; and he couldn't take it."

"Our mom – Beverly was her name – *was* rather heavy, and then she did lose a bunch of weight at some point. And her husband – the manager at Eola Village – *was* 30 years older than her; so all that sounds right. I'd always suspected that she was mistreated, since she filed for divorce a few months before she was killed. Most people, who have a happy life, don't go filing for divorce. But you're the first person to confirm my suspicions."

We spent an hour and a half with Gary and his wife, Linda. Like everyone on this journey, they were extremely nice and amazingly helpful at sharing information they had and in guiding us to others who were equally helpful.

From my phone, I showed Gary several of Beverly's Eola Village photographs I'd gotten from Aunt Barb. He took us to various places on the property to show us where the photos had been taken. In one photo, there was a prominent tree by the house in which Beverly and three of her children (Ricky, Jackie and Steven) had all lived. Gary and Linda had lived in that very house when they first purchased the property, and he described it to us in great detail. He also told us that the tree in the photo had fallen some years back and had crushed the house – but that the tree stump was still there and new growth was coming out of it.

Before we left, Gary took a photo of Theresa and me next to that fallen tree and another as we stood on the sidewalk that once led up to the house where our mother lived. In some mystical way, we had found our way back to a place we'd never been.

After we left Gary and Linda, we drove back into Amity to visit the tiny cemetery where Ricky, Jackie and Steven are all buried. We had no idea where to look for their graves, but we quickly found a large

"Cronk" stone just inside the gate and a tiny stone with Jackie's name and nothing else. Stuck into the earth, just above Jackie's name, was an aluminum stake with Ricky's name spelled out in letters that looked like they could have been pressed in with type from an ancient off-set press.

The next morning, Theresa and I slogged through rain-washed streets in McMinnville to the funeral home that had handled Jackie and Ricky's funerals. We ordered a proper headstone to mark the single grave that these two close siblings will forever share. It just seemed like the right thing to do.

We had to look a long time before we found Steven's headstone, which turned out to be about a hundred yards into the cemetery a couple of rows behind a large tree that was the natural focal point of the place. As Theresa and I stood beneath the tree, in plain sight of the three graves, it occurred to us that this was the first time ever (and likely the last) that all five of Beverly's children were together in the same place. We looked into each other's eyes and choked back tears in silence.

A few minutes later, as we still stood next to Steven's grave, we

noticed a woman enter the cemetery through the same gate we'd come through 30 minutes earlier. She wandered around the cemetery following roughly the same paths that we had taken and eventually came within about ten feet of where Theresa and I were standing. I

227

glanced back as she walked, and our eyes met.

The woman stared at me for several seconds, and then said, "Are you Craig?"

Taken aback, I stammered, "Uh, well, yes I am. And you are?"

"My name is Carol, I thought you might be Craig — you look like Beverly. I met your mom in 1963 while we were both in the hospital in McMinnville giving birth. We both had girls. Your mom gave birth to your sister Jackie and I gave birth to my daughter Susan.

"Well, it's certainly good to meet you, Carol. This is my sister, Theresa."

"I saw the newspaper announcement of your mom's memorial event today over in Willamina, and thought I'd stop by here on my way to collect some information for you. I see you've found it on your own," Carol said with a genuine smile.

Carol told us about how she and Beverly had shared a room at the hospital for three or four days after giving birth, and how they'd quickly become friends. She told us how they used to write letters back and forth in order to share news and photos of their young daughters. She mentioned several times the two families had been in each other's homes during the three years between when they met, and when she learned of Beverly's murder. Carol's husband had been significantly older than her, as was Beverly's; and Carol's husband's name was Alvin, which was also the name of Beverly's first husband. I wondered aloud if these simple coincidences might have contributed to Beverly and Carol's rather fast friendship. Carol also mentioned that she didn't think that Beverly had been treated very well in her marriage and that Beverly's husband had often made fun of her because of her weight and didn't seem to respect her. But

Carol was quick to add that she and her husband had always enjoyed Beverly's company.

We talked with Carol at the cemetery for an hour or so, then we all headed over to the tavern in Willamina for Beverly Day.

When Theresa and I arrived at the tavern, we met Carolyn, the current owner of Dillon's, who had done so much to make this day appropriate for honoring Beverly after 48 years. Carolyn had moved the juke box and had created a corner to commemorate the occasion. There was a lovely cake, a bottle of champagne for a toast, a poster as a marker for Beverly's birth and death, and there were two vases of gorgeous flowers. Carolyn had really outdone herself. Theresa and I arrived for the start of the event at 1:00 p.m. and we wouldn't leave until nearly 9:00 that night. There were so many people to talk to, stories to listen to and the kindnesses of written words preserved in a special guestbook for the occasion.

One of the first people we met at Dillon's was Jack, a man who looked to be in his late 60s whose parents had owned Benny's Tavern in 1966 – Jack's dad *was* Benny. Jack worked at the tavern back in the mid-sixties and he was there the night of the murder.

Jack told us that, several years after the murder, Benny's Tavern sold, changed names and moved next door (where Dillon's still is today) and everything about it changed. But Jack took us to the original site and described, in great detail, the decor and layout as it had been – right down to the vinyl booths, the ancient painting on the wall and the circa 1800s bar that stood proudly just to the right of the entrance.

The tavern was smaller than I had imagined it. I didn't measure it, but I'd guess it was about 25' wide by 75' deep. The front entrance, the one the killer came through that night, was on the main street. The only parking was also on the street.

Jack remembered where Beverly was sitting on her last night, and he remembered at least one person she was with. As we walked in through the front door, there would have been several booths along the wall at the left – directly across from the antique bar on the other side of the room. Beverly was sitting in the third booth from the front, under a large, framed painting. One of the three people sitting in the booth with her was a fellow nick-named "Gilley," who lived in an apartment directly above the tavern and was still living there when he died in 2013. One of Beverly's friends worked behind the bar; and it was this friend whom Beverly had come to see on that last night. Unfortunately, Jack could not remember her name, and therefore had no idea where she might be now.

Beverly had only been coming to the tavern for a few weeks, presumably since she'd met her new bartender friend. But she'd made quick friends with the regulars there. "We all liked her. She was young, pretty and got along with everyone. She was outgoing. Everybody treated her with respect. I think that's why she liked coming here – she just wanted to be treated right." Jack told us.

"Everybody knew that guy she was married to; he had a terrible reputation around here and he didn't treat her right – everybody knew that. So she started coming here after she left him and people started treating her with respect. That's all she really wanted, I think." Jack said.

So Theresa and I had been in Oregon for only a few hours, and already we'd heard several independent reports of Beverly's mistreatment at the hands of her husband. Her story was becoming much clearer to us as we talked with people in the area. We found that anyone who was roughly 70 years of age and who had lived around these small rural towns their whole lives, knew the story of our mother. Everyone we spoke to recounted – in approximately the same way – Beverly having been abused and ridiculed, her husband's jealousy, and the circumstances surrounding her murder.

It came as some comfort to me that not a single person recalled the murderer with even a solitary sympathetic comment. It's not that I want to vilify him, but it seems to me that he caught every legal break and benefit-of-the-doubt that could possibly have been tossed his way … and that Beverly got nothing of the kind. Perhaps history's verdict about our mother's murder differs sharply from the men who passed verdict on her killer. Maybe, in the end, this crime *was* more about a bad man, than about her being a "bad" woman. At least so far as the locals recalled it, the "Willamina Tavern Shooting" had less to do with "the reputation and history of the decedent," (as the court documents had conjectured) and more to do with the man who "wholly failed to cooperate with the authorities;" and the "insanely jealous" man who stole her life.

"I'd been here that night. I was 19 and worked here to pay my bar tab. My folks owned the place. My mother was here all night and witnessed the whole thing. But I left around 10:30, 'cuz I was going fishin' the next morning, and needed to get some sleep. I lived in an apartment across the street, so I didn't hear anything. I didn't know it had happened till I got up the next morning and saw the police tape everywhere. I went over and talked to my mom and she told me everything. We were just shocked; it was just terrible."

As he spoke, Jack often looked deeply into our eyes as if searching for clues about how much we really wanted to know. Or, perhaps he was hoping for Beverly to look back at him one last time with her winsome smile – the one he'd clearly come to appreciate. In either case, what looked back at *us* were Jack's eyes – filled with moisture and genuine pain.

Seven of us stood on the sidewalk in front of the entrance door to where Benny's had been in 1966. Jack, Marguerite, Carol, a member of the historical society, the private investigator I'd hired several months earlier, Theresa and me. Jack told us the eye-witness account that had been passed to him from his mother regarding the night of the murder.

"The guy who killed her parked his car here." Jack gestured to a spot about two car-lengths up the street from the front entrance. "He just walked in and went right over to where your mom was sittin' in a booth over there – and they got into it. He was demanding that she come home with him. It was like he didn't even see the other people in the tavern, or the three people sitting with your mom in the booth. He just yelled at her like she was his kid, wanting her to come home with him. She said she wasn't going to go anywhere with him. He just kept yelling and demanding and she kept refusing. She didn't ever get up out of the booth." Jack said.

"Then he stormed out the door and everyone thought the whole scary scene was finally over. But then, just a couple of minutes later, he came back in and walked right up to her – she was facing toward the back of the room, so she had her back to the door – and he said something and shot her right in the chest. The gun jammed, and he worked it to get the cartridge free and it went off a second time. Then a bunch of folks rushed him and were trying to help your mom, but he turned on them, waving the gun at them and yelling at them to 'stop, or you'll be next.' When he saw how bad your mom was hurt, and saw that the bartender was calling the sheriff, he ran out of the place, jumped in his car and sped off. Someone called the doctor, who had an office just across the street over there, but it was late at night so he wasn't in. They called him at home – he didn't live too far – but by the time he got here there was nothing he could do. He called for an ambulance, but in those days an ambulance was basically a station wagon with lights and a siren. They didn't have any fancy equipment in them back then. There wasn't anything anybody could do."

Jack paused as if he might be finished with this part of the story. But then he said, "I don't know if you want to know ... but your mom didn't die right away."

"After she was shot in the chest, she got up out of the booth, screaming and staggered across the room, bleeding, and went behind the bar. Maybe she was going toward her friend who worked here? But then she fell behind the bar and, after a while, she died right over here." Jack walked across the room and stood on a spot of tile and pointed at the floor.

"She lived maybe ten minutes after she was shot."

Theresa and I stared, paralyzed, at that spot on the floor for a pregnant minute, as the truth of these events sunk into us like a slow bullet lodging into our own hearts.

Finally, our gazes broke and we again made eye contact with the stunned folks around us. Jack's expression seemed to be questioning the universe to try to find meaning from the story he'd just retold – or maybe he suddenly wondered if he'd done the right thing in telling it at all.

After a few minutes, I looked at Jack and asked, "So you mentioned that second gun shot. The newspaper article at the time said that it 'went wild.' Is there a hole in the floor around here somewhere from that shot?"

"Well, no. That shot went up and it hit the wood frame around a big picture that was hanging on the wall above where your mom was sitting – right about here." Jack gestured toward the wall and drew an imaginary rectangle with his pointing hands. "The bullet skidded along the frame and left four deep gashes along it. Those gashes were in that frame for as long as the bar was here. Every time someone would ask about those grooves in the frame, someone would tell the story about what happened to your mom that night."

So it seems that back in Iowa, where the rest of Beverly's family lived on, in shock and loss, folks rarely uttered her name and had only the vaguest notion of what had really happened to her. But here, more than 2000 miles along our migratory route, where Beverly's life-light burned only briefly and then was senselessly snuffed out, folks hadn't stopped talking about her in 48 years.

There was more stunned silence as we all seemed desperate to try to take all this tragedy in, and find some soulful tool to process the images Jack had painted. I'm not so comfortable with long silences, so I asked a question just to eliminate the hush in the room. "So, do you remember what the picture in the frame was?"

Jack's voice hesitated and cracked a little as he said, "It was a painting of *Custer's Last Stand.*"

That last evening in Oregon, Theresa and I drove through the country looking for Bethel Road, the stretch of road where Jackie had lost her life in a car accident in 1977. The drive was awesomely beautiful as the sun set over the freshly plowed fields, seemingly eager to receive the seeds of new life.

We found the remote spot where we imagined the accident had occurred. Initially our gaze was insular, with eyes focused on a curve and a ditch and a utility pole. But after several silent minutes, our focus shifted outward to the horizon. The view was spectacular, serene and pastoral and a peace swept over us like the gentle breeze that blew past. Without sounding too morose, it seemed to me that there could be few places more beautiful in which to die.

We drove back toward our hotel in virtual silence, both of us processing the reality of our mother and sister's deaths, and our own tragic lives, in a way more real than we had ever had to before. As we drove slowly along the narrow rural roads, mechanically moving our heads  from side to side like bobbleheads, we were jerked back to life in the present by a new and spectacular scene that seemed to us to be a message of approval and completion from beyond.

RIP

I am in State Center, Iowa on Memorial Day Weekend 2013. Beverly's grave is just a mile from the bed and breakfast where I'm staying.

I'm here because Beverly's sister, Barb, will be in town for her high school reunion, which welcomes all students who ever attended Clemons High School. It will be only the second time I have seen Aunt Barb, and I long to continue to talk with her, as she is the caretaker of the planet's most vivid memories of my biological mother.

I checked into the B&B with the help of Jeffrey, the owner of the Remarkable Rose just down the street. We've met two other times when I was here previously doing research. His mother, Connie, and uncle, Richard, were both in Beverly's class at Clemons. They all moved elsewhere before graduation.

Jeffrey has been interested in my family research and he asks about my progress as he shows me around the comfortable, retro 70's B&B and identifies its dozens of light switches. I tell him of a possible connection between his family and mine. He is intrigued.

I tell him that I have found an on-line conception calculator that indicates that Beverly got pregnant with me on September 29, 1959 – plus or minus three days. I told him about her being in Fort Dodge when Ricky was sick at nine months old. I mention the records that I solicited from Trinity Hospital that show that Ricky was admitted on

September 25 and was released on October 2 of 1959. Therefore, it is likely that she got pregnant while in Fort Dodge.

I tell Jeffrey of Beverly's propensity for older men. As noted earlier, her first husband, Alvin, was 5 years older; her last husband, Clarence, was 30 years her senior. I mention that Beverly had dinner at Jeffrey's grandparents' house, old friends of hers from her years in Clemons, during the week she was in Fort Dodge. At the time Beverly was 19; Jeffrey's grandfather, Merle was 43.

Jeffrey makes the connection. He tells me that his grandfather had a penchant for younger women and left Jeff's grandmother for one of his employees – a woman younger than his own children. Apparently Merle had a reputation.

Jeffrey says, "What *you* need is DNA."

"I really do. In fact, I brought a DNA kit with me and plan to drive up to Fort Dodge to see if Merle's son, Richard, will give me a cheek swab."

"Yeah ... I'll bet he won't ... but I will."

"Seriously? That would be wonderful."

I then learned that the kit I brought would have worked with a sample from Richard, but wouldn't work with a sample from Jeffrey because he's related to Merle through his mother. Having female DNA in the middle makes it impossible for Identigene (the laboratory who made the kit I bought) to say if Merle might be my father.

After some frantic Internet research and several phone conversations with technology specialists at various DNA laboratories, I eventually learn that AncestryDNA has a test that will work, so I arrange for them to send a kit to Jeffrey directly. A few weeks later Jeffrey returned the kit to AncestryDNA and we'll have to wait several weeks for results.

Jeffrey and I walk back to the Remarkable Rose and I buy some flowers for Beverly's grave and for the grave next to hers that belongs to her parents.

Out at Hillside Cemetery I wander around looking for Beverly's gravestone. I thought I could remember where it is, but walk up and down the rows of graves without initial success. As I walk, reading the names and dates of one marker after another I see one with Jeffrey's Grandfather's name and notice that Merle is buried next to his second wife, who was four years younger than Beverly.

A few minutes later I find Beverly's grave only a short baseball toss from Merle's. How ironic.

I secure the bouquets of flowers artfully at the corner of both stones, Beverly's and her folks. The name on her stone is her maiden name, not the married name of the man who killed her. Her sister, Sherri, tells me that her father protested the convention of being buried under one's current legal name. "I'll be damned if I have to look at that name on her grave," he'd said. And so it will be her maiden name for all time.

Flowers in place, I walk back to my car and pull out a baseball from the sports equipment that is always with me. I sign it with a personal message just for Beverly and leave it at the base of her stone. I stand there alone for a long time, as tears stream down my cheeks – cheeks that look so much like hers.

Time Machine

Reflecting on all of this family death and tragedy is overwhelming.

Even now I want to get into a time machine and go back to find Beverly in the middle of June, 1962. I want to sit down with this teenage mom, apparently as abandoned by her family as I was by mine. I want to take her to the little café in State Center, Iowa and I want to buy her a cup of coffee and a cinnamon roll.

I want to look intensely into her eyes and ask her what's going on inside her. I want to listen deeply and give her time to get in touch with herself. I will wait. I want to be a safe haven where she can put into words whatever she is feeling, maybe find words for the first time ever, and then speak them out loud with no fear of judgment or shame. I want to hear her pain. I want to know her fears. I want to absorb her doubts, her insecurities, her depression and her sense of being caged by three screaming kids and one silent husband.

I want to coax out her dreams. I want to be her friend, her confidant, her priest and her pack. I want to affirm her and tell her that she is smart, articulate, outgoing and capable and can do anything she sets her mind to.

I want her to know that the world will change and will accept her as she is, and as she will be, if she'll only persevere. I want to offer to help her imagine a new and better destiny than the one she can see from here. I want her to know that she has options, lots of options. I want to be Jesus for her.

I want to see a light go on through the gathering tears in her eyes and watch hope get birthed there. I want to watch the tears flood out down her plump cheekbones that look so much like mine. I want to get up from my chair and silently approach her and embrace her with love, with understanding, with empathy and with forgiveness.

I do not want to ever let her go.

I want to hold her while my own body quakes in harmony with her sobs. I want to sob for her. I want to sob with her. I want to sob for all that will happen, because I do not have a time machine.

Beverly after the disappearance

Alvin, Beverly's first husband

Beverly's Iowa-born children,
Craig, Theresa and Ricky
weeks before the disappearance

Beverly's fourth child, Jackie

Beverly's fifth child, Steven

Craig and Theresa
the weekend of the State Fair

Part Three

A Journey for Father

And the cat's in the cradle and the silver spoon.
Little boy blue and the man on the moon.
When you comin' home, son?
I don't know when, but we'll get together then, Dad,
You know we'll have a good time then.

Harry Chapin

Lost

My life is rich with purpose, full of love, abundant with friendships, deep with meaning and overflowing with good things. I am one of the lucky ones. Statistics indicate that most children who are orphaned don't fare very well.

But fulfilled and happy as I am, I do carry scars in my heart and mind that will likely be there for as long as I'm on the right side of the grass. And because of those scars, I find this journey to be healing.

At times I feel like a detective on the trail of a high profile case sleuthing for clues, interviewing strangers, discovering new threads that may lead to treasures or dead ends. When I'm in this mode, I find myself mostly dispassionate and able to look at information in a neutral or detached manner. Because I don't have conscious memories of any of the people from my original family, being unattached emotionally is easier.

But it's not always such … sometimes it's not so much detective as lost little boy.

Once, when I was about seven, I went with Mom and Dad Steffen to Des Moines to visit my mom's brother and his wife, my Uncle Bob and Aunt Lynn. We always went shopping when we made the 85-mile trek to the "big city," since the variety of goods and prices were so much better than in the tiny rural towns around where we lived. On this particular visit, just before Christmas, we were shopping in a store a couple of orders of magnitude larger than any store around home. I was distracted by sounds of toys in the adjacent aisle and wandered over to investigate. Before long I realized that I was surrounded by scores of people, but none of them was my dad. Panic immediately set in and I started walking up one aisle and then another, frantically looking for a familiar face. I found none.

After what seemed like hours, though I'm sure it was only minutes, I was in full tears-and-snot-meltdown mode. I made my way back to the front of the store and found a person in a red smock and blubbered an explanation of my predicament. This kind, empathetic soul took my hand and led me to a counter, picked up a microphone and announced to the world, "We have a lost child at the front of the store. He is seven years old and his name is Craig. If you know this little boy, could you please come to the courtesy desk at the front of the store and retrieve him?"

After a few minutes of continued abandonment anxiety, I saw my dad emerge from the crowd. At the moment our eyes met, I was flooded with two emotions. First was the wonderful feeling of being found. Second was the frightening feeling of being found out. I knew I was in trouble for wandering off, but I was so happy to be found.

Sometimes in this journey to find out how my original family lost me, I still feel just like that. And subconsciously I think I've been waiting for decades for a father to appear from the crowd and claim me as his own.

Proof

After Dad Steffen died and after the grieving and responsibilities were complete, I had a strange sense of emptiness. I doubt that this is unusual, especially after the last parent is gone, but for me there was a lack of finality about the emotion. With the nagging suspicion that I might have other family out there somewhere, I wasn't able to simply rest after my adoptive family was gone. What if Alvin were not my biological father? What if, my actual biological father is still alive? What if he never rejected me – what if he just never knew about me? Wouldn't a father want to know about a child – especially one as wonderful as me?

Even though I had suspicions about my paternity, what I needed were facts and proof. The most definitive way to do that would be to get DNA from my sister and have a lab compare it with my own. They'd be able to tell if we shared a father or not. And, unless one of us was switched at birth, we knew we shared the same mother. The problem was, of course, since Dad Steffen died, Theresa wouldn't talk to me. If she wouldn't talk to me, there was very little chance that she'd give me a DNA sample.

Ignoring the obvious barriers, I did some research about DNA labs and found one that seemed to cater to my particular problem. Many of them seemed focused on paternity lawsuits and dead-beat dads. That wasn't really my problem. Sibling comparisons were barely mentioned on most DNA lab websites. So when I found Identigene, I was heartened to see that they had developed a specific protocol for comparing sibling DNA. I ordered a kit for $395.00.

During my next trip to Iowa, I asked one of Beverly's sisters and one of Alvin's sisters to provide a DNA cheek swab to be sent to Identigene for analysis. The challenge would be to see if Theresa would agree to see me and, if so, to see if she'd provide a swab to compare with mine and our aunts'.

I drove to Southwest Iowa to arrange a meeting with Theresa. We agreed to meet for dinner in Atlantic at Oinkers, but she didn't show up. I ate alone and did more research from my phone as I sat there like a date scorned. I seriously considered just getting in my car, driving home and shaking the dust of this little town off my feet forever.

The following day Theresa and I did connect at her evening place of work. Though I could tell that she would prefer to pretend as if nothing had happened between us, I told her how much it hurt me that Kenny would accuse me of stealing from Dad, and that she had apparently joined his opinion by refusing to return my calls and texts. Eventually she apologized and we hugged and reaffirmed our love for one another.

We spent the rest of the evening together, had some dinner and then headed back out to her place in the country. I shared photos and documents I'd been uncovering about Beverly's early life and included her in all that I'd discovered earlier in that same trip to Iowa. We talked about Beverly's sister Sherri and how I'd met her for the first time and had dinner with her and her husband, Steve, a few nights earlier. Theresa told me of when she had met Sherri a few times back in the 1970s and early 80s.

Finally, just before midnight, I directed the conversation to my questions about my own paternity. This was not a new topic between the two of us; I'd wondered aloud on a few previous occasions. Eventually I got around to talking about DNA and the kit I'd brought with me. I asked if she'd be willing to help me get an answer to this question that had been nagging me for decades.

She said, "Well, yeeess, but he's your dad too. You're my brother."

I assured her that, regardless of the test results, she and I would always be siblings because we shared both a mother and a childhood. Nothing could change that.

After a couple of months of waiting for the lab, I got the results of the DNA comparison on-line.

Summary and Interpretation of Results:

The alleged father of Theresa and Craig is Alvin Lorraine Shepherd, who is deceased. Tested in his place was his known biological sister, Kathy S, along with Sherri S who, it is averred, is the full sibling of Theresa and Craig's biological mother, who is also deceased.

1) Based upon the genetic data, the Combined Full vs. Half Sibship Index is 0.040 to 1, which means that these data are 25 times more likely if Craig and Theresa's fathers are unrelated, untested men from the Caucasian population than if Craig and Theresa share both parents in common. If the averred relationships are undisputed, this corresponds to a 3.8% probability that Craig and Theresa share the same father.

So the verdict is finally in. My instincts about this subject are now scientifically proven to be correct. Alvin is definitely not my father. But, if *he's* not, who in the world *is*?

Fatherless

My wife has a theory that God reveals himself to the world as Father not because God is male but because that is the human relationship that is most often estranged and broken; hence God comes to reveal himself as healer to that relationship. It's an interesting theory.

As a child who grew up without a biological father in my life, I have long fondly embraced the Christian doctrine of adoption. In this doctrinal theory, God presents himself as "a father to the fatherless." Additionally Jesus, the revealed son of God, declares that his followers are adopted into his family as sons and daughters of God and are given equal inheritance with him in the vast family of God. As a kid who never knew his biological father, and who felt estranged from his adoptive father most of his life, this doctrine provided me another, more promising paternal option. The idea of God as father was so compelling because I had this sense that if God was omniscient, as theologians claimed, then he alone understood me and my quirks in a way that no other being in the universe could.

In my house and our church, this idea of God's omniscience was typically used as a control device to keep people vigilant in their sin management. After all, if God knew your every thought and what was done in secret, you stood the real fear of being punished and rejected as a result of your dalliances into evil thoughts. But somehow in my young heart I understood, though I could not have articulated it, that God's omniscience was not so much a tool of fear and control, as it was a reason to take comfort that God knew me completely inside and out, and yet loved me unconditionally still. Now *that* is some serious good news.

253

I recall many times having fights with my parents over some difference between what they thought was appropriate behavior for a Christian and what I thought. Usually these disagreements ended up with me being exasperated beyond tolerance, because I could not get them to see that my perspective was not evil – only different from theirs. At the end of these arguments I would go to (or be banished to) my bedroom where I'd sob and scream into my pillow and find my only comfort in the concept that God understood my heart far more thoroughly than my parents did. God understood that my heart was NOT "deceitful above all things and desperately wicked" (an old covenant declaration) as my parents asserted, but rather that it was "a new heart, a heart of flesh, not of stone," (a new covenant promise) placed there as a gift by my loving, eternal Father. This was my only comfort.

One example of this kind of exasperation came during my sophomore year in high school. My life was changing dramatically as a result of my new relationship with Jesus and my new school. Instead of being known as a "burn out" or "loser," as I had been previously, my new nickname was "preacher." I walked the halls with a New Testament in my front shirt pocket, and was often found reading it during study halls and between classes. The moniker came because reading wasn't enough for me; I also had to tell other people how far short they were falling from the standards of the Bible. What I know now, but didn't know then, is how unwise and immature this behavior is. In fact, the scriptures call it "zeal, not according to knowledge." Put simply, I was ill-advised to behave like this because, as eventually became evident, it was the opposite of the loving and inclusive way Jesus engaged with people. What my judgmental behavior really revealed was how ignorant I really was of the way of Jesus.

As a natural outcome of this kind of Christian aspiration, I got invited to a special youth meeting at a Baptist church my friend Barb was affiliated with. I asked at supper one night if I could go to this youth meeting with Barb. Based on Mom and Dad's reaction, you'd have thought I'd asked to attend a communist rally or, worse, had told them that I was joining a rock band. I was flatly told I was not allowed to go because this was not an event affiliated with our exclusive church community. The Baptists might as well have been hippy, drug addicts so far as my parents were concerned. If pressed, they would likely have conceded that the Baptists MIGHT be able to get to heaven, but only "without rewards" and after the burning away of their "wood, hay and stubble."

Having met many of the people who would be at this youth meeting, I simply couldn't easily dismiss their faith as my parents seemed to. Lots of shouting ensued, and my father eventually retrieved an ancient 3/8th inch thick yard stick (they don't make 'em like that anymore) from atop the refrigerator and began hitting me about the head and shoulders. With each blow, the stick shattered into a shorter and shorter weapon. Bruised and bloodied, I retreated to my bedroom, slammed and locked the door and commenced weeping and screaming into my pillow. Again, my only comfort was that my eternal Father understood me and my heart better than anyone on earth—and he still liked me.

It was my belief then, and still is today that, as an abandoned child, I had a greater appreciation for the Christian doctrine of adoption than others who had not received the orphan wound as I had.

But even with this appreciation for my Father in heaven, at age 50, when my earthly adoptive father died, I longed for a father who was real, tangible, three-dimensional and one who loved and understood me in a way that no earthly father had yet done.

In the spring of 2012, while sitting on the back deck at my home, I had an epiphany. For the first time I realized that the hole inside me was shaped like an earthly father.

The dots had been there all along, but for the first time I found them getting connected inside me, as if someone else was operating an Etch-A-Sketch. I was longing for a parent's love. But, more specifically, I was longing for a FATHER's love.

Most of you are probably saying, "Well, duh." But honestly it had never occurred to me before — that the hole inside me could only be filled by a father's love, understanding and acceptance. At that moment I made the decision to do some research about fatherlessness and its symptoms that manifest in adults like me.

The books I've read since, on the topic of father-loss and the orphan-wound, agree that a few of the common struggles are fear of conflict, rejection and abandonment anxiety, extreme self-reliance, and anger issues aplenty.

My wife will tell you that each of these things is true in my life to one degree or another. There is no question that the wounds that were created in me as a youth are still present even now. None of these things has driven me to debilitation or dysfunction, but I confess to them being ever-present.

I know that I'll never be able to talk with my mother; she's been dead since I was five. My guts always told me that Alvin wasn't my father and DNA analysis has proven that instinct. And something inside me tells me that I need to keep searching with the tenacity that those of you with father-loss can surely understand.

I journey forward without fear for my tribe, my pack.

Tsunami

It took me by surprise. I'm sure it's obvious by now, Cindy and I love film. A few nights ago we sat down to watch *The Impossible*. It's a true story about the unlikely struggle and ultimate survival of a family encountering a tsunami while vacationing in Thailand in 2004. I didn't think the film was particularly well done, but the story itself was compelling. The fact that it was true made it more engaging from my perspective.

An author I've read rather extensively, John Eldridge, writes in at least one of his books that we go to the movies to "find *ourselves* in the story." I find this is typically true when I go to the movies, and it is the primary criterion on which I base my subconscious approval or disapproval of the film. If I can relate well or deeply with a character or with the story itself, I find that I come away with a really positive opinion of the film. But if there is no one or nothing with which I can connect and relate in the movie, it is very likely that I will leave the theater with a negative sense of the film – even if I can't immediately articulate why.

On this night, I found myself in tears on two occasions during the film. But it wasn't because I could relate to a particular scene or character in the film. Rather, it was the opposite – it was because it suddenly occurred to me that I had absolutely no emotional or intellectual memories in my own experience that could allow me to truly empathize with what was happening on the silver screen. And once I realized this, perhaps for the first time, I simultaneously became aware of tears seeping involuntarily from the corners of my eyes.

The family in the film had been separated by the trauma of the tsunami. Against all odds, the mother managed to find the eldest of three sons. The father was able to find and reconnect with the two younger boys. Husband and wife each try in vain to find the other during a long and difficult journey. Finally, almost serendipitously, the eldest son spots the father amongst a hoard of confusion near a hospital and screams, "DAD? DAD; DAAAAD," then runs desperately to find him. In the dramatic manner of films attempting to capture such rare emotional moments, the son falls into his father's embrace and is engulfed there in battered, but powerful arms as both weep massive tears accompanied by sobs of joy and catharsis.

The father, played by Ewan McGregor, tenderly holds his son in the midst of an ocean of chaos and wounded humanity while stroking his head tenderly. It is the personification of the Biblical parable of finding "the pearl of great price."

Watching this scene a near-audible switch clicked in my head. The scene illuminated a deficit in my soul and exposed the unkind truth that I have never had a father/son experience anything like this. As a child, I was intellectually aware that my adoptive father loved me, though this awareness was based solely upon his exemplary hard work, responsibility and temporal provision for my needs. I don't have a single memory of a moment where I felt "so loved," as the father God declares and demonstrates in Jesus in John 3:16. I am aware that many sons have never felt this depth of love from their fathers but, at that moment of the film, I came face to face with my own existence bereft of being the object of such zealous exuberance.

Later in the film, the father and son reconnect with the entire family and there is a reunion bliss that is palpable. As a group hug ensued, I found myself wet-faced a second time quite by surprise. In this moment my own loss took a deeper turn as I came to grips with two more realities of my own life story. First, I realized that not only have

I never experienced the depth of a father's love, but I'd never experienced this passion from either of the mothers in my life either. And second, I was literally jolted at the sudden awareness that – I likely never would.

Renwick

I think my curiosity to learn the identity of my biological father is natural. Many of my friends and acquaintances have questioned my mental health regarding this issue, fearing I have, or will become, obsessed with the search – or massively disappointed by it. "Why don't you just leave it alone?" "You have had a wonderful life. Why risk messing that up with information from the past?" "Are you looking for a father figure, or just curious?" "I don't understand why you care about finding someone who didn't care about you."

My standard retort is simply, "Most people know who their parents are. You know who yours are, right? So how can you question my desire to know something that you've known all your life?"

I journey forward without fear.

Since this quest began late last year, I've assembled a pretty long list of men who were in some kind of relationship with (or proximity to) my mother in roughly the time frame of my conception. Of course, I have such a tiny snippet of information from that time of Beverly's life, there's no way for me to assemble a comprehensive list. But at the time of a conversation with Beverly's sister, Barb, in November, I had six names on that list ... a seventh nameless possibility. And, unbeknownst to me, there was about to be an eighth name added.

1)   Alvin Shepherd, whose name is on my original birth certificate
2)   Dr. Harding, Beverly's doctor
3)   Dr. Dannenbring, Ricky's doctor in Fort Dodge

4) Richard, Beverly's school friend

5) Merle, Richard's father

6) Jack Hiner, my sister Jackie's father

7) The farmer(s) who had employed Alvin, whose name(s) I did not know

The family members of the farmer for whom Alvin was working back in 1959 were candidates because this is where Beverly was living at the time of my conception; not that there was any other reason to suspect them. I'd been trying to figure out who these people were, but so far no one could remember a family name – only the name of the tiny town.

I came home from a client's office one afternoon in March with energy to do more research. I took the name of that little town and searched to see if it ever published a newspaper. It did. I searched to see if that newspaper had ever

The Renwick Times

Your Newsy Home Town Newspaper

VOLUME 76 — RENWICK, IOWA — PRINTED THURSDAY P. M. DISTRIBUTED TO THE READING PUBLIC THURSDAY, April 2, 1959 No. 14

Easter dinner guests of Mrs Rose Hefty were Mr and Mrs Chester Ogan of Livermore, Mrs Anna Krause, Mr and Mrs Clarence Hefty and family and Mr and Mrs Lorain Shepherd and children. Guests for supper Monday were Mr and Mrs Ed Zweifel of Titonka.

Mrs Rose Hefty visited in the Ray Zweifel home at Fenton Tuesday.

been digitized and therefore would be searchable on-line. Amazingly, it had been and was. I searched for the last name of "Shepherd" and narrowed the search by the date range 1958-1962. As easy as that, I found this little tidbit in the social column of the paper that answered my question:

I'll confess right now that my first reaction was, "Oh dear God, let's hope that's not my biological origin. I don't think I can tolerate the combination of my current girth with the last name "Hefty."

I spent several hours doing internet research and found a 2007 obituary for Mr. Hefty, a dairy farmer. After following dozens of leads embedded within that obituary, it certainly appeared that some of the family was still living in Iowa and that the matriarch of the family may also still be living, at least so far as Google was aware. I couldn't find any phone information for any of the family, so I resolved to drive to that part of Iowa during my next research trip out there. That next trip occurred in May.

I reviewed the information on the family I'd gleaned months earlier and decided that a son named Fred was the most likely to still be in the area.

My GPS took me to the area without difficulty, but I had no idea how I might find Hefty family members. I looked around for a library, but didn't find one. Glancing down one street, I saw what appeared to be a school and thought a logical place for a library might be near the school. But as I approached the school building it was clear that it was no longer being used for that purpose, as the parking lot was filled with new and used farm equipment. There was also nothing resembling a library.

What better place to find out where a farmer might live than to ask around at a farm implement dealer? My little Toyota Prius was as conspicuous in that lot as a Siamese kitten at a St. Bernard dog show. I could see people staring at me as I slowly turned in and got out of my car.

As I approached two employees conversing in the parking lot I decided to lead with the obvious. "So, I'm not from around here."

The two guys glanced at each other and cynical smiles hinted on their faces.

"I'm looking for a guy named Fred Hefty. His family used to farm around here back in the 60s, but I don't know if they're still here," I explained.

"Oh sure, Fred still lives on the family farm. It's just outside of town. You see those grain bins over there?"

I looked through house tops into the distance a few miles and saw sun reflecting off silver metal.

"Just head out that way and stop at the second house on the right. I doubt he'll be around though; he works at a factory over in Clarion. The farm is rented out these days, but he lives in the second place, not the old farmhouse."

So I thanked these gents for their help and headed off in the general direction of the grain bins to see if I could find Fred.

I slowly coasted down the gravel driveway toward a newer blue ranch house that I was sure didn't exist when Beverly and Alvin were here. There was a man on a ZTR lawn mower in the front yard eying me suspiciously as I got closer to him. I stopped my car and emerged, waiting for the man to complete his swath and arrive at my location. I waved and greeted him with gestures, as he shut down the mower and removed his ear plugs.

"I'm looking for Fred Hefty."

He raised his right hand as if being sworn in to testify and said "That's me," with a suspicious insinuation of a smile on his face.

I explained that I was doing some family history research and told him that my folks had once worked for his folks. I didn't see any obvious physical resemblance to me, as I starred inquisitively into his round, red face.

Fred said that he'd have been about 10 years old back in 1959 and that he thought he did remember Beverly and Alvin, but not too much. I showed him some old pictures of both of them and he was sure they were familiar, especially Alvin since he'd worked alongside him in the dairy barn.

Fred showed me where the little farmhand house would have stood where Beverly and Alvin would have lived. "It was blown away in a tornado back in 1979. That's when we built this one." He gestured toward the blue ranch.

Fred and I talked for over an hour. He went inside the house at one point, and got a couple of family photo albums and I powered up my computer so that I could share a few more pictures of Beverly and Alvin. Fred and I sat in my car and thumbed through photos, told stories about our respective history and reminisced about farm life from decades ago.

"So Fred, I noticed in the old newspapers that your father died in 2007. I'm sorry for your loss… Is your mother still living?"

"Yes, she's in a nursing home over in Clarion."

"Is she still mentally sharp?"

"Well, some days she is and some days we just wonder where she went."

"Do you think it would be worth my time to go visit with her?"

"Well, sure. Give it a try. Maybe she'll be having a good day."

So Fred and I said our goodbyes, and I thanked him for his time and information. I backed down the driveway and drove back into town where I pulled over and plugged in "Clarion, Iowa" to my iPhone GPS and headed out following SIRI's pleasant voice.

As I drove the 20 miles toward Clarion, I pondered the information and pictures Fred had shared. I concluded that it was very unlikely that anyone from the immediate Hefty family was responsible for my birth. Fred's father's nickname was "Red" because of the color of his hair. Everyone in the family had red hair. They were a rather devout Christian family from a rather conservative branch of the evangelical tree – ironically, pretty near where the church of my youth would have been located on that tree.

I thought it was pretty safe to mark the Heftys off my list of potential biological families. So I wasn't sure why I was driving to Clarion to talk with Anna Hefty, but I just wanted to talk with someone who might actually remember Beverly first hand.

I found the nursing home, let myself in and wandered about looking for an employee who could direct me to Anna. A pleasant woman showed me to her room. Anna was seated upright in a powder blue recliner, vintage 1970, almost certainly brought directly here from the farmhouse in Renwick when she moved out. Her eagle white head was professionally coiffed and she looked straight ahead watching *The Price is Right* at an uncomfortably (for me) loud volume. As I entered the room, her gaze alternated from the staff member who led me here and my face. She was clearly excited to have a visitor, while at the same time searching my features in a desperate attempt to decipher who I might be.

"I'll bet you weren't expecting a visitor today were you?" I said with a big smile. "My name is Craig Steffen."

Anna seemed bright and engaged.

"I was just out at your farm talking with your son, Fred. He told me you were here and suggested I stop in and talk with you. I'm doing some family research. My folks used to work for you and your husband back in the late 1950s and early 60s. Do you remember Alvin and Beverly Shepherd?"

After only the slightest hesitation, Anna brightly said "Oh sure, I remember them. Alvin was so good with the cows. He had a way with them that kept them calm."

After talking about our mutual connection around Alvin and Beverly I said, "My research seems to indicate that Alvin and Beverly didn't work for you and your husband for very long. Is that true?"

Anna looked at me, cocked her head as if recalling a dark secret and said, "That's true … AND there's a REASON."

Sensing that she was about to tell me something unexpected, yet critical to my quest I said, "Oh really. Do tell."

Fuller Brush

Anna is out working in the yard in the autumn of 1959. As she ambles through the verdant grass picking up sticks after a storm she notices how lush this grass always is, growing out of northern Iowa top soil that is three feet deep. "We should plant corn here," she thought.

The slender Anna is wife of a dairy farmer, mother of a young family and still pretty in her early 30s. She works her way farther from the main house, a classic, white, two-story cube that once had a coal burning furnace and still sports the single large discharge grate in the center of the lower level that feeds "gravity-heat" to the entire structure. As she gets farther from her own house she moves closer to the little one-story, structure built on a slab in the lowest spot in the yard. It is in this structure that Beverly and Alvin have lived for nearly a year while Alvin serves Anna and her husband as a farmhand.

Lost in her own thoughts in the midst of the mundane collection of fallen debris from last night's wind, Anna is interrupted by a sound she cannot immediately identify. Though the storm has long passed, the wind in this part of Iowa is nearly constant, so it is hard to sift the target sound from the wind's natural howl. But there is definitely something… something disturbing and unnatural… something that sets off her base maternal instincts … the cry of a child.

As if by divine remote control, Anna's body moves toward the cry and she finds herself standing on the step of the tiny farmhand house. Inside, the walls vibrate with the screams and sobs of multiple children in sick harmony. Concern and compassion fills Anna's chest. With three children of her own, she recognizes the alarming difference between a fussy cry and a desperate one. She knocks on the door. The cries grow louder, but there is no perceptible stirring inside the house. She knocks louder and more frantically. Still, no reaction to her pounding can be heard from within. Anna calls out and pounds the door till her fist hurts, "Beverly ... BEVERLY!"

Finally it occurs to her, "This is my house; I'm going in." She flings open the unlocked door and moves through a perfectly clean and ordered abode toward the pungent excrement and sobs of abandoned children, all the while calling Beverly's name. There is still no answer.

She finds the children and speaks softly to them, comforting their fears and wiping their wet, snotty, terror-filled faces. "Where is your momma, little ones?"

Theresa is about two years old and soon stops crying and clings to Anna's leg with the grip of a linebacker. Ricky, less than a year old, cannot be consoled. His face is magenta, his cries raspy from over-use and his back arches stiff in anger. At times he stops breathing and his face morphs to a frightening blue-gray. Anna holds him, speaks softly to him, rocks him tenderly and longs for him to find calm. His little body convulses. He breathes again, gasps for life-giving air and each breath is then rudely interrupted by a hiccup. Ricky aspirates, vomits and sobs on.

Anna's furious emotions alternate between panic and rage. "Where in hell is these children's mother?" She thinks, but is too proper to speak the question aloud.

After hours of comforting, the children calm and the worst of this storm subsides from their infant-sized perspective. But there is still no word from Beverly. The storm inside Anna is gathering fury.

Anna has lived in this tiny north central Iowa community for years. Her husband and his family have been here all their lives. They know everyone – literally. She picks up the phone and begins to make inquiries. She knows who to call and who is likely to have information. Before long she has learned that Beverly isn't on her death bed. Nothing criminal or terminal has befallen her. That is the good news.

The bad news is that Anna has also learned that Beverly is out with a man – not her husband. They'd been seen by many, and according to the locals, this man has quite the reputation for trying to ensnare bored young women with the allure of his "man-about-town" ways. He is a door-to-door salesman.

When Anna hears his name she knows exactly what has happened. She instantly recalls a time a year or two earlier when this same salesman knocked on her door and flirted with her. When his flirts had lost their subtlety, she threw him out and told him never to return.

Anna is 12 years older and much wiser than Beverly and knows how to see through to the emptiness and trouble this kind of man is peddling. But Beverly is still a teenager and already has two children. She'd come from "town-living" and is now stuck alone on a farm with a silent and constantly working husband. The bellowing dairy cattle and bawling children sound more and more the same to her. There is no escaping the smell of bovine and children's feces. She is bored. She is looking for some action.

As Anna weaves the details of her amazingly vivid recollections of those days, the story crystallizes in my imagination.

On a pleasant autumn morning, Beverly is lounging in the tiny house's most comfortable chair, with a magazine in one hand, a cup of coffee in the other, and an empty breakfast plate beside her. The kids are asleep in the bedroom and Beverly loses herself in the incomprehensible worlds of *Look*.

There is a startling knock at the door, which happens approximately twice a year in this remote and private rural area. Beverly jumps up eagerly and turns down the music on the radio. As she rushes for the door, she pauses for a few seconds in front of the worn, beveled mirror on the wall. She pushes on her hair two or three times, with no discernible result, and brushes some crumbs from her blouse. The knock recurs.

She opens the screen door which hangs loosely from its ancient and rusted hinges, screeching like a hawk from its neglect.

A distinguished older gentleman stands on the step dressed sharply in a pressed blue pinstriped suit, starched white shirt, a paisley tie and shiny black shoes. A freshly waxed 1957 Chevy gleams in the driveway behind him. It is a cheery mauve color that Beverly has never seen before.

"Yeees, how can I help you?" Beverly asks.

"Good morning, ma'am. My name is Bill, and I'm your Fuller Brush Salesman. I have here many quality items that will make every day go better. What might your name be, ma'am?"

"I'm Beverly."

"May I come in to show you how I can change your life?" Bill recites cheerfully for the thousandth time.

Beverly tries to mask her elation over this unexpected human contact.

"Sure, come on in. You can have a seat here at the kitchen table." Beverly gestures. "So, Bill, how are you going to change my life?" Beverly asks in a friendly tone.

Bill removes his fedora revealing perfectly groomed hair and releasing the distinctive aroma of hair tonic.

"Well, I've got hair brushes, vegetable brushes, toilet brushes, brooms, feather dusters, carpet cleaners, stain removers and detergents, just to name a few. Ma'am, I can see that you keep a mighty clean house here. Don't you just hate those little trails of dirt your broom leaves behind when you sweep the kitchen floor? I've got a highly engineered broom in my car that will solve that problem once and for all. Or how about the spot you just can't get out of your favorite blouse?" Bill responds as if an actor playing the role.

Bill opens his well-worn black leather case and pulls a small jar from inside with the flare of pulling a rabbit from a hat.

"We've got this Fuller spot remover that will save your husband a lot of Hamiltons on clothes. Does your husband ever complain that you spend too much on pretty blouses, Bev? May I call you Bev?"

"Sure, you can call me Bev. My husband doesn't really say much about anything."

"I might even have something in my bag that can help you with that problem."

Smiling mischievously, Bill reaches into the bag and places a decoratively cut bottle of Leading Lady perfume on the table. A ruby pump bulb seductively tempts Beverly to reach for it. But she resists showing interest.

"I just use the same brush for everything around here," Beverly grins. "We don't have money for more than one brush, so in the morning we always brush our teeth and hair BEFORE we clean the toilet." She jokes with a giggle.

"Well these products are hand-made and we've been selling them for over 50 years. I've got customers who are still using the same brushes they bought when Al Fuller started the company back in 1906."

"Wow, you look old, but you don't look like you could have been selling brushes for 50 years, Bill." Beverly goads the salesman while wearing a sarcastic grin.

"Well, I didn't say that I was the one who sold the original brushes, Bev. I'm not *that* old – old enough to be your daddy, but not *that* old."

"I don't really have a daddy," Beverly says in a barely audible tone.

"You know, I met Al Fuller once at a training meeting. He's a millionaire many times over; fascinating guy. I think I'm a lot like him. I might be a millionaire someday too. Whataya think?"

"Maybe you will, Bill. You've already got a nice car and a snappy suit of clothes. If your wife doesn't spend it all, you just might get there."

"I never let the little lady keep me from getting what I want." Bill responds. "She's earning me money right now working at my other business. I own the dry cleaner's in Clarion. I keep her busy – that keeps her from spending my money." Bill smiles.

"Maybe you *will* be a millionaire then, Bill."

A baby begins to cry from the corner bedroom.

"I guess you have a baby."

"I have two. The girl is almost two and the boy is, let's see, about ten months. You got kids, Bill?"

"I have a son. He's twelve," Bill says, seeming uncomfortable revealing personal information.

"Geez Bill, I thought your kids would be married by now. Did it take you a while to figure it out?" Beverly teases.

Bill blushes, unconsciously flips the latch on his case open and closed, then gets a bit defensive.

"Oh no, I 'figured it out' a long time ago. I can still 'figure it out' with the best of them. It's just that Norma, err, my wife, she can't have kids. But we 'figured it out' a lot before we knew she couldn't," Bill says, a cocky smile emerging.

"Can you show me how that spot remover works? I dripped a little coffee on my blouse this morning. I'll bet your little tube of goo doesn't really work."

Beverly gestures to a barely detectable, dime-sized mocha spot just below the top button of her ecru blouse. Opening the jar of spot remover and sliding it across the kitchen table toward Beverly, Bill offers verbal instructions.

"Just put a little dab on the tip of your finger and rub it into the spot in a circular motion. Then get a clean dish cloth, wet it, and dab away the spot. It's really easy, and it *will* work."

"Oh no, I don't know how to use this stuff and if it doesn't work, you'll just say I did it wrong." Sliding the jar back toward Bill, she says, "YOU do it."

Acting every bit the showman, Bill stands with the open jar in his left hand and offers his other to Beverly, helps her to her feet and leads her toward the kitchen sink.

"Where do you keep your clean dish cloths, Bev?" he asks, his eyes searching the premises.

"They're down here in this drawer." Beverly bends at the waist and slowly retrieves one, handing it dutifully to Bill as if assisting in a magic act.

Bill spreads his legs apart to shorten his stature and is now eyeball to eyeball with Beverly, close enough to smell the coffee on her breath. Following his own instructions, he dabs a bit of the cleaner on his left index finger and grasps the buttoned area gently in his right, allowing two fingers to slide inside the blouse to apply pressure from behind the spot.

Beverly stands stock still as a dutiful child, her gaze never leaving Bill's face as he gives all his attention to her. Her nostrils flare at the scent of after shave. It is a scent she should recognize, but in the intoxication of this moment, she cannot recall its name. Beverly feels noticed and dangerous.

Bill retreats to his case and removes a small circular brush and repeats the rubbing process, this time with the soft brush he holds expertly in his left hand. Two fingers of Bill's right hand slide expertly back inside Beverly's blouse. After rotating and spinning the brush for a few seconds, he discards it and reaches for the moist cloth lying next to the sink. He presses the cloth firmly into the spot over and over again to remove the gooey paste and then rotates the cloth to use the dry portion to press away the remaining moisture.

"There it is, Bev. Your spot has been taken care of and your pretty blouse is as good as new." Bill announces. "I just saved you money on your wardrobe, darlin'."

More than 30 minutes has passed since the cries from the bedroom had first been heard. Neither Beverly nor Bill seemed to hear their constancy, but they have now intensified to a decibel that can no longer be ignored. Ricky's cries have woken his sister, and she is whining and calling for her mommy. Annoyed, Beverly realizes that she's going to have to go deal with them.

"I guess I'm going to have to play mommy again now, Bill. It's never ending. But I *am* interested in the magic potions you're selling Bill, but I don't have any money right now. Can you stop back some other time so we can complete what you started here today? And I'll take a jar of the spot remover and one of those little brushes. Leave me a catalog, Bill and I'll see what else I can't live without."

Bill removes his order book and scribbles "Beverly" at the top. Beverly watches him draw a little star next to her name. In the lined form below he records the numbers 758, 855 and 384.

"Well Bev, I'd certainly be eager to stop back by in a few days to take care of you. When would be a convenient time?" Bill asks.

"Why don't you try at the end of the week, Bill. We don't have a telephone, so just stop by about this time of day and I'll have some money for you then. Maybe you can show me some other things from your magic bag."

As Beverly talks, Bill gathers his wares, returns them to their leather case and grabs his hat from the kitchen chair. Placing it deliberately on his head, he retreats to the door, swings it open and swaggers to his shiny, mauve Chevy.

Her children wailing in the background, Beverly lingers with one hand on the door until the cloud of gravel dust disappears from down the country road.

She lets the door slam behind her. Catching a hint of Regatta aftershave still lingering in the air she grumbles, "You stupid kids ruin all my fun, damn it – he liked me."

Three days later Bill returns. Beverly has been waiting and listening since his amazing car disappeared in a cloud of dust days ago. She is dressed up as if going to the city or to the theatre, though she doesn't own the kind of clothes to really pull off the look. She's "taken care" of the kids too. She's put some cough syrup in the kids' bottles and put them down to sleep. She meets Bill at the door a little too eager – but doesn't really care.

"Good morning, Bev. Are you ready for me to change your life today?" Bill asks with a smile.

"I certainly am," Beverly smiles. "But first, I wonder if you could do a favor for me?"

"If I can, I will. What do you need?"

"Oh, I'm pretty sure you can. I wonder if you can give me a ride into town in that beautiful car of yours?"

"Well, sure. I'm planning on heading there right after I give you the items you ordered from the Fuller catalog. What is it that you need?"

"Our car's down at the oil station being worked on, and won't be ready till tomorrow, so I thought I could get a ride from you – if you're up for it."

Bill takes a step toward the door with a small, lidless box in his hand. Inside the box is a jar of spot remover, a small circular brush and a sponge.

"Just put that stuff over there on the chair, Bill. Here's your money. Now can we go?"

"Aren't you an eager one?"

With his right hand he places the box on the chair and with the left he accepts payment ... something like a prisoner exchange.

Beverly heads for the door and is certain Bill will follow.

"Aren't you going to open the door for me, Bill?" she says as she breezes toward the Bel Air.

"I certainly will."

He rushes to the passenger door and, for the first time, notices that Beverly is dressed smartly. She has a light full-length coat on, with a black purse over her arm and she's put on white gloves while she walks toward the car. Her naturally curly hair is done up tightly and he catches a whiff of a sweet perfume as he brushes past her and opens the door. Beverly slides onto the seat and waits for Bill to close the car door behind her.

Bill walks quickly in front of the car and gets into the driver's seat, looking over at Beverly who is smiling.

"Did you buy this car new, Bill?"

"Yes, Bev, I've had it for a couple of years now. I got it from Cambier's in Clarion. Have you been there?"

"No, we never go to places like that. Car lot cars are too expensive. We always buy from people. It's cheaper. I've only ridden in a new car once before in my life. My friend, Sharon, and me stole a car down in Clemons once and took it for a joy ride," She blurts with obvious pride.

"Well, Bev, you didn't tell me you were into grand larceny. Should I be afraid? You got a gun in that purse? You gunna force me to commit a crime with you today, then steal my car?"

Bill is toying with Beverly, but deep in his mind he realizes that he doesn't really know anything about this girl. He's not even certain now that she's "of age." She says she has a husband and two kids, but he's never actually *seen* them. Come to think of it, where are those kids today? Maybe she's just a dropout baby sitter?

"I've never seen a car this color before. What do they call it?"

"It's a 1957 Chevy Bel Air."

"I KNOW it's a Chevy Bel Air, 'DAD.' What I don't know is what they call this COLOR." Beverly's words drip with playful sarcasm.

"Oh. Uhh, I don't remember for sure. It's something 'Pearl' or 'Coral' or something like that. Why does it matter what it's CALLED?

"I just like it, that's all. When you like something, you want to know its name, don't ya?"

The two drive around in the Chevy for over an hour stopping in at Basham's Phillips 66 station for a fill-up and to buy a couple of Frostie Root Beers. Later Bill and Bev make a conspicuous stop for lunch at the Townhouse Café in Belmond. As they drive east of Clarion on Highway 3 with the windows down, feeling wild and free, Bill sees a new sign for the Evans-Kay Motel. Without conversation, Bill pulls into the small gravel parking lot, shuts the motor off, turns in his seat and looks Beverly in her pretty green eyes.

"Bev, do you want to have some real, grown-up fun? I know the guy who just bought this place. He's from Minnesota; I met him at a Council meeting. He owes me a favor; we can do this without anyone ever knowing."

Beverly notices that Bill's voice is softer and more uncertain than it has been before.

"Don't be such a fraidy cat, 'DAD.' I don't give a shit if anyone finds out. I'm going to change YOUR life. Go get us a room. And bring that magic bag of yours; you're going to need some of the stuff in there for this 'Leading Lady.'"

As it turns out, Bill is 43 and Beverly barely 19. He is two years older than Beverly's father. Anna knows him well, both by reputation and by relationship. Anna is a first cousin of Bill's wife and knows them both to be "trouble."

More than five hours later, Beverly returns to her little house and cannot find her children. She is not panicked. She takes the time to change her clothes, and to make a snack. Then she simply strolls, nonchalant and barefoot, through the lush grass to Anna's house.

Anna is not kind or inquisitive. She confronts Beverly with the truth of what she's already discovered through her phone calls. Beverly is incredulous and defensive and chooses belligerence over humility.

"This is NONE of YOUR business!" Beverly claims. "You run your life and I'll run mine!"

"It IS my business – that's MY house you left those kids in. When you force me to take care of the kids you neglect while you're out doing God-knows-what, you MAKE it my business." Anna snaps.

Theresa and Ricky hear their mother's voice and begin to cry in the downstairs bedroom.

Apparently discretion and humility are not strong suits of Beverly. She continues her uncomely defense and paints herself into a corner.

"Well, Beverly, I wasn't going to mention this to my husband or to Alvin. But you leave me no choice. I know EXACTLY what you did today – all of it. You grew up in a small town; you should know by now that you can't get away with anything. People snoop, people talk. I'm just afraid you might get pregnant – have you thought about the consequences of THAT?"

Anna has been prepared to keep Beverly's indiscretion to herself, even though she is repulsed by the action and the resulting child abuse. Anna remembers being 19 and restless, and she remembers the lascivious salesman. But when Beverly chooses to lambast her and feign false innocence, it is more than Anna can abide.

"Let's just see what my husband has to say about all this," Anna draws a line.

Later that night Anna and Beverly are together again, this time in the presence of their husbands. Anna spells out the whole sordid tale and Beverly finally, far too late, realizes how caught she really is.

"This can NEVER happen again, Beverly. You cannot run around with men while your husband works here. You cannot leave those children in our house all alone. You must take your motherly responsibilities seriously and you can't jeopardize our reputation in this community just because you act upon your every whim. If anything like this happens again, Alvin will be fired and you'll both get thrown out of our house. Is that clear?" Anna says indignantly as her husband nods consent.

Alvin is mute in the face of this heart-wrenching revelation. He may have been among the quietest humans alive. But later, in the privacy of the milking barn, he asks Anna's husband for information regarding local lawyers he might contact. So far as I can determine, he never acted upon that information.

For Beverly's part, it seems clear that she did understand their mandate. She was a bright, articulate woman after all. But it is also clear that she really didn't "give a shit," as she'd said, about their desire for a quiet and peaceable life. Somehow she had managed to make it to age 19 without regard to the moral constraints of her culture or the religious sensibilities of her employers. And though she grew up in a home with younger siblings, it is apparent that she did not aspire to any part of maternity. She was without natural affection.

Just a few days later, Beverly left the kids behind again, ran out with Bill again, was betrayed by the screams of abandoned and terrified children again: and encountered the indignation of her husband's employer again. But she did not receive leniency again. That night, Alvin and Beverly packed up their stuff, and their frightened children, and headed south, back toward Marshalltown. They were unemployed and homeless again.

Anna told this story with such clarity and familiarity that it was obvious she had told it many times. But, as I sat in the nursing home listening to Anna recount these memories from her deep past, she kept looking at me with sad eyes, going silent, and slowly shaking her head from side to side as if she were devoid of the ability to understand what could cause this kind of behavior in Beverly – or any mom.

"I was afraid he was going to get her pregnant." Anna said, reliving her past.

"He might have, Anna. He just might have. Maybe that's why I'm here."

Daddy?

I left the nursing home armed with two first names and a place of employment; Bill, who was married to Anna's cousin Norma, and they both worked at the Rainbow Cleaners in Clarion. Anna told me that the dry cleaning business was still there and still operating after all these years. I decided to drive there and see if anyone could tell me what Bill's last name might have been.

It was closed. I arrived at 4:30 on a Friday afternoon, and the sign in the window said they were open till 5:00, but the door was locked, the lights were off and no one emerged when I knocked.

I stood in front of the dry cleaning business that was within a block and a half of the center of town, located at 216 N. Main Street. I looked around at the surrounding businesses, and was clearly conspicuous as many folks stared at me, but none asked if they could be of assistance. Given the reputation for hospitality these small Iowa towns have, I found this a bit strange.

As I looked to my right, I noticed the library just across the side street. I walked over, ascended the ancient staircase as if entering a medieval castle and found two middle-aged, female 'subjects' at the top of the stairs behind the information desk.

"We're about to close; is there something quick we can help you find?" One of the women said.

I could tell from body language that they were eager to get out of there and on with their weekend. I had to think fast.

"How would the two of you like to help me solve a MYSTERY?" I asked in my most enticing voice.

The two women looked at each other and smiled. I knew I'd hooked them.

"What kind of mystery?" they both said in near synchronicity.

"I'm from Ohio and I'm here in town doing family history research. I'm on the trail of a man who might be my biological father. He used to own the Rainbow Cleaners here in Clarion back in the late 1950s and early 1960s. His name was Bill and his wife's name was Norma — but I need to find out his last name. How would I do that?" I asked in my most winsome way.

The two women began to toss possibilities back and forth. They recalled the current owners, and the ones before that and one from the late 1960s, but couldn't go back far enough to solve my mystery. One of the women called her husband, but he didn't remember. Then she called her brother-in-law, but he didn't remember either.

The second woman flipped through a local history book, but found nothing. Finally, she slammed the book closed and, as if receiving divine inspiration said, "Let's call Judge Draheim. He's been here forever."

She grabbed a phone book, found the number and dialed all in one fluid series of motions.

"Hey Judge, its Nancy down at the library. We've got a man here from Ohio who's doing some family research and he's trying to find out who the owner of the Rainbow Cleaners was back in 1959. He thinks his name was Bill, but doesn't have a last name."

I could hear a male voice coming through the receiver from 15 feet away. I couldn't distinguish every word, but it seemed like this gent had some information.

"Ok, well, let me just put him on the phone and you can tell it directly to him," Nancy told the judge.

She handed me the phone.

"Hello, my name is Craig Steffen. I'm from the Dayton, Ohio area and I'm told you're the town historian."

"Well, I think what they meant to tell you is that I'm old as dirt, so I've been around for most of the town's history," he joked. "I think the name you're looking for is Epping. Bill Epping owned the cleaners back in the late 1950's and early 1960's. I remember it well because my father actually bought Rainbow Cleaners from Bill. So I remember him."

"Just so we're clear, did Bill have a wife named Norma?"

"Yes, Bill and Norma. They lived here in town a long time. And they had an adopted son too, but I don't remember his name. Bill moved here in the early 1950's from somewhere up northwest. Some town that started with an "S" I think. Storm Lake or something like that. Don't hold me to it. No, that doesn't seem right. Ohhh, I can't remember for sure. Northwest though I think," the judge said, as if a stream of consciousness.

"What else do you remember about Bill? What kind of person was he?"

"Well, he was a nice enough fella, I guess. He sold Fuller Brush, was a Scout leader and was pretty active in town business over the years. He's been gone a long time now – 30 years or more I'll bet. I think he and his wife are buried over at St. Johns," the judge offered.

"Anything else I should know about Bill?"

"Oh, some people thought he was quite the man-about-town, or at least HE thought he was. Always flirting with the young ladies and acting like a big shot, ya know. I don't know about all that, but that was sort of his reputation anyway."

I felt like I was beginning to impose upon the kindness of strangers at this point, so I resolved to wrap it up. The clock on the wall said 5:05, so I knew the ladies were eager to shut the place down and get out of there this Memorial Day weekend.

"I sure appreciate you taking the time to talk with me. You've got a terrific memory – I see why these ladies think of you as the town historian."

"Now wait just a minute. You tell that girl who handed you the phone to behave tonight. Tell her I said so, now." I could hear the smile on his face.

"The judge told me to tell you to behave yourself tonight," I said with a smile so that the judge could hear that I was complying with his instructions.

"She had a questionable upbringing, so I have to keep her in line. Lord knows what she might do if it weren't for my watchful eye," the judge continued.

"Well, she says to mind your own business," I said with a laugh. "And have a great weekend yourself. Thank you again for all your help."

"Thank you so much, ladies. You were ever so helpful. That was just what I was looking for."

"You're welcome. Good luck in your search," Nancy said.

Three teenage girls entered at the bottom of the stairs.

"We're closed, girls. You can't come in now," the first woman said.

I took this as a cue, thanked them profusely and let myself out.

"Bill Epping," I thought as I walked to my car. "What is YOUR story? I've got a bunch of research to do tonight."

I spent every spare minute of the next few days searching the internet for information about William Epping.

I discovered that he was born in 1916 and died in 1981. I found that his wife's maiden name had been Archer and that she was two years younger than William, but died four years before him. Both are buried in a cemetery near Clarion where they had lived at the time of William's alleged dalliance with Beverly.

I confirmed that William and Norma had an adopted son named Gordon. I was able to locate a person likely to be Gordon living in eastern Iowa.

I also found some photographs of William and Norma from a newspaper archive. I can't say I see any resemblance, but they are very poor quality photos.

In a few days, I would be driving back to Ohio and I'd be within 20 miles of Gordon's residence. I endeavored to take a slight detour and stop by for a visit and see what else I can learn about this William Epping.

A few days later, just before dark on a rainy Saturday evening in May, I found Gordon's house in a nice, recently developed neighborhood. I knocked on the door and a middle-aged woman (presumably Gordon's wife) answered. I asked if Gordon were home and she went to get him. Gordon met me at the door and I introduced myself and handed him a business card hoping to set his mind at ease.

"My name is Craig Steffen. I'm from Dayton, Ohio. I've been in Iowa the last couple of days doing family history research over in the Renwick and Clarion areas."

"Ok."

"I'm assuming that you are the Gordon Epping that is the son of William and Norma Epping. Is that correct?

"I am. Yes."

"While I was up there doing family history stuff, I found what might be a connection between your family and my family."

"Hmm. Ok."

"So, my mother and her husband at the time, not my father, were living over in Renwick back in 1959 when I would have been conceived. They were farmhands for the Hefty family – I don't know if you know them?'

"No."

"A few days ago I spoke with the woman they were working for at the time. That woman is now living in the nursing home at Clarion and has a remarkable memory. She remembered my mother and her husband quite well and relayed a story about my mother, and I hope this isn't a difficult subject, that my mother and your father may have had a relationship."

"I doubt it. I'm adopted and I don't think that was ever the case. No. If it was, it was long before he married my mother, not my birth mother obviously. It wouldn't have been anything after that. That was in the 40s. I was adopted in '47."

"This would have been after that. They were living up there in 1959."

"No. Not that I'm aware of anyway. There was never any word or news that I ever heard anyway. '59, I would have been twelve."

"The story that this woman told me was that your father called on my mother, in his role as a Fuller Brush salesman, and that they became romantically involved for a short time. She said that she found out about the affair and terminated the employment of my mother and her husband as a result of the indiscretion. Apparently people were talking about it and this woman and her husband were concerned about their reputations."

"Well, Dad sold Fuller Brush, but I can't believe any of the other stuff is true. He and my mom couldn't have kids, Mom's health wasn't so good, and they adopted me through Catholic Charities. There was a young woman in Albia, Iowa who had gotten pregnant, and my dad, who was Catholic, arranged to adopt me."

"Have you ever found your biological family?"

"Nope. I never had any desire. It never bothered me one way or another."

"I understand. I never did any searching until after my adoptive parents were gone. I never wanted to show them any disrespect. Do you keep in touch with any of the Epping family?"

"No, I've pretty much lost touch with them. Last I ever saw them was when my father passed away and they came to the funeral. None of them live around here. Nope, I haven't had any contact at all."

"Gordon, thank you for taking a minute to chat with me."

"Well, good luck on your search."

"Thanks. You have a great night and enjoy your dinner. I appreciate you taking the time to talk with me about this. I know it's an awkward topic, and I hope you know that I'm not trying to stir up any trouble for you. I'm just trying to find some answers in my own life and wanted to follow the lead of this nice woman in Clarion."

"Alright, good night."

Gordon proved to be a nice fellow, but as I suspected would be the case, he didn't have any breaking news to share with me. And, unfortunately, he's not close to the Epping family, so I don't have any new leads for folks that might be able to shed light or donate DNA.

When I got back to Ohio, I did considerably more research about the Eppings and found a person on LinkedIn who seemed as if he might be related. I called Tim and shared my story. He turned out to be the grandnephew of William and was quite connected to the rest of his family up in the Sandborn, Iowa area. In fact, he was heading to a family reunion the next weekend and said he'd ask around about my story.

I didn't hear back from Tim for a few weeks so I decided to give him a call. We had a nice chat, but his relatives hadn't been able to shed any more light on the situation either. All the folks who had known William well have since passed away. What's left is a collection of poorly documented legends and stories that don't include any skeletons in the family closet.

So I asked Tim if he might be willing to provide me with a DNA sample, since we'd show up as related if William's affair with Beverly had been a fruitful one. He was understandably hesitant, not knowing me from the proverbial "load of coal." He said he'd get back to me after he'd had a chance to think about it.

So I wait. I'm planning another trip to Iowa in July for my thirty-fifth high school class reunion. If I haven't heard back from Tim by then, I'll plan to head up north to Sandborn and knock on a few doors.

Doctors

I've always liked science. I remember sitting at the dining room table while in the 7th grade, pouring over the 1956 World Book Encyclopedia my Uncle Bob had salvaged from the dumpster at the school where he worked. I was fascinated by science and that year I was taking Earth Science from Mr. Wallace. I must have written a dozen or more papers for extra credit, just because I found it all so fascinating.

Where does this scientific curiosity come from? The thought occurs to me that perhaps one of the doctors Beverly was in contact with back in September of 1959, when I would have been conceived, had accepted some alternative form of payment for services rendered.

From the hospital documents I received from Trinity Medical Center in Fort Dodge, Iowa, I learned that the referring physician was Dr. Harding from Eagle Grove, Iowa. And the attending physician was a Dr. Dannenbring from Fort Dodge.

My research indicated that both doctors were now dead. Dr. Dannenbring passed in May of 2006, and Dr. Harding died in July of that same year. I was able to find on-line photographs of each of these men, and neither jumped out at me as my doppelganger.

I called the libraries in Fort Dodge and in Eagle Grove respectively to gather additional information about these two to see if something might set them apart as more or less likely to be a candidate for father-of-Craig. The Fort Dodge Library was less helpful, in that they never followed through on any of their promises to search for information I was requesting.

The Eagle Grove Library, on the other hand, was very accommodating and quickly sent me a packet of information they had researched and copied from their archives. When I traveled to Renwick in May, I stopped into the library and had a nice conversation with one of the librarians. She told me that Dr. Harding was famous in Eagle Grove for his many years of service in the community and a bit infamous for having left his first wife and for moving to Montana with a younger woman who worked in his office. Having told her my story, the librarian winked and encouraged me not to give up on the good doctor as a candidate for my paternity. Apparently he had a bit of a reputation. I left them a small donation for all the help they had given me and endeavored to do more research when I returned home.

That research turned up a couple of descendants of Dr. Harding, one of whom, Randy, seemed to be living in a little town in Illinois called Morton. I knew this town well as it exists at approximately the halfway point along my typical route back and forth between Ohio and Iowa. I've often spent the night there, or stopped in to grab some food or fill up with fuel.

I decided to set aside Dr. Dannenbring as a paternal candidate for a while, since information about him had been difficult so far, till I'd had a chance to check out Dr. Harding. I planned to stop at Morton during my upcoming July trip to Iowa.

Coincidentally, Dr. Dannenbring's wife was from Xenia, Ohio and is buried less than 10 miles from where I now live. Dr. Harding's second wife is called "Punky," the same term of endearment I use to refer to my wife, Cindy. Neither of these details means anything, but it does cause an eyebrow to lift and make me say, "Hmmm."

DNA

It is fifty-one years after the disappearance.

On this scorching July day, I am driving 700 miles to my thirty-fifth high school class reunion.

I left Ohio at 2:00 p.m. after a partial day of work. My first stop will be in Morton, Illinois to see if I can meet the son of the doctor Beverly first went to when Ricky was sick back in 1959, Dr. Harding. However unlikely, he was in proximity to Beverly at the right time frame to be a paternal candidate.

The rise of cell phones has made contacting people much more difficult. One used to be able to simply pick up a phone book or dial 411 and request the phone number of virtually anyone in the country. During all my research, I've found that about 90% of the time the phone numbers available through Internet research or directory assistance are wrong or disconnected. More and more folks are ditching their landlines in favor of full-time cell phone use. Such was the case when I tried to call the person I hoped to be Dr. Harding's son. So, my plan is to find Randy Harding's home, knock on the door and begin a conversation eyeball to eyeball. Let's hope he's home.

It was early evening when I pulled into Morton. I filled my little Prius with gas and activated the MapQuest App on my iPhone. Within a few minutes I arrived at an attractive, well-landscaped home in a nice, middle-class part of town. I drove slowly past the home and then turned around to pull up on the other side of the street.

I parked and sat in my car a few minutes to assess the situation, looking for clues about who this person might be and watching for signs of life. Cute as the house was, I didn't see any sign that someone might be home. There were no lights evident inside the house, no car in the driveway and no sign of people out in the yard.

My hope was to get a DNA sample, at least eventually, after meeting this son of someone who knew Beverly. But I had a strong and unexplainable sense that this was not the right timing for this contact. I suspected that no one was even home, but it was more than that. I really felt like this wasn't what I was *supposed* to do, at least not at this time.

So after sitting there conspicuously for about ten minutes "discussing" my options with the *sense* within me, I put the car in gear and drove back out to I-74 and continued west toward Iowa.

I rationalize that I will go to Iowa, do some research in Fort Dodge on Dr. Dannenbring, travel up to the northwest part of the state and see if I can meet some Eppings from Sandborn, enjoy my class reunion and see if I can get just a little less manic about this unlikely paternity research. After all, my "evidence" regarding each of these paternal candidates is purely circumstantial. All eight of the men on my list is a "candidate" simply because I can track their proximity to Beverly in September of 1959. That's all I have to go on. I really have no desire to jeopardize the reputations of any of these folks just because they were in the same room with Beverly approximately at a time that corresponds to my own conception.

The next day, as I continue my journey to my reunion, I pull my car into Nevada, Iowa. Thirty-eight years earlier I came to this town for the first time in my life. It was in this town in 1975, when my sister, Theresa, brought me to the steps of a trailer owned by Alvin

Shepherd and I heard the words, "Craig, this is your father." Since then, I have returned to this town only one other time — three months ago.

I am to meet Beverly's sister, Sherri, for lunch. Minutes earlier she texted to tell me she'd be a few minutes late. So when I arrive at her office on this sweltering Thursday, I make the choice to sit in my air-conditioned car and check my email – it is a work day.

When I thumb through the mail on my iPhone screen I see a message from AncestryDNA.

My heart literally skips a beat.

I click to open the email. I click again to "view results." And there it is. Of the hundreds of thousands of DNA donors to AncestryDNA, Jeffrey's closest relative in their database is Craig Steffen. So close, in

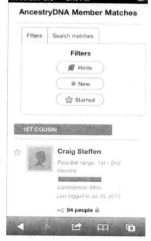

fact, that Jeffrey and I share the same grandparents.

In my head, I hear words that are nearly audible. Words that have hung in this central Iowa air for nearly 40 years – and now echo again inside me ... "Craig, this is your father."

Nearly fifty-four years ago, my nine-month-old brother, Ricky, started crying and only stopped when he passed out. Fifty-four years ago, my mother drove him to Fort Dodge,

Iowa and spent a week in this strange city trying to learn what was wrong with him. Fifty-four years ago, she got bored and hooked up with one of only two men she knew in Fort Dodge. On September 29, 1959 (plus or minus three days) it would seem that Jeffrey's uncle, Richard, and my mother made a baby.

Disbelief

It didn't go as I had hoped; this first conversation with Richard since discovering, with DNA confidence, that he is my biological dad. What I had hoped/imagined/intended was to call and make an appointment to meet with him *in person*. I hoped to gently share the process I've been through getting to this latest piece of information. I imagined sitting again around his kitchen table to show him the AncestryDNA data, explain and directly answer his questions and read his eyes as he processed.

It is Friday, the day after I got Jeffrey's DNA results. I've passed the morning with angst and uncertainty, sitting alone in a stale little room at the Super 8 in Atlantic, Iowa. I keep flashing to a scene I'm imagining in my head that involves my own conception. It's a scene filled with appropriate awkwardness and the disturbing imagery of the sexuality of one's own parents.

Just after noon I touch the keypad of my iPhone 10 times and listen to two plaintive rings. Richard answers in a questioning tone, "Hello?"

"Hi Richard, this is Craig Steffen. How are you today?"

"Oh, pretty good."

"Good. Hey, is this a good time to chat?"

"Yeah, I could talk for a little bit. Why, what's up?"

"Well, hey, I have gotten some new information, and I wanted to see if perhaps I might be able to stop by and talk with you about it. I'm in Iowa this weekend for my thirty-five year class reunion."

"Well, this weekend we're going to be gone. Ah, so I don't know, this wouldn't be a very good weekend; this weekend."

"Ahh. Well, I'm just in Iowa this weekend. Of course it's a long drive out here from Ohio, so I thought, wow, maybe I can ..."

"Well, what'd you find out?"

"So, let me give you some background. I got some DNA information yesterday that indicates that your nephew Jeffrey and I are closely related ..."

"I can't see how this could be, I really don't"

It seemed to me that Richard's generally friendly tone changed. I couldn't tell if what I was now hearing was simple incongruity, utter disbelief or a perceptible shift to adversarial mode.

"Well, all the more reason why we need to talk ... I was in Iowa back in May and I was meeting up with Beverly's two sisters, Sherri and Barb. Barb was back in central Iowa to attend her class reunion – the Clemons Reunion there at the end of May. I stayed in State Center at the Bed and Breakfast that your nephew, Jeffrey, manages for a friend of his, and while I was there, I was telling Jeff the story of how Beverly's hospital stay in Fort Dodge, when my brother Ricky was sick, corresponds to my own conception date. So I said to Jeff, 'There's this possible connection between your family and mine.' And, at the time, I'm thinking this is perhaps a story about your dad and Beverly – as you and I had spoken before. And Jeffrey said, 'Well what you need is some DNA.' And I said, 'Yeah, I know, and I'm here this weekend and I'm thinking about stopping in and talking to Richard and seeing if he'd be willing to do that.' And Jeff said, 'Well,

I'd be willing to do it.' So Jeffrey gave a DNA sample, and he sent it in, and yesterday I got the results back from AncestryDNA and it said that Jeffrey and I are first cousins – with 99% certainty.

"Well, I just don't see how it can be myself ... I really don't. So Jeff gave you DNA?"

"Yes."

"And it says that you and Jeff are cousins?"

"First cousins, yeah. So, as I understand it, first cousins share the same grandparents. If Jeff's grandparents are the same as my grandparents ... that would indicate that you are my father."

"Ahh, that can't be...something's screwy somewhere. It can't be."

There was clearly agitation in Richard's voice. I tried to put myself in his shoes. What if some kid was claiming paternity for me – especially over the phone where I couldn't look into his eyes? Had I pushed too far too fast? I imagined Richard pacing, tethered to the short cord on the phone hanging from his kitchen wall.

"So, I guess, there's a one percent chance that they could be wrong ... according to their statistics. But I'm happy to show you what they came up with and, um, if you still think that's not biologically possible, then I guess you and I could just do a test between the two of us – and then we'd know for sure."

"Whataya, what's a DNA test consist of?"

"It's basically a saliva test. You spit into a little plastic tube and mail it into a laboratory."

"And who tests it? I mean, there's gotta be a charge or something – they don't just do this for free do they?"

"No, no, it's a hundred dollars per person. I did mine months ago, and Jeff did his back at the end of May, I think it was Memorial Day weekend, and I just got his results back yesterday."

"Well, I don't know … I just can't figure out how that could be… Well, we're going to be gone up to the lake this weekend, my son's got a place up there, we're going up there."

"Ok."

"So we won't be around this weekend."

"That's Ok. We can do this testing remotely. We can have further conversations …"

"Did Jeff get these results back too then?"

"Yes, Jeff and I met yesterday afternoon and I showed him the results on my computer. He saw enough to convince him that the results were accurate."

"Well, I don't know what to do. I just can't see … I don't, I don't see how it can possibly be. I think there's gotta be mistakes made somewhere."

"Well, I'm not sure how the DNA lab could link Jeff and me together without there being some genetic reason to do so."

"Well, let me talk to Jeff cuz I just can't see how this can be. There's gotta be something going on here."

Was he accusing *me* of something?

"Ok, well, I understand how this is a serious bit of information here. I'm not trying to complicate your life, I hope you understand that to be true. I'm just trying to get information about what my DNA background is."

"Ahh, let me talk to Jeff and see what he's got to say."

"Sure. Sure. Alright, well, give me a call back when you've got some time to chat. I know you're heading out of there now. But I'd like to continue the conversation. And if we need to get another set of DNA tests done, I'm perfectly happy to pay for it."

"Ok, well, let me talk to Jeff first and see what's going on."

"Ok, well, I hope you have a great weekend."

"Yeah, goodbye."

I disconnect the call and notice my hands are shaking. Then I notice my heart is pounding and I feel completely disoriented. I don't know what to do with myself. Just sit there and think? Lie down and think? Call Cindy and process this conversation?

The universe has shrunk to the size of a 10 by 12 foot hotel room, and I'm its only inhabitant. But regardless of the universe's size, my questions are still the same. Who am I? Where do I come from? How did I get here? Does my life have meaning?

I feel as if I've just called someone out of the blue and tried to sell them life insurance or something, and they've shut me down and called me a con-artist. I feel a little sick to my stomach. I have a profound sense that this call did not go well, but it's more than that. I feel, honestly, like I've done something wrong, like I should have kept this new DNA information to myself, like I have no right to intrude upon the life of this old friend of Beverly.

But WHAT have I done wrong?

I want to believe this person. I want to think that he's really telling me everything he knows.

Because I want to believe him, I find myself spending most of the rest of the day imagining all sorts of convoluted scenarios by which Richard's DNA could find its way to me through Beverly. Some way, I mean, that doesn't involve the time-honored, pregnancy-causing activity we've come to know as coitus. I discover just how creative (and twisted) I can be, all because I want to believe the man I now think is my biological father.

Old School

Three weeks have gone by since my brief DNA chat with Richard. I had asked him to call after he talked with Jeff, but I haven't heard from him. I'm not surprised. He seems conflict-averse. I'm thinking that he's going "old school" on me. Back in his youth, it would have been enough to simply deny a claim of paternity. There were no scientific means of determining paternity definitively.

Maybe Richard has a science degree – I have no way of knowing. But he and I do share an Iowa High School education. If his experience there was something like mine, it is likely he took only one or two science classes in the 1950s. I'm pretty sure there would have been little, if any, mention of DNA in those classes. It is true that the concepts of DNA go back to the late 1860s, but the first double-helix structure of DNA and its role in heredity weren't confirmed until the early 1950s. When I went to high school in Iowa, 120 miles southwest of where Richard graduated, we were routinely using textbooks that were 6-10 years old. I'd bet money he never once heard of DNA in science class.

So back in the 1950s, testing blood types was still the most common "paternity test." Blood-typing was used to try to eliminate paternal candidates – but it could never positively identify anyone as the father of a child. Back then, it was always one person's word against another. One could always get some people to "take your side" in disputes of this type. If they were a white male from a good family, it was pretty likely that whatever they claimed to be the truth, was accepted as the actual truth. It usually came down to *her* obvious baby-bump versus *his* plausible deniability – case closed.

But DNA has changed all that. Fittingly, at least from my perspective, it was on my 40th Birthday that U.S. President Clinton and U.K. Prime Minister Blair held a joint press conference to announce that the Human Genome Project (HGP) had completed a "rough draft" of the human genome. Three years later, in 2003, the project was considered "complete" – even though significant and deeper work continues even now.

The completion of the HGP changes everything. It's entirely possible Richard doesn't even know about these scientific advances and the mapping of the human genome; most people don't. Up until the 1980s it wasn't possible to eliminate more than about 40% of the male population when "scientifically" trying to determine paternity. But with the advent of readily available DNA testing it is now possible to determine paternity with 99.99% accuracy.

Risking fear of understatement, the topic of paternity has come a LONG way from the "his word against hers" world in which Richard grew up back in the 1950s.

Having said all that, I really don't think that Richard ever knew that his night(s) of carnal pleasure with Beverly resulted in anything more than teenaged guilty pleasure. It seems likely to me that Beverly returned to Renwick after Ricky was released from the Fort Dodge hospital and never had contact with Richard again. Sure, Beverly got pregnant – but she was presumably having sex with her husband. And then there was the fling with the Fuller Brush salesman in that same time frame. It is quite likely Beverly had no idea who the father of this unborn child might be. There were, after all, at least three equally likely candidates. And in Beverly's world of 1959 rural Iowa, heart of the "Bible Belt," it would have been prudent to let the world assume that the reason she was pregnant was as obvious as the husband at her side. What could have been gained by trying to claim otherwise?

Beverly didn't even have a telephone in her home at the time. She didn't have a car either. But she did have two children under three years old to tie her down and she did live in the country, about two miles from the nearest town, all of which would have kept her from a payphone. So her best chance at communication would have been by mail. But it was a small town, and a letter to a male friend from high school, placed in the box at the end of the driveway, would have been conspicuous at the least – but more likely dangerous and/or scandalous.

So my conception and gestation was almost certainly accompanied by secrets, silence and selective ignorance. Beverly seemed to be trying hard to convince her sister, and maybe herself, that her husband was the father of the child she gave birth to in Marshalltown, Iowa on the morning of June 26, 1960. The following day, she wrote a birth announcement and mailed it off to her sister Barbara. In it she wrote:

June 27, 1960

Dear Barb,

Hi! Well, I've finally got it over with, and is Lorain ever proud of his big boy!

We came to the hospital at 4:30 Sunday morning & he was born at 10:26 A.M. He isn't a pretty baby but very few are. He has blue eyes, and not a whole lot of hair.

I feel fairly good, but today, the after pains have been terrible! I think I'll probably get to go home Thursday.

I'm about to cook here in this room. Right now, I'm head stuff, with no roomate. Katie Lewitz is right next door to me.

Sure do wish I had the buggy at home. It sure was dumb of us, neither of us thought of it.

Well, Barb, come over & see us. Write!

Love,
Bev.

I find it revealing that Beverly felt compelled to go back and add the color of my hair, squeezing a miniature "brown" parenthetically in between the lines. It is as if she is trying to offer latent "proof" of my paternity, by lying about my hair color – since my hair and skin were both the color of larva until I was five years old.

Leading with how proud her husband is of "his big boy" is also a nice, but guilty, touch to the note written to the suspicious sister, in whom she'd confided about a mysterious sexual dalliance in Fort Dodge.

Documentation

I sent Richard a letter today. Apparently patience isn't one of my great virtues.

Jeffrey's words keep ringing in my ears, "They're probably suspicious of you."

Intellectually I understand this – I really do. To Richard and family, I'm either a con-artist or, at best, I'm a ghost from the past and I've shown up unannounced in the present. It must seem that I'm here to upset the natural order of things, the familiar, all that has ever been believed and acknowledged as truth.

But emotionally, I don't like it. I don't like knowing that anyone in the world may think I'm a scam-artist, trying to deceive in order to gain some temporal advantage. It would bother me even if it were some random person on the street who held to that kind of suspicion, but it bothers me more to know that people who share the same DNA with me might believe that.

I have the right to remain silent, but I don't have the ability. So I wrote this letter, hoping to set the record straight with as many facts as I have. And hoping to dispel the temptation that Richard may have to think I am something sinister and manipulative.

The letter is too long. Perhaps worse, it's too business-like. I've been negotiating business relationships, patent licenses, joint venture companies, terms sheets and the like for over 20 years; this letter is written with too much of that bleeding through. I re-read this thing dozens of times before finally dropping it in the mail. But I sent it anyway, wondering what effect it might have on the universe.

Craig A. Steffen

August 5, 2013

Greetings Richard:

I do hope that you and Berniece are having an enjoyable summer. I so appreciate the kind welcome you both gave me in your home last fall as we talked about your memories of my mother, Beverly.

It has been nearly three weeks since our last communication. I apologize for the awkward phone conversation on that day. The telephone is such a poor medium for discussing matters of this type. It had been my hope that we might be able to meet personally but your weekend plans with David made you unavailable. I wish we'd have been able to talk face-to-face during my brief visit to Iowa.

Now that I'm back in Ohio, I thought I'd send you a bit of information that may serve to answer some of your questions.

I completely understand how confusing and upsetting my call would be to you. It has been nearly 54 years since you last saw Beverly, and now her son shows up asking lots of questions and eventually turns up with DNA results. When I imagine myself in a similar situation, I know that my own emotions would be running high. And I'd be questioning how something like this, if true, could take 54 years to reveal itself.

When I began this journey into my biological roots, I declared that it was a quest for truth. I simply wanted to know, as most people do, where I come from genetically. I'd spent more than 50 years with the gnawing lack of knowing why I needed to be adopted, why I was different from my siblings, who my "tribe" is and what kind of blood runs through my veins. I imagine that, from your perspective, it may just seem that I'm trying to cause trouble. But, if you can slip into my shoes for a moment, I hope you can see that what I'm doing, in the most gentle way I know how, is merely to answer some of those gnawing questions.

I knew that my mother was dead when this journey began, so there was never a chance that I could have a relationship with her, no matter what truth I found. It has, however, been a blessing to get to know Beverly's three sisters and several of Beverly's friends through this process. Once I discovered for sure that Alvin Shepherd was not my biological father, I had very little hope that I would ever find out who might be. My only hope throughout the quest has been that others I met along the way would be as interested in the truth as I am.

It has been an amazing journey of discovery that has led to this communication. And now my quest has brought me to a place where I need to ask you for your help in finding those answers and relieving my nagging, life-long wondering.

First, let me share with you the chronology of my quest to learn about my biological family. What follows is a bit tedious and reads like a manual of sorts. I apologize for the length and tedium in advance, I just couldn't come up with a more creative or succinct way to answer the many questions you must certainly have.

1.   My adoptive mother died in 2003 and my adoptive father died in 2011. Once they were gone, I felt free and motivated to learn what I could about my genetic origins.

2.   I reconnected with Beverly's sister Sherri in January of 2012 and began to learn about Beverly's family. Sherri is 14 years younger than Beverly and so doesn't remember much about her. She tried to connect me with her sister Barb, but initially Barb didn't want to connect with me because of the painful memories Beverly's murder conjured up in her.

3.   Because of the many physical, emotional and cognitive differences between my older sister (Theresa), brother (Ricky) and me, I had long suspected that they had a different father than me. I was the third born child, and Beverly abandoned us in June 1962, less than two years after my birth (See Attached, Page 1) and by September the three children were placed in the Annie Wittenmyer Children's Home (See Attached, Page 2).

4.   In July 2012, I traveled to Iowa to do research about Beverly, to meet Sherri for the first time, and to talk with anyone who might have known Beverly.

5.   During that trip, I met with Theresa in SW Iowa and she provided me a DNA sample so that we could determine scientifically if we had the same father. When the results came back October 23, 2012, DNA proved that we did NOT share the same father. (See Attached, Page 3)

6.   I shared the DNA results with Aunt Sherri (who had also provided a DNA sample for comparison – as did Theresa's Aunt Kathy) and Sherri, in turn, shared the results with her sister Barb.

7.   In late October 2012, I decided to write a letter to Aunt Barb to ask her to reconsider her choice not to meet me and, therefore, not to re-open the painful era of her life that included the death of her beloved sister.

8.　　　I returned to Iowa in November 2012 to do additional research, meet more people and try to piece together information. It was during this trip that I met with several people who knew Beverly from her school days in Clemons. I met with some of them at the Remarkable Rose in State Center, and met Jeff for the first time. Jeff overheard portions of my meetings with people from the area that he knew well (Katy Lively for example) and seemed intrigued by my quest. He helped me connect with other people in the area who knew Beverly. During our conversations, I learned he was the son of Connie, whom I knew had been a classmate of Beverly's. After these meetings, I drove to Fort Dodge and met you and Berniece for the first time as well.

9.　　　When I returned to Ames from Fort Dodge after my visit with you, I met with Sherri again and she told me that she had received a tearful call from her sister Barb the night before. Barb had received my letter and was touched by it and decided to talk with me after all. Barb and I had a long phone conversation that day and, by the end, had agreed to meet in person.

10.　　　Late that afternoon I headed to Missouri to meet with Barb and her husband Dale, finishing the trip the following morning when I arrived at their home in time for breakfast.

11.　　　We spent the day together and, as expected, she had a wealth of information about Beverly and their family that I could not have learned from anyone else. During the many topics we covered over the course of 8 hours of dialog, the subject of my DNA test with Theresa came up. Barb revealed to me that she had never thought that Beverly's husband (Alvin Shepherd) was my father. She told me that when she met me for the first time when I was only a few weeks old, she looked at my white skin, thin blond hair and blue eyes (See Attached, Page 4) and said "Uh Oh." Alvin, Theresa and Ricky all had very thick dark hair, dark skin and deep brown eyes.

12.   Aunt Barb told me the story of when Beverly was at the hospital in Fort Dodge (the same story you had shared with me during my visit to your home a few days earlier). Aunt Barb told me that when Beverly returned from that trip, she told Aunt Barb that something sexual had happened while she was in Fort Dodge and that Beverly said with a wink and a smile, "I think he still likes me." Aunt Barb told me that she had always taken this to mean that you and Beverly had rekindled an earlier, high school relationship during Beverly's trip to the hospital in Fort Dodge. Aunt Barb added, "Then nine months later you were born." She gave me a birth announcement Beverly had sent to her after my birth. (See Attached, Page 5)

13.   Uncertain what to do with this new information; I did nothing for a couple of months. Then, in late December 2012 or early January 2013, I called you. I picked a bad time to call as you were dealing with your Mother's admission to the nursing facility. Kindly, you called me back within a day or two and I asked you about what Aunt Barb had told me. You told me that nothing sexual had happened between you and Beverly, and we wondered out loud if perhaps Beverly might have been referring to your father instead.

14.   After our conversation, I went on-line and found a conception calculator that backdates from one's birth date using human gestation norms, to predict conception date assuming a full-term birth. At 9 lbs. 7.5 oz, I think it is safe to assume I was full-term. ☺ The calculator predicts my conception at September 29, 1959 – plus or minus a few days in either direction (See Attached, Page 6).

15.   At this point neither you, nor Aunt Barb could remember when Ricky may have been in the hospital. I began significant research to try to uncover this information. Eventually I had several phone conversations with the hospital in Fort Dodge and was able to get them to provide me with waiver forms to sign so that they could send me the medical records from Ricky and Beverly's stay there.

When I received those documents, I learned that Ricky was admitted to the hospital on September 25, 1959 and was released about a week later on October 2, 1959 (See Attached, Page 7).

16.   So the combination of the conception calculator and the hospital records indicates that it is likely Beverly was in Fort Dodge at the time of my conception.

17.   I had been using Ancestry.com to do a lot of my family history research and I noticed that they also did DNA testing in order for their customers to learn about their ancestral heritage as well as to connect with other Ancestry.com members who might be close or distant relatives. Upon researching their process, I learned that their test was far more extensive than the one Theresa and I had used last year (See Attached, Pages 8 & 9). They had already collected tens of thousands of samples. In April 2013 I decided to buy a kit and send them my DNA sample as well, in hope of finding clues to my own genetic history.

18.   I traveled back to Iowa over Memorial Day Weekend at the end of May 2013 because Aunt Barb was to be in town to attend her 55 year class reunion. I actually attended the first part of the reunion as well and was able to meet several new people who had been friends of Beverly during her years at Clemons High School. It was quite enjoyable. During that trip, I stayed at the B&B that your nephew Jeffrey manages in State Center. Jeff and I spoke at some length and he asked about my quest that he had become familiar with during my previous visits. I shared with him the possible connection between his family and mine based on the conception calculator and hospital records and the 1959 conversation between Beverly and Aunt Barb. We agreed that the only way to get a definitive answer was to get scientific proof via DNA testing. Jeff volunteered to provide me with a DNA sample. It seemed clear to me that Jeff felt the connection between his family and me was unlikely at best and that by providing a DNA sample he could protect you and his

mother from potentially uncomfortable conversations, while at the same time helping me to eliminate your extended family from my search.

19.   Coincidently, my own AncestryDNA results were completed while I was in Iowa over Memorial Weekend and I was able to find several people/family trees to whom I was related from my mother's side of the family. AncestryDNA provides this information confidentially on-line. It is accessible only by signing in with a password. It is updated every week as new people submit DNA samples from all over the world. The screen shot I show in the Attached, Page 10 is how the page looks today (it includes Jeff's results now) not how it looked back in May when I first got results.

20.   Jeffrey's DNA kit was shipped directly from the AncestryDNA lab in Utah to Jeffrey in State Center. By the time it arrived, I had long since returned to Ohio. The kit required Jeff to provide a saliva sample into a small plastic container and mail it directly back to the DNA Laboratory in Utah. The Kit did not contain Jeff's name or personal information; it was traced only by a complex tracking number on the kit. The kit was never in my possession.

21.   In early June, Alvin Shepherd's brother, David (whom I had only recently learned was still living) volunteered to give me a DNA sample, because his sisters still believed Alvin to be my father. Though I felt I had already answered this question with the DNA samples with my sister, I was grateful for his willingness and I had learned that there were several different kinds of DNA testing processes. The one my sister and I had used was based only on Y-chromosome testing and was therefore limited because the samples I had sent involved three females – no female possess the male Y-chromosome. The AncestryDNA test is far more sophisticated looking at 700,000 DNA locations, rather than the 40 or so places that the Y-chromosome tests examine (See Attached, Pages 8 & 9).

So I had AncestryDNA send a kit to David to get confirmation. In early July, David's DNA results came back and confirmed that David Shepherd and I are NOT related (See Attached Page 11). Theresa has since provided an AncestryDNA sample and it will prove or disprove whether or not Alvin Shepherd is her father, as we both suspect he is. I have not yet received those results.

22.   On Thursday, July 18, I checked my email while sitting in my car waiting to meet Aunt Sherri for Lunch in Nevada, IA. I had traveled to Iowa to attend my 35-year class reunion in SW Iowa, and was having lunch with Sherri and her husband Steve on my way through. I opened an email from AncestryDNA which told me that Jeffrey's DNA results had been posted to their website (I had paid for the kit, so they notified me). It was then that I learned that, according to the AncestryDNA Laboratory, Jeffrey and I are first cousins. The AncestryDNA Lab is 99% certain of this result.

23.   I called Jeffrey before leaving Nevada, IA and we met the afternoon of July 18 in State Center. I showed him the full results from the AncestryDNA website (See Attached, Page 12) and he confirmed that several other people the site listed as his relatives are, in fact, related to him.

24.   The next day, I called you. I really didn't want to have this kind of conversation on the phone, as I felt it would be clearer if I could actually show you the results as I had done with Jeff. Understandably, you seemed confused by the conversation, so I thought that I'd send this documentation to help to make sense of it all.

The scientific data indicate with 99% certainty that Jeff and I are close genetic relatives. Stated another way, statistically speaking, there is virtually zero chance that you and I are genetically _unrelated_. Clearly the AncestryDNA Laboratory thinks, with 99% certainty, that Jeffrey and I share the same grandparents (See Attached, Page 13). But they do acknowledge that other relationships might theoretically, in rare cases (ie 1%), yield similar results (See Attached, Page 14). But if you study those scenarios, you'll see that neither is possible in Jeff's case.

So we now have scientific proof that Jeff and I are closely related. Obviously I am inferring a genetic relationship to you based on the AncestryDNA Lab's scientific results, along with all the anecdotal information I've outlined above. But in our phone conversation, you contended this is "not possible."

So long as there is any doubt or hesitancy about my genetic origins, I want to continue to seek truth that will eliminate that doubt and hesitancy. It seems to me that neither you nor I can be fully satisfied until you provide your own DNA sample to be compared with Jeff's and mine. Only then can we both know for certain what the truth is.

It is my hope that you will be willing to take this next step to get to the bottom of this mystery once and for all. Somehow Jeff and I are closely related and you and I need to know for sure how that is possible.

I understand that you would be naturally suspicious of some stranger knocking on your door out of the blue. I'd be concerned about you if you *weren't* suspicious. I know I've said this to you before, but I want to express it here again in writing. I'm after <u>nothing</u> but truth. I have no need of money, organ transplants or any other tangible thing. I don't believe the law would ever entitle me to any of these things anyway, but I'm even willing to sign a legal document that expresses this if it alleviates concerns on your part.

I don't have any skeletons in my closet, addictions, or scandals in my past. I have a Master's Degree and am Ordained in the State of Ohio (See Attached, Pages 15 & 16). I'm a successful business owner, with a long history of devotion to my wife of 29 years and to the ways of Jesus. I have provided for my own future and have no debts I could not pay off tomorrow if I chose to. I am well regarded by my many friends and associates. All of this is verifiable with a nominal amount of research on the internet. Given my past questions and recent DNA claims, I hope you have already researched me, but if you have not I welcome you and your family to do so (See Attached, Page 17). I have nothing to hide.

I'm not necessarily seeking relationship with my biological families, though I am open to them if they develop. As I mentioned earlier, it has been wonderful to develop a growing relationship with Beverly's sisters (feel free to contact your old friend Barb if you so desire). I have only ever been interested in knowing the truth about my genetic origins.

And now we get to that part of the letter where I ask you for your help in answering the gnawing questions I mentioned several pages back.

I'm proposing that you provide a saliva sample for a final DNA test. Please review the video links I've provided to learn more about what I'm requesting from you (See Attached, Page 18). If your DNA test confirms Jeff's DNA test results, I hope that you and I can then talk about what that means for our futures. But if, at the end of that talk, you prefer not to have a relationship with me, I promise to honor that request. I have no desire to intrude upon your life. If Jeff, or others in the family, wish to have a familial relationship with me, I'll pursue that only with them.

After you have had some time to review this information, and discuss it with your family, I'd like to have a phone conversation to determine the mechanics of the next step toward both of us finding trusted, verifiable truth via a final DNA test. I will be happy to cover all the costs associated with the test. If I haven't heard from you in a couple of weeks, I'll give you a call.

Thank you for thoughtfully considering all these pages, and my request for your help. I really do believe, as Jesus once said, "The truth will set us free."

Warm Regards,

As you can see from the references to attachments, I sent along 18 pages of documents to substantiate the facts I was putting forth. I didn't want to leave any claim open for scrutiny. If there would never be an acknowledgement from Richard about how his DNA ended up flowing through my veins, I at least wanted him to know that I already had enough evidence to be as certain as anyone can be about their paterfamilias.

Waiting

Then I waited.

I hoped Richard would read the letter and the supporting documentation, digest it, talk with his family, maybe a friend or two, and then he'd call me and we'd have an adult conversation.

A week went by, but I had been traveling so I really didn't have much time to think about it.

Two weeks went by and I began to have a bit of trepidation. Did he actually get it? Did it create unintended problems for him? Did he pitch it in the trash in a fit of rage?

Three weeks went by and I thought about calling him. But I was busy and decided to keep giving him a chance to do whatever preparation he needed.

Five weeks went by and my patience ran out. As I contemplated initiating the call, I was both disappointed that he hadn't taken the lead and nervous to the point of really wanting to avoid this conversation altogether. I was short of breath, forcing myself to take deep, intentional breaths as I looked up his number and held my finger hovering over the keypad of my phone. My heart was racing as if I'd just finished an aerobic workout.

Finally I let my finger drop onto the telephone keypad, more from gravity than intent. The phone rang several times, but I got his voice mail. I didn't leave a message.

With the same angst-filled prelude, I called again the next night with the same result. I called again later that night and this time I decided to leave a message. It was his wife Berniece's voice on the machine, so I said:

"Hello, Berniece and Richard. This is Craig Steffen. Richard, I just wanted to get in touch and follow up on the letter I sent several weeks back. Please give me a call when you have some time to talk."

I heard nothing. So, two days later I called again and left another message:

"Hello, Berniece and Richard. This is Craig Steffen. I hope that our inability to connect is the result of you two being away enjoying a favorite vacation spot. I just wanted to follow up on the letter I sent several weeks ago. Please give me a call when you get back."

I heard nothing. Another week passed.

At the six week mark I called again. I was surprised to find all the same physical anxiety each time I geared up to make these calls. From the time I decided I should dial the number till the time I actually did was often fifteen minutes or more. I'd think, "Oh, my phone battery's almost dead, I should charge it before I call." Or, "That fan is too loud, I should shut it off before I call, but it's pretty warm in here, maybe I should wait till it cools off." Or, "Hmm, I don't want Cindy to call while I'm on the phone, so I'll call her now to let her know what I'm doing." I devised a seemingly endless number of delay tactics. But I'd eventually take several deep, intentional breaths and dial the number.

This time I called in the morning, hoping that calling at a different time of the day might find him home and able to talk.

It worked. Berniece answered:

"Hi, is this Berniece?"

"Yes."

"Hello, Berniece, this is Craig Steffen."

"Yes."

"Hey, is Richard around?"

"No."

"Do you know when he might be back?"

"Probably later this afternoon."

"Ok, well, I'll call back this afternoon then."

"Ok."

"Bye Bye."

It was short and to the point. I couldn't tell if there was attitude behind the short answers, or just introversion. But to an extrovert, it *seemed* like attitude.

I called back around 5:00 that evening. Berniece answered again:

"Hi Berniece, it's Craig Steffen calling back."

"Yes."

"Is Richard home yet?"

"Yes, just a second.

I literally forgot to breathe. This conversation was finally going to happen. I steeled myself for adversarial responses.

Richard got on the line:

"Hello."

"Hey Richard, Craig Steffen here."

"Yeah."

"How are you doin?

"Well, not too bad."

"Good. Glad to hear it. ... Hey, I just wanted to check in with you and see if you got the letter and packet of information I sent you a while back?"

"Yeees, I got it." Sigh. "Well, I'd like to talk to you in person if you ever get back."

"Ok."

"Uh, but I don't think there's any need, prolly, for a DNA test. Uhh, I can kina fill you in on what happened."

"Ok."

Buick

Once it started, it all happened so fast. Mom and Dad were sitting around the table talking with my paternal grandparents when Mom began to feel all the familiar signals that there was going to be a baby. She already had my two older siblings, so experience told her what was happening.

Rather abruptly, they decided it was time to go to the hospital. Fortunately, the hospital wasn't far, but they hadn't thought to bring anything for this occasion. Neither of them imagined that this would finally be *that* night. So, completely unprepared, they gathered their things and headed for the car.

It was unseasonably chilly, and Dad tried to be chivalrous holding his jacket up around her to keep her warm. It wasn't as choreographed as it is in the movies. It was awkward and they both felt every bit like the teenagers they still were. They were both just 19.

Pressures were building. Emotions were running high. There was a sense of urgency growing as they settled into the car, got the motor running and headed down the street toward the hospital.

They talked some; even laughed a little, but after only a few minutes it became clear that they weren't going to make it to the hospital – regardless of their best intentions. This was going to happen, and it was going to happen now. Nature couldn't be stopped, or even slowed-down. Mom knew that once these hormones were released, there was no turning back.

So, instead of getting to the hospital, they pulled off down a dark, quiet side road along the river. He slid the front seat all the way back and arranged his jacket like a makeshift pillow in the spacious front seat. He helped her to get comfortable there, where they both found room to maneuver. As she lay down, he kissed her.

The rest is a blur of adrenaline, elevated heart rate, nonsensical communications, pulling off obstructive clothing, trying to find the most comfortable positions, emotions spiraling ever upward.

And then it happened.

Right there in Dad's car, on a cold night in 1959 Fort Dodge, Iowa — I was conceived.

Of course, neither of them knew that conception had occurred — but no precautions had been taken either. Though the persistent person could obtain them, condoms were actually illegal in the USA until 1965.

When the act was done, Richard dropped Beverly off at the Fort Dodge Trinity Hospital where Beverly's second child, 9-month-old Ricky, had been admitted a few days prior for pneumonia and a seizure disorder. Richard and Beverly never saw or spoke to one another again — ever.

It wasn't supposed to happen this way. These two had known each other since grade school and there had been crushes and puppy-love. Richard sometimes got teased about Beverly making "googly-eyes" at him in their tiny school back in Clemons, Iowa. No doubt some of their friends had uttered the classic love poem,

Richard and Beverly
Sitting in a tree,
K-I-S-S-I-N-G.
First comes love,

Then comes marriage,
Then comes baby
In a baby carriage.

But all these childish ideas of love ended abruptly when Beverly's parents moved away from Clemons. Not long after, Richard's parents moved to Fort Dodge and Richard and Beverly didn't see each other again until that one, cold September night in 1959, just after Richard had returned from a stint in the Army.

For Beverly the evening may have produced fear. Was this her first indiscretion since marriage? The foundation of her life may have cracked that night. Her life was hard and boring and she likely felt trapped – but it was predictable and there was shelter, food and a little money. A mistake like this in a time like this could end all certainty as she knew it. She could be labeled a "tramp," could be forced into divorce, could lose the children and could, literally, be on the street.

For Richard, the evening likely produced a flush of head-spinning and conflicting emotions – the joy of reconnecting with an old friend – the exhilaration of an unexpected sexual encounter – the danger of being with a married woman. He had the luxury of processing these emotions in the confines of his own mind, or maybe with a trusted friend. But, not ever being aware of the conception, if he had any sense of ignominy, it was produced only from internal sources.

Beverly, on the other hand, would soon feel a child growing within her and would have to deal with that reality and all the unanswered questions *that* child represented. She was surrounded by people with whom she could never reveal those questions and the certain angst this unborn child brought to her.

It seems as if she cast off all restraint after her indiscretion in route to the hospital. A few days later she returned to her home, her husband

and her children in Renwick, Iowa. Shortly thereafter, she began the whirlwind fling with the Fuller Brush salesman, which resulted in her husband, Alvin, losing his job and the whole family being homeless for a time.

And though I speculate about the thoughts, feelings and emotions this encounter and subsequent conception produced in Beverly and Richard, I am certain of only one thing. The evening produced me.

Only the most dedicated fatalists would venture to portray this evening and the child it produced as being part of an ideal plan. Yet here I am; and I am grateful to be alive. Furthermore, I am grateful to be this particular blend of DNA that makes me exactly who I am. Without those awkward, stolen moments in the back of that car and all the angst they may have created, I would not have been created.

Sure, I wish I were a little taller. I could do without the slow metabolism I got from Beverly. I wish my hair were a bit more tightly rooted. Being a little more handsome has always seemed like a good idea. A healthier dose of athleticism would have spared me from some childhood embarrassment. But, all in all, I could have done a lot worse than the 50/50 blend of DNA donated and mixed on that clandestine September night. I'll take it. I'll take life. I'll take this particular life. Thank you, Beverly and Richard, for my life that wasn't really "supposed to be."

Resolution

After Richard told me this story, we talked for another half hour.

He now seemed resolved to the fact that what I had been claiming *was*, in fact, possible. At first, he sounded like a man caught – finally submitting to the evidence presented. It seemed to me as if he saw himself as being in an interrogation room with bright lights in his eyes, and a "confession" was his only way out.

And even though it had been more than six weeks since he received my letter, he hadn't yet decided how (or perhaps if) he would tell anyone else. At least three times he said some version of, "I'm just trying to figure out how to tell my kids."

Finally I offered, "Well, Richard, I can't imagine that they will think any less of you. After all, they were 19 years old once too."

By the end of the call, we'd agreed that I'd check my calendar and see when might be a good time to get out to Iowa and sit down face-to-face to have a discussion.

Several days later, I called and left a message on his voice mail proposing some dates in November a few weeks in advance of Thanksgiving. It's been three days since I left that message, but I haven't yet heard back from him.

Maybe we'll have a chance to sit down like two mature adults and have an honest dialog. Maybe it will be the first of many talks. Maybe it will be the last conversation we ever have. Or maybe, he won't call me back. The wait continues.

Kids

A week had passed since I'd left a few potential dates for a visit to Iowa on Richard's answering machine and that face-to-face talk he'd offered. I'd spent the weekend down at our farm in southern Ohio and was now on my way back to the Dayton area. It was Sunday, September 29, in the early afternoon – exactly 54 years to the day since my conception (plus or minus three days).

I'd been on the road less than 30 minutes when my phone rang. It was Richard.

After a few pleasantries, we agreed on some dates to meet in Iowa in November, a few weeks prior to Thanksgiving.

During the call, Richard told me that he had talked about me with his son David on Friday evening and his daughter Suzie just last night.

"How did those calls go?"

"Pretty well," was all he said.

We concluded the brief call with dates on our calendars and, I'm guessing, a fair amount of shared angst about our next meeting six weeks hence.

My mind was swimming with disparate thoughts coinciding with a surge of wildly variant emotions. I tried to call Cindy, but she did not answer. I left a message and was left alone to deal with all the chaos in my veins, soul and synapses.

About 10 minutes after the call ended, I pulled up to a stop light on my way home and pulled out my phone as a distractive tactic to pass the time. I opened Facebook and saw that I had a friend request notification. I touched the screen and saw a request from an attractive young woman named Suzie.

I didn't recognize her, so the request was curious. Having just gotten off the phone where Richard had told me about a phone conversation he'd had the night before with his daughter, Suzie, I suspected there was a connection. I didn't know Richard's daughter's last name, but the timing was too proximal to be a coincidence.

I clicked the profile and saw that Suzie and I had one friend in common, my new cousin Jeffrey. This had to be Richard's daughter — but what was her intent? Was she simply checking up on me, trying to figure out if I was a good guy or not? Was she doing Internet research at the behest of her dad? Or was she reaching out to say hello? There was no message associated with the request, just Facebook's automated announcement that someone was looking to connect with me.

I clicked "accept."

At the next stop light, I sent her a private Facebook message that simply read:

"Greetings Suzie, nice to 'meet' you. Thanks for reaching out."

And then I waited to see what kind of message, if any, might come back from this never-met-stranger — who was also my new little sister.

The following morning, at about 9:00, I got a reply. It read:

"Nice to meet you! Wow! God works in mysterious ways ... I look forward to meeting you in person in Nov. I am not a big

Facebook user...my email is _____. I'm not quite sure what to say other than thank-you for your determination, you must be a very courageous man! Not surprising though, if you are letting God run your life! Have a wonderful day!"

So this is the type of person my little sister is – kind, thoughtful, understanding, spiritual, welcoming, empathetic and sweet. Since this first simple dialog, Suzie and I have exchanged several emails and photos in a distant and sometimes awkward attempt to get to know one another, despite the hundreds of miles and years of secrets that have separated us all our lives.

Fathers

It is unlikely I'll ever forget that day in the summer of 1975, when Theresa and I stopped at a non-descript trailer in Nevada, Iowa and I heard her say, "Craig, this is your father." We spent that weekend together at the Iowa State Fair and I slept on the floor of that trailer. The memories of waking up the next morning to watch my sister make breakfast for her father, and the liberal pepper coating on the eggs she prepared, are fixed in my familial history.

I met Alvin Shepherd only five or six times in my life. By the time I saw him the second time, he had lost most of his right leg to a blood-clotting disorder. And in the brief episodes where I would see him and attempt conversation, I'd ask questions about him and tell stories about myself that were designed to probe the origins of my true self.

I was always disappointed though. I never found another connection between us. Slowly I began to believe that our mutual propensity for pepper was just a coincidence. There were SO many differences between us. He looked so much like Theresa and Ricky, and nothing at all like me. The three of them were slender and dark and introverted. I was none of that. Each subsequent visit revealed we had literally nothing in common – except pepper.

While on a business trip to California in the late 1990s, I got a call from Theresa to tell me that Alvin was in the hospital in Bakersfield, CA. He and his wife, Darlene, were there visiting her family. While there, he'd had another clot and had consequently lost his other leg to amputation. Ironically, I was then working as the Director of Marketing for an internationally known manufacturer of prosthetic legs for amputees. I rented a car and drove from Los Angeles to Bakersfield to visit him in the hospital and to discover if there was anything I might do to help him, given my connections within the prosthetics industry.

He didn't have much to say. He never did. I could never tell if this had something to do with me, or if he was just unusually quiet and introverted. In either case, we spoke mostly about the amputation and I committed to getting him access to products that would make his life easier and more comfortable. I shipped him cases of comfort-related products over the remaining years of his life.

By the time Alvin died in 2002, he'd had multiple amputations of his lower extremities. All that remained of his legs were residual limbs of about six inches in length. A few days before I learned of his death, I had landed a big client for the new company I had started a few months earlier. My first strategy session with them was scheduled for the same day as Alvin's funeral. I had angst because of what my wife calls my "overly developed sense of responsibility."

In the end, I chose not to go to the funeral of my first dad. As terrible as the reason now seems, I had bills to pay. I feared that if I tried to reschedule my client event, I risked having that client label me a "flake" and walk away from our business relationship. I didn't want to risk that with such a fledgling new company.

 But it was more than that too. I suspected that Alvin was not my father and something inside me told me that *he* knew this too – but never admitted it, even when asked.

A few months after the funeral, I got a photo in the mail from his surviving wife, Darlene. It was a picture of Alvin's tombstone. When I saw it, I was flooded with the feeling that I had misjudged or misinterpreted all the differences between us. And, for several years, I wondered if I had been the one who had built a wall around my heart and had kept Dad out. Maybe the differences were my own fabrication? In case you can't make out the first words at the top of the tombstone, they say, "Gone Fishing." My name is the last thing on the stone. This is the closest Alvin and I will ever be to fishing together.

Of course, I've since learned that the differences were real – and for a good reason. Alvin was not my biological father, though he took care of me for the first two years of my life. There were no DNA connections between us, and there were no personality or emotional connections either.

I'm not 15 anymore. I'm a responsible adult, a leader in many ways, a business owner, a husband. I'm a person that others often seek out for perspective or advice.

But I have a confession to make.

Now that I've discovered that Richard, not Alvin, is my biological father, I find all those old familiar questions rising within me afresh. The questions run the whole gamut from philosophical to ridiculous.

Several years ago I read a scientific article about a hypothesis proffered by a geneticist who had formulated the concept of a "God Gene." That geneticist, Dean Hamer, wrote a book titled, *The God Gene: How Faith is Hardwired into our Genes*. A few days ago, as I read a book about theology, I found myself drifting from the words on the page to ponder in my head if my love of God and theology might come through Richard's DNA that I now know flows through my veins.

What about my quirky sense of humor, my monogamy, my entrepreneurial penchant, my laugh, my health? What is Richard like? Am I, in any way, like that?

Yesterday I put some vitamin E on a mole on my arm and wondered if he has a mole like this on his triceps? What about baseball and fishing? Does he love baseball like I do? Who is his team? Did he pass these loves onto me and to his other children? If so, will we all ever go fishing or to a game together?

Questions like these pop into my head multiple times per day. When they emerge, like an intrusive trivia game, they create an ache in my chest. Will I ever learn the answers to these questions? What other origins, wondrous and disconcerting, will I discover when/if that dam of silence breaks?

And on those mornings I grab breakfast, I always wonder if Richard likes pepper on his eggs.

Anticipation

It is fifty-one years since the disappearance.

In 20 more days, I'll be on a long drive to meet a new family – again.

It feels like a déjà vu of that hot July 23rd day in 1963, when the Steffens picked up Theresa and me from the Annie Wittenmyer Home.

In many ways, I feel like the little boy who left The Home and its cottages behind and traveled with strangers to a farm far away. As then, I have no idea what the future holds. This time, I'll travel with a different girl who loves me – Cindy instead of Theresa. This time, I'll leave from my own home, or from the cottage we own in the woods. This time I'll travel as an adult with the ability to comprehend what is happening around me. This time I'll travel by my choice, instead of the will of others. This time I already know the identity of the characters who await my arrival.

But I don't know – can't know – how the journey will end. Will this trip result in long-term relationships as the first one did? Or will it begin and end on this one November day?

Will the father I meet be as faithful as the father I met at age three? Will the father I meet this time understand who I am in a way that the first one never did? Or will he be silent, cool and aloof?

Will this new sister and I share an unconditional love? Or will we grow distant over time?

Will this new brother and I connect deep in our souls? Or will he feel I am some kind of threat, or will he just be uninterested?

Will this grandmother I meet be kind and gentle and accepting like Grandma Steffen and Grandma Gardiner? Or will she resent me for upsetting the natural order of the family?

Will the aunts and uncles I meet accept this new boy into the family and send me thoughtful birthday cards, as my first new extended family did? Or will they even have the inclination or curiosity to get to know me?

Will the cousins I meet become fast friends, with life and stories to share, as several in the 1960s did? Or have I come too late to their lives for them to care?

I'm trying hard to reign in my expectations. My new sister, Suzie, has reached out to me and we have exchanged several email messages. She has been so wonderful it's hard not to let that singular experience skew all my other expectations. I have to keep reminding myself that, statistically speaking, it is unlikely that everyone in the family will have her sweet personality and welcoming spirit.

I want to control the get-together. I want to put together an agenda complete with topics to discuss, memories to share, photo albums to thumb through. I thought about doing a Power Point presentation – really. Secretly, I want to do all the symbolic things I've never done with family before. And I'd like to get them all done in this first weekend.

Intellectually I know it's completely unrealistic – impossible really. But emotionally I feel like a kid on Christmas morning. Here are just a few of the questions swirling in my head that I want to ask:

To Richard:

- What was your relationship with Beverly over the years? Was she ever your girlfriend? Or was it all platonic until that one September night in 1959?

- What happened that ignited the fire between you, as you drove her back to the hospital to be with Ricky?

- What were you feeling when you dropped her off at the hospital later that night?

- Did you ever call or write after? Did she?

- Did you ever wonder if that night of passion resulted in a pregnancy – in a person – in me?

- What did you feel when you found out about Beverly's murder?

- After you met me, at what point did you begin to wonder if I were your son?

- Why did it take so long to finally tell me the Buick story? What did you fear?

- Does your mind wander as often as mine does to thoughts about what our future might look like?

- Do you think about things you want to know about me?

- Do you want to do things together? Baseball? Fishing?

- Do you want to go places together?

- Will you ever think of me as "family" and include me?

To David:

- I want to discover all the ways that we are alike – and different

- I want to toss around a baseball, a football, shoot some hoops and play some golf and racquetball

- I want to watch "the game" (any game), drink beer and eat

junk food together
- I want to talk about life, about work, about women
- I want to laugh with you
- I want to get deep with you
- I want to help each other build or fix something

To Suzie:

- I want to talk about our shared experiences:
- Being extroverted
- Losing our mothers
- Being misunderstood
- Being "rebels"
- Leaving home young
- Finding Jesus
- I want to talk to you on the phone for hours like new teenage friends
- I want to send you greeting cards
- I want to listen to you and understand deeply
- I want to be a good big brother to you
- I want to host you in my home, make you feel special and grant you refrigerator rights

But I'm WAY ahead of myself, I know. We haven't even met. We haven't looked into each other's eyes yet. We haven't even acknowledged that we share DNA – at least not out loud, in person.

We haven't gotten past the first awkward silence. We haven't stumbled into the first forbidden topic – unaware. We haven't shared our first emotion together – will it be a laugh, sadness, reminiscence, a smile, regret, relief, fear, hope or joy?

We haven't been spontaneous with one another. If we've talked at all, it has been for a purpose or on a schedule or before we knew or before we acknowledged.

We have not touched. There has been no physical contact, no reaching to comfort, no hug, no nudge, no pat on the back. No sense of comfort that would prompt even an unconscious pluck of lint from a shoulder.

We have not connected. We have not sought, nor have we found something deep inside us that might, someday, reach out and find that corresponding puzzle-piece in each other. We have not linked together in some universal, yet indescribable way, as families sometimes do.

Family ties, if they are ever to exist, cannot be scripted or controlled. I can't put them on a to-do list to be accomplished. I can't manipulate the stars to align at my own behest.

I can't control this. I shouldn't try. As in a relationship with the Almighty, I must get comfortable with mystery, the unknown and the unknowable. I must cease striving and relax into these relationships. I must be *me* – take my time and give it space.

I must seek and find the empathy to see, feel, and care about what is going on inside of each of these new sharers of my DNA.

But even though I know this, I admit that the questions continue to swirl in my head. They sneak in at every quiet moment. Sometimes they derail other trains of thought and take them down a dirt road. Occasionally, they interrupt so rudely and loudly I do not hear the people right in front of me.

Do these new sharers of my DNA have a list of burning questions inside of them, as I do? Do they see a preferred future as I see? Am I in it? Are they being drawn to this meeting as a moth to a light, DNA whispers in their ears?

Perhaps they are pushed by mere obligation? Or could it be more like the prurient curiosity that drives one to slip under a circus tent to catch a glimpse of some freak of nature?

Though the questions are a bit more sophisticated than those that plagued me at age three as I sat in the back seat of the '57 Ford with the Steffens, they feel the same. And, like then, it will take decades for the relationships to gestate and for the future to give birth to yet unwritten possibility.

In a few more days, a new life chapter will be underway.

It seems like a year since the dates were set for our trip to meet my paternal biological family – but it's only been six weeks. The day for the journey to begin has finally come, Wednesday, November 13, 2013. The time for first contact has finally arrived. Cindy and I head out toward Iowa on this sunny, but chilly early afternoon, with a hope of getting to Davenport yet tonight.

The plan is to spend the night there, then get up tomorrow and return to the Annie Wittenmyer Home for a fresh look around. It has been nearly 25 years since Cindy and I first visited The Home after our car broke down near Davenport in 1988.

Then, Thursday afternoon, we'll arrive in State Center, Iowa, meet up with my new cousin Jeff at his store, The Remarkable Rose, and check into the Bed and Breakfast he manages in town. Friday afternoon we'll meet up with sister Suzie, brother David and their spouses. And, finally, we'll meet my biological dad, Richard, and his wife Berniece Saturday for lunch.

Mixed in will be dinner with maternal Aunt Sherri and Uncle Steve on Thursday night and breakfast with Aunt Barb, Uncle Dale, Aunt Sherri and Uncle Steve on Saturday morning.

It'll be a busy few days with both sides of my biological family. Cindy will be meeting everyone for the first time.

Wittenmyer

Our stop at Annie Wittenmyer brought back profound and stark memories from the first time we'd been to the orphanage since Theresa and I left for the Steffens.

It was 27 years after the disappearance.

Cindy and I had been in Iowa visiting the Steffen side of our family for Thanksgiving. We headed back to Ohio on a Sunday afternoon after attending church and grabbing a quick restaurant lunch with the folks.

We cruised along Interstate 80 heading eastward in our 1985 VW Golf. But after about 200 miles, the car began to make some strange noises and exhibit even more troubling behavior. The slightest bump on the road would set the front end to shimmying and the movement could be heard inside the car and felt through the steering wheel. I determined that this was not the kind of mechanical problem that should be ignored. Tie rods? Ball joints? Wheel bearings? I slowed down and started looking for exits that might offer some mechanical services.

We ended up getting off the interstate on exit 295 and looked for a hotel to stay the night, since car dealerships wouldn't be open on a Sunday evening. We checked into the Blackhawk Hotel in Downtown Davenport. The first order of business was to pull out the thick phone book from the nightstand drawer of our room and look for a Volkswagen dealership.

Serendipitously there was one not too far away. I thumbed to the city map at the back of the phone book and charted a route. It didn't seem too hard. I jotted down the address and phone number on the hotel stationery and then picked up the phone and dialed the number, hoping that they'd have a recording that told me when their service department would be open in the morning. Seven a.m. was the answer given by the professional voice on the machine.

I was up at 5:30 a.m., quickly showered and headed to the dealership determined to be the first car in line, since I had no appointment.

As trips to the service department go, this one turned out to be about as painless as they come. These folks were sensitive to the fact that I was traveling, competent in their diagnosis of the problem and efficient at repairing it. For you mechanical types, it turned out to be a loose tie rod.

By ten o'clock I was back at the hotel and hungry. Cindy and I went down to the hotel restaurant for some breakfast before hitting the road for another 500 miles toward home.

As we sat in the restaurant, I began to tell Cindy that Davenport was the town where I had been in an orphanage with Theresa and Ricky. She had heard the story before, but it was impossible not to recount it while we sat here in a place so near to where the orphanage had once stood.

As our waitress filled our water glasses, she overheard me telling the story.

"Are you talking about the Annie Wittenmyer Home?"

"Yes, I was placed there as a child back in the early 1960s. Was it anywhere near here?"

"I used to work there years ago before the orphanage closed, about a dozen years ago. But the buildings are all still there. It's not far from here – only a few miles."

"REALLY?" I asked astonished. "We're from Ohio now, but I had heard that it was torn down years ago. So it's really all still there?"

"It sure is. I drive past it every morning to come here to work. You should go there if you've got some time. It'll only take a few minutes to get there."

"I was only two or three years old when I was there, so I don't remember much about it."

I exchanged glances with Cindy who sat engaged and curious across the table. It was clear that these two women were in agreement with what I *should* do.

The waitress grabbed a napkin and sketched out a crude map and wrote directions that would take us to the, now mostly abandoned, campus of my former residence.

It was a bright, calm autumn morning as we drove down the winding concrete drive toward the big main building that looked as if it could have been at the center of an old university campus.

There were thousands of the largest acorns I'd ever seen, fallen from ancient oaks that were already long-time residents when I walked these grounds at two and three years old. Old friends were we.

At first, I could only stand and rotate slowly in order to take in the macro view of this now barren campus and imagine it full of parentless children playing tag or kick ball outwardly, but curled up in an emotional ball inwardly.

I was drawn, like a kid to candy, to the row of cottages that extended out from the right of the main building down the length of the campus and formed a U at the other end.

So *these* were the cottages I'd heard about all my life.

These were the cottages in which I had once lived. These were the cottages to which the Steffens had come to get a daughter to raise with their existing son. These were the cottages that had housed not just a pretty little girl named Theresa who had stolen their hearts, but cottages that housed her little tow-headed brother as well. We were a brother and sister pair that would not be separated.

Cindy and I walked about the campus, hand-in-hand, quietly talking about my childhood connection to this place and conjecturing about how each building might have looked and been used 27 years ago. We stopped at each cottage and peered in through dirty windows to see empty rooms or rooms filled with stored junk. We walked around the cottages to find round, metal fire-escape tubes that could have provided endless fun in a playground, but were relegated to more serious duty at the backs of the buildings.

After nearly an hour of exploration, I could feel the pressure of a 500-mile journey still on the agenda for the day. On my way back toward the car, I slipped in between two of the cottages to get a look inside from a side window. I rubbed a clean spot onto the surface of the glass and looked through into a room caught in time on the other side of the pane. Like staring at a proverbial train wreck, I could not look away. Tears poured down my checks without permission. My chest convulsed and heaved with such force that Cindy became alarmed about my health.

"What? What's happening?" she said, too loud, from just a few feet away.

She rushed to my side, put her arm around my shoulder, pulled my face away from the breath-fogged window and directed it toward her own.

"What are you experiencing, my love?" she asked with a soul-merging earnestness.

I could not contain the emotions that poured out of me like a sudden volcanic eruption. I'd never experienced any such emotional burst in all my conscious years.

Yet there it is. On the other side of that glass is the stanchion set before me like a cruel monolith. It is smaller than in my memory. It is made of old, ugly, unfinished wood. It is like a coffin stood on end, divided into three uneven sections. The middle section is big enough for more than two of me. I am overcome with sadness.

The base of the stanchion sits on the floor, and above the floor is a drawer. At the top of the drawer is a piece of wood that serves as a seat on which I once sat during morning instructions. I got splinters in the backs of my legs. I sat quiet facing out into the room. I am still alone.

There is an important shelf above my head. I can now see the dusty, spider-webbed top of the stanchion. There are many of these stanchions lining the walls of this small, linoleum-tiled room. Today, there are no kids in each stanchion looking blankly out into a room — and there are no strangers. But I am still frightened.

That memory that had lingered so long in the recesses of my mind instantly morphed from surreal, to so-real. The fog that obscured those memories, preserved since age two, lifted before my eyes. Everything about that room, 27 years later, fit into my memory as if it had been a long-lost key, turning now to secure forever my once uncertain childhood memories.

They WERE real — ever so real.

I HAD been here before. Not just some anonymous abandoned kid — ME. And all the emotions that I had felt then, I was feeling again now.

But today, I was able to give those emotions names in a way that I could not have done then. I knew:

- Fear
- Confusion
- Panic
- Hopelessness
- Loneliness
- Helplessness
- Exasperation

And today, I was able to give names to the personal violence that caused such emotion, in a way I could not have done then. I was:

- Unwanted
- Unloved
- Lied to
- Forgotten
- Abandoned
- Accused
- Dehumanized

Cindy held me as gently and lovingly as if I were yet two years old. She held me a long time until the intensity slowly melted from me, warmed by her own unconditional love.

And then, as I stoically turned to walk away, as one might after learning of the tragic death of a loved one, Cindy turned back toward the window, looked into the room, and lingered there as if studying the origins of my very soul.

**

And this time, when we returned on our way to meet the new family, we walked around inside the cottages and I was able to leave this imprint, and snap this stanchion photo. It's just not as scary anymore.☺

The Meet

The designated time for first contact has arrived. It's four o'clock Friday, November 15, in State Center, Iowa.

Cindy and I are sitting on the sofa of the B&B we've reserved for our stay. Candles flicker and release their sweet aroma throughout the room. The Beetles anthology plays on my iPhone and every familial fear and expectation I've ever had plays in my soul.

My eyes are closed, head down, in some kind of amalgamation of prayer, anxiety and attempt at emotional control. The nervous vibration within me is akin to what happens when one lights an M-80 fire cracker and throws it – perhaps not quite as far away as intended ... a fear, danger and excitement rush. Then you wait. And wait. And wait. And wait. Why isn't it happening? Where is it? Did the fuse go out? Is it a dud? Why isn't it going off? Does it need to be relit? Should I go look for it? Or should I just close my eyes and wait – not so patiently – for the explosion?

Then, boom, my phone rings. I'm startled by an adrenalin surge into a heightened alert. I glance at the screen and see the caller ID is from Missouri. I assume it is Suzie. I answer the call.

"Hi, Craig. It's sister Suzie. We're here with David at the nursing home seeing Grandma, and we're running a bit behind schedule. We should be there by about 5:00 though. Is that Ok?"

And wait. And wait. And wait ...

We haven't slept much. Cindy suggests that I lie down and try to "reboot your brain." My mind flashes to the popular TV commercial from the late 1990s of a family the night before a trip to Disneyland, images of Goofy dancing in their heads. A four- or five-year-old boy whispers to his slightly older sister, "I wonder what it'll be like?" She replies with a toothless grin, "There's even more exciting stuff now." Mom interrupts and tells them to go back to bed. To this the little boy declares, with a lisp and a winsome giggle, flopping backward onto the bed, "We're too exthited to thleep!"

Yeah. It's like that.

I do lie down, but I don't sleep. As five o'clock approaches, I get up and pace around the B&B, impatient as a puppy at supper.

And wait. And wait.

At 5:10, I hear voices on the steps to our B&B. "I wonder what it'll be like?" Then, boom, someone knocks.

There's a hug for Suzie who's been so amazingly welcoming from afar since the news of my existence broke. There's a hearty handshake for her husband, Bill, who's a "trooper" to drive these five hours from Kansas City to make this meeting possible. And there is a slap on the back for their grandson, Jordan, whose smile is as authentic and friendly as a long lost friend.

David and his Cindy are at the back of the processional and gather into the greeting line with big smiles and hearty handshakes. There are a conglomerate of words and greetings that my brain cannot now untangle completely, but included things like, "Well finally we meet" and "I can't believe this is really happening" and "This is unbelievable."

Unbelievable. Truly.

We move into the living room area of our basement B&B tastefully decorated in a retro '70s style with lots of red, black and white color and leather-slung period chairs on sealed concrete floors. We each gather around the faux fireplace and everyone chooses a chair to their liking. It feels a bit like visiting a house church for the first time – it's a little awkward, but we all have something important in common and words to share. We commence getting to know one another, an odd activity for siblings meeting each other for the first time – at an average age of more than 50 years.

Questions are flowing steadily. Answers lead to more questions or bump us down a rabbit trail so distant that we forget how we ever came to be there. Mostly we nip around the edges of who we really are – not knowing any of the 50 years of experiences and life that molded us and carried us to this place at this time. But at a deeper level, I sense that we all "get" each other. Awkward as it has been getting to these early hours in our first date, I feel a certain kinship, a certain tribal familiarity one might feel visiting with a relative from the old country.

Hunger sets in after an hour or two and we rise to walk a block down the street to St. Andrews Grill and Bar. We are seated at a large round table immediately to the left of the entrance. Our conversation continues unabated, despite the waitress's attempts to take our drink and food orders. There are 50 years to catch up on, and we have only this one evening, before David must travel back to his home. All my questions burn within me and new ones are formed from the scraps of answers left behind. It is clear that everyone has questions burning within them. We are engaged.

David takes the conversation toward a deeper place.

"Well, you know, Dad called me that night and told me that he needed to talk to me – something important. He said he'd stop by the next day and we'd have a talk. I said, what's going on Dad? Are you alright? Let's just talk right now. He said he didn't want to have this kind of conversation on the phone and that he'd be over the next day to talk. I said no, Dad, this sounds serious; we're going to talk right now. I'll be over in ten minutes. I got all worried you know – I thought he might be dying or something. So I got in my truck and drove over to his place. It's only about 10 minutes. That's when he told me – told me about you."

The chatter of our little family group grows quieter as the weight of what David is saying captures everyone's attention.

"He seemed nervous and maybe ashamed of himself. I assured him that stuff like this happens. I said, geez, Dad, you were only 19, this kind of stuff happens to 19 year olds. He said, 'Well, not to ME it doesn't.' I sort of laughed, because everything about Dad has been so ordered and deliberate and now there was this long lost kid coming out of nowhere. I could see he was shaken by it and didn't really want to admit it to me."

Suzie adds that she had sensed the same thing from her dad the following night when he called her in Kansas City to tell her that he had another son and that she had another brother.

David continues, "After he told me about you and what happened, he said that you'd sent him a letter and other documents. I didn't really know what to think of you. So I asked him to make a copy of these so I could see what kind of person you were. The next day he came over to the house with a copy of everything and gave it to me. I laid the pages down next to my chair and I didn't really pick them up for several days. Then one night after I got home from work, I got myself a cold beer and sat down and started to read. I read those pages most every night for several nights in a row, trying to let it all sink in. After each reading, I felt like I knew you, understood you, just a little better. After I'd read those twenty-something pages about six times, I set them down and I said, I want to meet this guy, this Craig, my long-lost brother."

Apparently feeling a little left out, Suzie says, "Wait, what letter? I didn't get a copy of any letter."

David and I both promise to get her a copy, wanting to make sure we are all equally informed.

"Well it's pretty obvious that you're a very determined man. You stuck with this a long time when most people, I think, would have just given up and moved on," David says.

"I think Cindy was a little worried about me at times, thinking that maybe I was obsessed with this. But I just kept feeling like, as long as there was a lead to follow, I had to keep going. If all the leads dried up, then I'd stop and feel like I'd discovered all that there was to know. Obviously my biological origins took place more than 50 years ago. A lot of information gets lost and forgotten when a half-century separates past facts from present tense. I hope I don't come off like some crazy person for sticking with the journey for this long," I offer.

"Oh no, not at all. I'm so glad – we're so glad – you did. This whole story is amazing," Suzie chimes in.

With some timidity, David asks me about my childhood. "So what was it like growing up in your family, and then the orphanage and being adopted? I hope it's ok to ask?"

"Oh, it's fine. I can't imagine a question that would be inappropriate; I'm really a very open person. I'll tell you about my bowel movements if you really want to know." I said laughing.

"No, no need to talk about that," Suzie inserted, smiling.

"Well, despite all the stuff that happened to me and the wounds and scars associated with it, I really think I've had a pretty wonderful life. Because I was less than two, I don't remember the disappearance of my mother. The orphanage was hard, but I was young so I have only a few memories of the place. There were a couple of foster homes that I don't think were good experiences, but again I was so young so as not to have much memory of it. Then the Steffens adopted Theresa and me and we finally had real stability in our lives. It was three square meals a day like clockwork, church three times a week and lots of chores and work to do on the farm. The most difficult part was that the Steffens weren't really warm, huggy people. They were older than my biological grandparents and survived the entirety of the Great Depression. They had their own wounds and scars. I know they loved us and provided for us but I don't remember ever being told I was loved and I don't remember ever getting a hug from them."

Suzie speaks up and says, "Well, if it's any consolation, we weren't really a huggy family either. I got my hug from Dad when I graduated high school. I think he was so shocked I made it that he forgot himself."

We all laugh … that kind of laugh that indicates the deep knowing of a thing, but not the accepting of the thing.

We close the place down and then wander back to our B&B. I had brought some of my homemade wine from Ohio and we open a bottle and continue to talk and laugh together. It is clear to me that we have lowered our guards and are communicating with greater ease.

At one point Bill says playfully, "So you're really a tenacious fellow, if we ever piss you off should we be worried that you'll hold a grudge forever?"

I start to respond to the question by explaining what a generally easy-going fellow I tend to be – most of the time...

But my Cindy breaks in and says, "Oh no, there's really only one thing you don't EVER want to do to Craig. If you do, you'll feel the full extent of his wrath."

I have no idea where she's going with this line of communication, but everyone else is egging her on to reveal this "dark secret" of mine.

She continues, "You don't ever want to cut Craig off in traffic and then respond to his honking at you by flipping him the bird, as if it's HIS fault. He'll absolutely go MONKEY on you."

Sheepishly I have to admit that this is indeed true. I even admit that one of my angry outbursts just happened a week earlier. I'm ashamed at my flaw, but enjoying the safety I perceive in this group to be able to be who I really am without the need for a "mask."

Slowly David raises his hand like a guilty child in a classroom. "Oh my God, I'm just like that – and so is Dad. I thought we were the only ones to be this crazy."

He tells stories about his own road-rage incidents and then one about Dad. Each story sounds suspiciously similar to the dozens of my own stories of roadway indignation. It's truly a surreal experience to see my own life reflected back at me through my biological brother and father.

Everyone laughs – maybe a bit nervously – at the stories we literally share.

I look at my Cindy and proclaim, "You see, you can't hold this against me anymore. There's nothing I can do about it – it's GENETIC."

As eleven o'clock approaches, David's phone rings and he answers it and walks into the B&B bedroom for privacy. A few minutes later he returns to the group and says, "That was Dad; he wanted to see how the big meet up went. He was surprised to find out that we're all still here talking."

"So, what did you tell him? How *is* the big meet up going?" I quizzed, replicating his dimply smile.

David takes a few thoughtful seconds before he says, "I'd say it's going great. I hope you agree."

"Oh, I totally do. You've all already exceeded my expectations."

The evening draws to a close. David and his Cindy have a 90-minute drive ahead of them and it is approaching 11:00 p.m..

The familial visitors gather up their jackets and other belongings and we congregate by the door to say our goodbyes. Everybody hugs everybody now with slaps on the back and conversation about when and where we might meet again.

In the midst of all the jovial conversation, eleven-year-old Jordan looks me in the eye, shakes my hand and says, with an authentic smile, "Welcome to the family."

I don't know how many others hear this inclusive statement, but it quickly sinks into my soul. What a great kid. What a wonderful evening.

My five visiting family members head out to the street for their departure, first contact complete. I follow behind, not really willing for this meeting to end.

Conversation continues as we stand in front of our cars on Main Street of this refurbished, historic Iowa town. I find myself standing alone with Suzie. We hug again. I look her in the eye and I speak from my heart, "Suzie, I just want you to know that the little note you sent to me on Facebook the day after you first learned of my existence has been so healing for me. When I read those welcoming words, I knew instantly that this whole journey had been worth it. If I never heard another word from anyone in my paternal family, the contents of that one note had already exceeded my wildest expectations of this journey into my past. THANK YOU ... you have made all this possible through your inclusive and welcoming heart that is so like Jesus."

She is such a kindred spirit. We have another long hug before everyone finally has to leave.

Back inside the B&B with my Cindy, we look at each other and our smiles glow in the candlelight. "Wow," I say. "I can't imagine how that could have gone any better."

"I know. They're really good people. I liked them. I'd like them whether they were family or not."

I'm sure we talked for a good while, reliving the events of the evening. But the friction from my repeated smiles must have scrubbed those memories from my brain, because I cannot now recover any of that conversation to share with you.

Obviously

The next day, Saturday November 16, we are scheduled to meet up with my biological dad, Richard, and his wife Berniece for lunch – and, I'm hoping, for the rest of the day. The SNAFU of the plan is that the restaurant we've chosen, unbeknownst to us, isn't open for lunch on Saturdays. Apparently, ALL the restaurants in State Center are closed at lunchtime on Saturdays. The business consultant and entrepreneurial spirit in me wonders why at least one of them hasn't seen this as a competitive opportunity. To be the only option, when there is no competition, is every business's dream – at least where I come from. But I digress.

Richard is meeting up with Suzie this morning and then visiting his mom who celebrated her 92nd birthday just last week. Last night, I left Suzie with the information about the closed lunch spot, so that Richard wouldn't be blind-sided and we could all start thinking about alternatives.

My phone rings around noon. It is Suzie's number on the caller ID, but it is Richard's voice when I answer. I have walked a half block down Main Street from our B&B to The Remarkable Rose to say hello to the proprietor, my new cousin Jeff. On the phone I suggest that Richard, Suzie and the gang just meet Cindy and me there when they are ready, and we'll decide on a lunch spot face-to-face.

They all show up about fifteen minutes later and I sense a collective sigh of culmination as Richard and I finally meet as father and son for the first time.

We sit around Jeff's store for over an hour enjoying coffee and snacks and just talk small talk. Richard and I end up at one table, Cindy, Suzie and Berniece at another and Bill and Jordan at a third. Jeff circulates amongst the tables, and with his customers as they come in and out.

I am a bit guarded, not quite knowing what to expect. There are no hugs and excited language as there had been the night before. On this early afternoon, it is handshakes and reserved, cordial conversation. "How was the drive? How long did it take? How was your mom this morning?" – stuff like that.

From where I am sitting, it seems like the girls are getting along just fine across the room.

Around two o'clock, hunger gets the best of us and we talk about lunch options – none of them all that convenient. We settle on driving back over to the historic Colo Motel where Suzie, Bill and Jordan stayed last night and where Richard and Berni had checked in this morning. This classic place is a remnant of pre-interstate highway travel at the intersection of the Lincoln and Jefferson Highways. Jeff and I had eaten breakfast at the Niland's Café here back in July, when the DNA results revealed Jeff to be my first cousin and therefore pointed to Richard being my biological dad.

Richard invites Cindy and me to ride over to the café with them. Small talk continues as we make the ten-minute drive west. We all stream into the back room of the vintage café, full of memorabilia, and choose a long rectangular table situated just in front of the shell of a 1939 Cadillac mounted in the corner of the room.

Each new venue seems to bring its own brand of awkwardness, reminiscent of a Sadie Hawkins dance, to the fledgling relationships in the room. We each sit at the table staring deeply into our menus, as if they might yield the secrets of the universe.

I'm not particularly comfortable with long silences, even though I've been around a lot of introversion in my life. So I look over my menu at Richard and say, "So, Richard, what was it like growing up around here? What memories of your childhood can you share?"

Richard leans back in his chair and lowers his menu to ponder six and seven decades into his past. After a few seconds a glint of a smile creeps into his eyes and he says, "Well, I was a perfect child, really."

Sitting at the opposite end of the table is Bill, who immediately lowers his own menu and looks Richard straight in the eye, then glances sideways at me and punctuates that deliberate gesture with a single word, "Obviously."

The whole table erupts in laughter and Richard's face turns deep red as he laughs heartily with us.

The waitress returns with our drinks and begins the process of taking our order. Everyone orders something different, no two orders are even close to the same – except Richard's and mine. He and I each order a pork tenderloin with cheese, lettuce and mayo and a side of fries to go with our diet Cokes already in hand. Hmm.

While we wait for our food to be prepared, light conversation continues. At one break in the discussion, I look at Richard and say with a smile, "Richard, you shared with me about how my mother had come to your folks' house for dinner that night and that you gave her a ride back to the hospital. I have to ask – what kind of car was it?"

He is a little taken aback and his face reddens again. But he soon responds, "Well, I think it was a 1957 Buick Century. I bought that car when I got back from the Army, so that's the car I would've had at the time Beverly visited. It was a really nice car. It was pea-green and panty-pink ... and fast. In fact, I think it was the fastest car I ever owned."

Seeing a fat, straight-change-up having been pitched in my direction, I interjected, "And Beverly was probably the fastest girl you ever had in it, right?"

For a second time the table erupts in hearty laughter and we all get just a little more comfortable with one another.

Suzie adds with a mischievous smile, "Too much information. I don't want to know about this."

Truth be told, I take this opportunity to interject humor into an uncomfortable topic because I really want to communicate to Richard that I have no disrespect for him based on what happened that September night in 1959 Fort Dodge, Iowa. It really was as David had said last night; they were only 19 years old. Things like this happen to kids who are 19 years old. And without the events of that night, I wouldn't be here. And, for the record, I really enjoy being here. I love my life.

We talk for nearly three hours around our meal. Generously, Richard picks up the tab for the whole table, and we express our gratitude. Richard and Berni are wanting to get to the 5:00 p.m. Mass in State Center on this Saturday evening. We make arrangements to get back together after Mass.

Suzie brings up the topic of Grandma Helen, and when would be the right time to tell her about me.

"I'm thinking we should tell Grandma and have her meet Craig and Cindy while they're here in Iowa."

Richard's face gets red again. "Oh, I don't know; I think it would be better if we wait till Berni and I get back from Florida. We're leaving in a couple of weeks and then she'd be here all alone with that information and nobody to talk to about it."

"I understand that. But Craig is here now and, let's face it, we really don't know how much time Grandma has left. I'm thinking we should tell her tonight?"

"Well, I'm just worried about how she might react. I don't want to give her a heart attack."

"Oh, Dad, I think Grandma can handle it. She's not that delicate. She's dealt with a lot more difficult news than this in her life. In fact, Jeff and Bill and I think she'd really WANT to know."

"I know she's not delicate, but she's a lot older now and I'm just afraid ..."

Bill adds his perspective saying, "I have to agree with Suzie and Jeff on this one. This is a small town. She's going to hear about this from someone, and I'd hate to find out how THAT would affect her, if she finds out her own family was keeping something from her."

Time has ticked off the clock and the stress level has risen like the two-minute-warning of an NFL game. Richard stands and Berni quickly follows. Clearly flustered, he declares in a tone uncharacteristic of his years, "Well, I guess I'll just have to go over there and tell her after church then."

"Oh, Dad, don't be like that. We're not trying to make this difficult for you. We're just trying to see this from Grandma's perspective. And if she hears this from the town gossip instead of from us, she's going to be PISSED."

"Right now we've gotta go to church. We'll talk about this after."

We make arrangements for Richard and Berni to drop us off back at the B&B. Suzie, Bill and Jordan are heading to the nursing home to see Grandma Helen. Richard and Berni will go to church first, and then to the nursing home. They'll call us later and arrange the details of what we'll do the rest of the evening.

In Richard's car, as we head back to the B&B I break the awkward silence with, "Richard, I just want to say that I'm not putting any pressure on you to tell your mom. I'd consider it an honor to get to meet her, but I don't know her at all – you do. So just be aware that I will be Ok with whatever decision you make about this."

I don't recall now if Richard responded verbally to my statement, but I wanted to make sure I wasn't being perceived as the new kid who comes into town to turn everything upside down. I don't want to be THAT guy.

But the tension in the car lifts, and we talk about things other than the elephant in the back seat. Before we know it, we're back at the B&B and Richard and Berni take off for evening Mass with a promise to call us later.

Back inside, Cindy and I feel a little numb about the way things had ended. It was awkward to be in the room while the family had been discussing how the new fact of my existence would be shared with Grandma. It feels as if this was a conversation that could have taken place before we arrived in Iowa – a definite plan laid out in advance. But it wasn't, so we have to deal with the tension and reality of not knowing what the outcome will be.

We spend an hour in a state of icky numbness. I really don't want to be the cause of tension within the family. I'm wondering if my presence here has already had a negative effect that can't be reversed.

Then my phone rings and it's Richard. Without much fanfare he says, "Well, we're here at the nursing home with Suzie and we've told Mom. Why don't you and Cindy come on down and meet her."

I ask no questions and simply say, "We'll be down shortly."

I brief Cindy who asks me several questions about what we're about to encounter at the nursing home. I can answer none of her inquiries because I had asked no questions.

About 15 minutes after the call, Cindy and I pull into the nursing home parking lot and see Bill and Jordan horsing around, all smiles, in front of the place.

As we approach them I ask, "So how did it go?"

"It was fine. She took it well. She was obviously surprised, but she didn't have a heart attack or anything. She's excited to meet you," Bill says.

The facility is considerably smaller than the nursing homes I've been in throughout Iowa and Ohio in recent years. We walk in and find the family gathered around a small table in the open area inside the entrance. Grandma sits in a wheelchair with an oxygen tank connected next to her. Her face exudes smiles, with a hint of nervousness. We reflect the same countenance back to her and greet her warmly.

Completion

After we left the nursing home, we all drove back over to the B&B and spent another three hours together. We looked at some of my family pictures on my computer including some pictures of Beverly when she was young. Mostly Richard and Berni looked at these pictures with me, but Suzie joined us from time to time.

We drank more of my homemade wine and told stories of our various childhood experiences. We talked about our health and various maladies we each have had over the years, all of us generally healthy. We talked about how we met our various spouses and talked about our education and employment. In short, we talked about things families talk about and I felt very much like I was being included in the family discussion.

It was nearly eleven o'clock now and everyone began to stir and talk of departure. And, like last night, I really did not want this experience to end.

As everyone grabbed for jackets and moved toward the door, we began to say our good-byes. By now our comfort level had improved and there were many more hugs than there had been 10 hours earlier at The Remarkable Rose. There seemed to be a collective sigh of relief that Grandma had been included in the discussion about this newly configured family.

"Now, Dad, you can go to Florida for the winter without the prospect of telling Grandma hanging over your head," Suzie offered with empathy and gentleness.

Richard nodded approvingly and with apparent relief in his eyes.

Berni leaned toward Cindy and I overheard her say, "I think he was just worried about getting in trouble with his mother."

I'm reminded that no matter how old one becomes, we are all about 10 years old to our parents.

We wandered out to the street and lingered a while longer talking as a few cars meandered up and down Main. Jordan got into the car awaiting his grandpa and grandma so they could get back to the motel for a good night of sleep. Seeing him there, I walked to the back of my car and pulled out a football. Last night I had mentioned that I'd toss the ball around with him if the weather permitted and here it was, the end of the day, and we hadn't yet had time to do it.

I held the ball in the air for Jordan to see and he quickly exited the car. We tossed the ball back and forth along the wide sidewalks in front of the stores in this throw-back Iowa town. We passed the ball around for 10 or 15 minutes, interrupted occasionally by a side conversation with one of the adult family milling about between cars on the street. It was like a scene out of a classic film, and I basked in its Film Noir feel as the street lights spilled jagged shadows across our faces while we talked.

Just before everyone left, I stood with Richard apart from the group. He asked about my education and I told him about going to college later in life, after I was married and was working full time.

"Where I grew up there wasn't much talk about going to college. Even though I was a pretty good student, I don't recall anyone ever mentioning that I should go to college. It was a rural community where most kids got out of high school and worked on the family farm or immediately got a job. That's what I did too. I worked a few jobs; then I bought a little sign company and ran it with a friend for a few years. Then we sold that and a few years later I bought another little company, a franchise janitorial company and ran it till 1990. It became clear to me that this was not what I wanted to do for the rest of my life. But as I imagined what other things I'd rather do, it also became clear that I'd never be able to do any of them without a college degree. So I went back to school and paid my own way to an Associate's Degree. Then I sold my janitorial business, took a job with a good company that had a 100% tuition reimbursement program. I was working 60-hours a week and going to school full-time – twice taking 23 credit hours in a semester. A couple of times Cindy sat me down for a 'come to Jesus' meeting, and we wondered together if I could keep up this pace and stay married too. But we did it."

"Well, you're certainly tenacious; I'll say that about you," Richard said.

"Where do you think I got that from? You said earlier that you worked all that overtime and rotating shifts for all those years in order to make a better life," I responded.

And then I reached out and put my arm around his shoulder, and he briefly put his around mine. I'm going to count it as, at least, half a hug. ☺

With that, Jordan sprinted down the sidewalk for one last pass. I waved him deeper and launched a perfect spiral into the street lights. The pass came down just a little beyond the spot Jordan was running toward. He leapt and simultaneously stretched for it with his right hand and hauled it in like a pro. Completion.

Na(ur)ture

I've talked with scores of people about my journey to discover where I come from and who I am biologically. After a few years of research, a common comment from those who have been engaged by my story is, "You know more about your origins than I know about mine."

Perhaps I do. It is clear that most people do not know – nor do they care to know – the circumstances of their own conception. The general lack of knowledge that most folks seem to have about how their parents met, the details of their parents' lives prior to their children's cognition, and the humanity and transitions of their parents has caused me to ponder my own discoveries on a deeper level.

Most folks would find it extraordinarily difficult to parse between nature and nurture. Why do they do the things they do ... think the things they think ... act the way they act? So intertwined in their own upbringing are both nature and nurture, it is nearly impossible to conclude where one ends and the other begins.

Is this habit I have one that I learned from a family member or is it mysteriously encoded in my DNA? Do I find that style of humor funny because I was exposed to it frequently in youth or because there is something in my double-helix that predisposes me to it? Where do my talents come from? Is my mechanical ability genetic or learned? What about my spirituality? Am I more likely to find faith in a Divine Being because I was taken to church by my adoptive parents from age three on? Or is the ability to embrace mystery and the unseen rooted in a part of my brain that is enhanced by something I've inherited from my biological parents?

Is who I am a cocktail of both nature and nurture mixed in random parts inside my soul, triggered by specific but indiscriminant timings and arbitrary people and events? Or is there a supernatural force that manipulated circumstance to predestine all that I am and do? And if the latter, what are the theological implications of a God who would take an active and intervening role in my little life, but has not done similarly in the lives of billions who have seemingly been left to the evil intent of others more powerful than they?

It is natural, when looking at family members, to peer deeply into their faces to search for exterior characteristics that mark them as originating from the same gene pool. I've shown pictures of my biological families to countless friends who ask about my research into my origins. They each glance at me, then at the photos, then back at me, scanning for something to recognize. Sometimes they say, "Oh, yeah, man, I can really see the similarity." Other times, they say the opposite.

When I look at pictures of my biological mom and her two sisters, I see my own visage in them. It is easy to see the same green eyes, the same prominent cheekbones, the same chubby face, smiling lips and mischievous expression.

But when I look at photos of my biological dad and my new brother and sister, I see far fewer of these exterior biomarkers. I'm pretty sure that if you put my biological dad's picture in a lineup with a dozen other men chosen at random, few people would identify the two of us as related. Having said that, I don't think his other two kids look much like him either. But I've seen pictures of my new brother and me when we were both toddlers and grade-schoolers, and I had trouble telling us apart – the resemblance is almost spooky.

When I first met Alvin, the man whose name is on my original birth certificate, I saw my sister, Theresa, in him, but I did not see me. During the half dozen, or so, times that I spoke face-to-face with Alvin Shepherd, I desperately wanted to find myself in him – to see him as my originator, but was never able to take that leap of faith in the sheer absence of any visible evidence.

But these are all external markers. What about the internal?

When I met my brother, Ricky, for the first time in 1997 I was struck by the similarity in mannerisms he displayed – they were so much like Theresa and Alvin. They had the same facial expressions, drank the same beer, smoked the same brand of cigarettes, ate the same favorite junk foods and displayed the same quiet introversion. They even laughed, coughed and talked alike.

Yet they hadn't been together since 1962. Are things as seemingly ordinary and mundane as these actually programmed into one's DNA? It seems ridiculous on one level, yet ...

My research indicates that there are more than three billion base pairs in a person's Haploid genome (the information that comes from the egg and sperm of the parents). That's a big number.

I doubt that most of us have a real, practical sense of just how many base pairs that really is. Here's a little glimpse into how many a billion is – if you began counting right now – one, two, three, four, five – as fast as you can and never stopped to eat, sleep or poop and if you could average speaking each new number aloud within an average of one second, it would take you nearly 32 YEARS to count to one billion. Of course, no one can count 24/7/365 because no one can go without eating, sleeping and pooping (not to mention the many other things in life worth doing). The first few hundred numbers could be counted aloud in an average of one second each, but very quickly one gets to numbers too long to speak in a single second. The actual average is likely about 5 seconds. (Time yourself reading this number out loud 742,667,957– seven hundred and forty two million six hundred sixty seven thousand nine hundred and fifty seven – it took me more than 5 seconds). And, of course, no one could start this counting endeavor at birth; they'd have to be 10 or 12 before their brains were sophisticated enough to comprehend numbers of this size. When we factor in all of these caveats (and there are so many more), it becomes impossible for a person to count to a billion in a single lifetime. It's probably more like five lifetimes to get to one billion. And that's just ONE billion. There are THREE billion Haploid DNA pairs encoding information about each human being.

Oh, and did I mention that there are also (i.e., in addition to) Diploid genomes in each person's DNA. The Diploid genome contains at least TWICE as much genetic information as the Haploid base pairs. (i.e. six billion plus three billion equals nine billion). Hence, if it takes five lifetimes to count to one billion, it would take at least 45 consecutive lifetimes to count to nine billion. Assuming an average lifespan of 70 years with counting beginning at age 10 and ceasing when the counter draws a final breath (i.e. 60 full years of useful counting), it would take 2,700 years (60 years times 45 lifetimes) of non-overlapping counting to reach nine billion.

So, imagine if Christopher Columbus had begun counting in 1492 when he arrived in what is now known as the North American Continent. That's about 525 years ago. And then allow that every subsequent generation of Columbus' had designated someone to do nothing in their lifetime but eat, sleep, poop and count. By now the Columbus family would be at roughly 1.9 billion. They'd be a bit more than 20% of the way to achieving their goal of counting to nine billion – the number of Haploid and Diploid genetic bits of info inside each DNA strand.

Nine billion is kind of a lot – let's just say.

So within these nine-plus billion bits of genetic information encoded into every double-helix strand of DNA, is it possible that things as seemingly unique to one's nurture and experience like attitudes, humor, preferences and propensity for learning are as likely as height, weight and facial features?

My personal experience would indicate that the answer is, yes.

Having just met my paternal biological family last month, they have literally had zero nurturing impact upon my life. They didn't know I existed, and I didn't know who they were until just a few months ago.

In the first two years of my life, all of my nurturing was done by my biological mom, Beverly, and her husband, Alvin. For a year after that, the orphanage staff provided whatever nurturing there was. And then since the age of three, the Steffens and Gardiners were the main source of nurture once I was adopted.

Getting the opportunity to completely separate my nature from my nurture is an interesting prospect – at least I find it so.

After spending a few hours with my new brother and sister, David and Suzie, Cindy asked them if they saw any similarities between me and my paternal family. David and Suzie looked at each other and nearly in unison said, "It's like talking to Dad. Craig's way of speaking, sense of humor and mannerisms all remind us of Dad."

David's Cindy added, "They even dress alike."

My Cindy chuckled, "Uh oh, maybe it's time to modernize Craig's wardrobe."

As the evening progressed, we talked about many things and found that we had so much in common. We enjoy many of the same favorite movies, music and foods. We all enjoy cooking and keeping a tidy house. We each have a strong work ethic and what we termed, "an overdeveloped sense of loyalty" toward our work.

We'd all been drawn to technical fields of work. Suzie spent 24 years as an ICU Nurse. David has been 26 years with the same employer as an engineering and laser technician. I've spent my career with scientists and engineers doing technology transfer, licensing, and commercialization, as an entrepreneur.

We each have a strong faith in God, but now express it mostly outside of traditional church environments. The three siblings are all pretty laid back and calm – most of the time. But we each discussed how, when pushed beyond our limits, we'll "snap" and go "a little crazy" in expressing our anger or exasperation.

We're all with partners who are older than us. We all enjoy professional sports, mostly football and baseball. We each love to be outside, hiking, camping, golfing, gardening and boating. We each left home at 17 or 18 and began making our own way in the world. We're all fiercely independent.

We've all taken a long view of our financial responsibilities, bought and paid off houses, and invested for the future. We all talked about how we never buy anything we don't absolutely need and, when we do, we research the purchase and buy the best product available in hopes that it will last many, many years.

And there is more. But we learned all that in just five hours of being with one another for the very first time. Nature or nurture?

The following day, after my first meeting with my biological siblings, I met my biological dad, Richard. I'd met him only once, a year prior, when I was talking to people who had known my mother. But this was the first time since we'd learned that he is my father.

Turns out Richard and I both played baseball (he in his youth and me till I was 51). We both enjoy golf and like to be outdoors doing most anything. We like the water; he in a fishing boat and me in a kayak. We enjoy investing and he gave me a few investment pointers in our initial meeting. He worked two jobs in his professional career, the first lasted just short of a generation the second lasted more than a generation – there's that over-developed sense of loyalty again. He has a self-deprecating sense of humor, like me, and we both love to laugh a hearty laugh. At lunch, we both ordered the exact same thing – including requesting options not listed on the menu. To quote a line from an old but favorite B-movie, "Kinda spooky-like."

That same night I met Richard's mother, my grandmother, for the first time. She too was a hard-working, loyal employee all her life. She was also entrepreneurial having run several businesses with her husband. She's 92 and sharp and enjoys technology – reading the news, following her Facebook page and doing her banking from her Kindle Fire and listening to music on her MP3 player. I wonder where I get it?

Nature seems to play a much bigger role than I ever gave it credit for.

Pinocchio

Something strange is happening in me since I met my biological family. Like Pinocchio, I'm starting to feel as if I'm not a real boy.

I'm back home now. I'm living my life. I'm with Cindy and our 8-month-old German Shepherd, Cyon. I go to work most days and deal with technology transfer and technology commercialization. I negotiate licenses and agreements and set strategies. I go to our farm in the forest of Southern Ohio on most weekends and I split wood for the fireplace, work on projects with the tractor, write and take long walks with Cyon.

Life is back to "normal."

But something is strange. With everything I do – everything – I think of my new family. I watch myself, as if in an out-of-body condition, do all the "normal" things and it all feels inauthentic. It feels not real. To say I feel like a fraud or a fake isn't too strong.

These feelings confuse me – take me by surprise. I do not understand their source. I am not a fake. I am not a fraud. I have been real and transparent and truthful with my new family and in life in general. There is no reason for these feelings of disingenuousness. Yet there they are.

I talked to my sister Suzie for two hours today. It's the third time we've talked, like school girls, since we met each other in November. I so enjoy her. We "get" each other.

After the call, I was hauling a few tractor-bucket loads of firewood up from the barn to the front porch. It's a mindless activity that gives my brain a chance to run free. I love this kind of work – at least sometimes.

As I perform my wooden chores, stacking firewood meticulously into its designated porch spot, beneath the bathroom window, a thought flashed through my mind. No one in my family has seen this place. They've never taken the tractor for a spin. They haven't enjoyed the warmth of the fireplace. In fact they've never seen me in my natural habitat at all. They've never witnessed me doing anything I do in my "normal" life. They literally have never experienced any aspect of who I really am.

It occurs to me that this is it. This is why I'm not feeling like a real boy. If a boy lives in the forest and there's no one there to see him, does his life make a sound?

Somehow nothing I do, nothing I have, nothing I am, seems real anymore. When I talked to Suzie, I told her I was at the farm this weekend – but it lacks authentication until she's been here too.

When I talked to my brother David last week, I mentioned how I enjoy getting on my tractor and doing various projects around the place. But it doesn't seem real until he sits on the tractor and engages the bush-hog.

I told Richard about being an adjunct professor at Indiana Wesleyan and tried to describe what I do in my work. But it seems more like novel than memoir, till I can introduce him to students and clients and have him watch me be me – watch me be real.

I've written letters to Grandma Helen and sent pictures from various periods of my life, but I don't think it will ever feel real until we can sit together, hold hands and share our stories, while searching each other's faces for the cues that make the stories come to life.

I talk about my life. I answer questions about my life. I describe my life. But the Pinocchio in me believes that none of it will truly be real until I SHARE my life with this new family of mine.

Perhaps my life is so unlikely, given the darkness of many of the stories I've told here, that I can't conceive of anyone believing it without actually witnessing its details with their own eyes. Perhaps I don't even trust *my* own eyes, and I long for someone else, someone from my pack, to reassure me that my natural habitat really does have some "normal" and some "redemption" written in.

Beginning

It is fifty-one years after the disappearance.

I sit in a nursing home in front of a ninety-two year-old woman in a wheelchair. Tiled floors act like piano keys, sending every heel strike echoing. Odors of disinfectant, medicine and excrement co-mingle in my offended nostrils. Hopelessness is seen on every face I encounter. It is the first time I have ever seen her, and I am concerned it may also be the last. Until this moment, when we look deep into each other's eyes, searching for ourselves in each other's visage, she did not know I exist.

She is dressed nicely in earth-tones and her hair is coiffed neatly. She stands out from the other residents as if she is the only character in color in a classic black and white film. Her countenance shifts nervously from big smile to bewilderment.

I bend at the waist and draw close to her, "It is an honor to meet you, Grandma Helen." She extends a hand, and I hold it atop my left palm as if I might be about to slip a ring on it. We stare deeply at one another for a long time, and for a moment I think I can see my life played back in reflection off of her bespectacled eyes.

She is surrounded by her beloved family, now expanded by the presence of a newly revealed grandchild she'd never heretofore imagined.

"What do you think of this news?" I ask with a big smile.

393

She works to extract a few new breaths from the oxygen tubing in her nostrils. "Well, I'm … I'm kinda … stunned I guess." She punctuates the statement with another big, dry smile.

We talk for twenty minutes or so. I ask about her childhood, which took place in this same part of Iowa. She tells a story about a time when she was a little girl, learning to drive a Model A Ford in the pasture of their farm with her siblings. Somehow, accidently, the Ford hits and kills a pig. Fearing the wrath of their father, they work hard to cover the evidence. They break up sticks and arrange a makeshift scaffold and prop up the pig, mannequin-style, in the pasture, hoping to avert the attention of their father. Predictably, the childish attempt at deception fails, and they are punished for their carelessness. All of us in the room laugh and revel in the tale.

She asks me what I do for a living. I explain that I work with technology transfer and commercialization. "I hear that you like technology too. You have a Kindle that you use?"

"Well, yes, but I don't have it here."

Suzie reaches into her purse and retrieves an MP3 player and headphones that she has brought so that Grandma Helen can listen to music, and a 20-year-old recording Suzie has found of Helen's great-grandson in a school play.

We talk briefly about Beverly and how she lived with her family just down the hill from Grandma Helen in Clemons. "She was a fire-cracker, she was," she declares.

Helen is visibly tired; she struggles to stay mentally present with us. With her family in town, she has missed her afternoon nap. Even though it is only 7:00, she is fading. Suzie takes her hand and draws close to her like a best friend. "Grandma, you tell us when you're too tired for this and you want to go to bed."

"Well, I'm tired. I want to go to bed."

Slowly we all rise and gather closer to say our good-byes. I say, "It was such a pleasure to meet you. I'll bet you didn't expect to get another grandchild at this stage of life?" She laughs and smiles her big smile. As Cindy moves alongside me to say good-bye, Grandma Helen says, "Well, no. But it's wonderful. I guess we'll have two more people to invite to the family reunion next year."

I point out that I noticed a card pinned to her bulletin board announcing the now past 67th annual family reunion. She looks at me and says, "I didn't get to go to that one. I was in here."

It is clear that this fact pains her, and it is equally clear that she doubts she'll be able to attend any future reunion that I may be invited to. It reminds her of her age and her condition. Sadness sweeps across her face, as if a cloud has obstructed the sun.

As the rest of the family begins to move toward the door, I take her frail hand in mine again. I look into her face and she matches my smile. I stoop forward and kiss the back of her ancient hand, as if we have been swept away to chivalry for just a moment.

I move to the door. As Suzie leans in to Grandma to give her a hug, I hear Grandma say, "He really does remind me of Richard."

A few months later, I am in this same room with Grandma Helen and Suzie again. Since our first visit, Grandma Helen and I have exchanged letters and photos by mail. In her first ever letter to me, she is quick to express her love to me and laments the years that have passed without our knowing one another. Then it is my turn to be stunned. Stunned at her authentic acceptance of this one-time orphan. Stunned at the love she demonstrates in word and deed. Stunned at how quickly she has drawn me into her heart and how quickly she has found her way into mine.

I have brought her more childhood pictures of myself and she notices, as Suzie and I have already, how much my new brother, David, and I looked alike in our first several years. Her smile beams out from her but, somehow, it is accompanied by a certain sadness.

"I wish I could kiss your feet." Grandma says as she beams her sadness into my eyes.

"Kiss my feet?" I question as I alternate glances from Grandma Helen to Suzie, searching for clues as to the meaning of this abrupt declaration.

"I always used to kiss the feet of my children and grandchildren after I changed their diapers. I never got to do that with you, so I wish I could kiss your feet."

I laugh out loud at the image in my head of this fragile saint kissing the feet of her new 53 year-old grandson. "I'm pretty sure it wouldn't be quite as endearing an experience now as it would have been when I was a baby." Suzie and Grandma join in my laughter.

"Ever since I met you, I've been thinking about what it would have been like if you had been with me when the grandkids used to come to my place along the river. We used to have so much fun in the summer, fishing and skipping rocks and exploring along the river banks. I wish you could have been with us."

Every cue emanating from her eyes, expressions and body language scream of her authenticity and the genuine longing of this verbal sentiment. Just as Grandma Steffen had been able to communicate true love to me during the "pot roast incident" so many years ago, now this grandma is reaching me in a long vacant place deep within my soul.

A few months later, on my birthday, a box arrives in the mail. Inside is a letter from Suzie explaining that she and Grandma Helen wanted to give me something special for my first birthday as a member of the family. Searching through the box's contents, I find a gift certificate for a tree – a tree described in the letter as a "family tree"— which they request that I plant in my yard as a reminder of my new family status. Also in the box is a plaque intended as a permanent marker for that tree which reads:

Family Tree
Although we are apart
You are in my heart
Love,
Grandma Helen

I am moved to tears. I am overwhelmed by this remarkable display of welcoming, inclusion and love.

I sit down at the desk in my home office and write a thank you card to Grandma, feebly attempting to express the swelling gratitude of my heart. In that card, I tell her that I am planning another visit to her in Iowa the third weekend in August. Knowing that Grandma Helen is an avid Chicago Cubs fan, I have noticed on their schedule that they will be playing my Orioles on that weekend. Because they play in different leagues, and because of the complexities of the interleague play schedule, the Cubs and Orioles have played one another only six other games in history. I consider it great fortune that they will play less than two months from my birthday. With humor, I write to Grandma Helen that we should also invite Suzie to join us in August so she can play the role of umpire to keep us from fighting.

But only a few days after Grandma Helen would have received that card, I got a call from my new dad.

"I wanted to call and let you know that Grandma's not doing very good." He'd said. He went on to explain the details of her day that brought her from "as talkative as she's been in months," to "unconscious and unresponsive." He punctuated those details with, "It doesn't look good."

A few days later, I was on my way to Iowa for Grandma Helen's funeral, and a tearful, heart-wrenching good-bye to this saint of a woman who had welcomed me so well and so completely into her heart and into her family.

The circle of life has taken another lap ... and will again.

Endings beget beginnings.

Beverly and Richard
side by side in the 1952 yearbook

Craig, David and Suzie
the first time we ever met.

Suzie and Craig
while visiting Grandma Helen

Richard, Craig and Berni in Florida

David, Richard, Suzie and C
at Grandma Helen's funeral

Epilogue

I am not my wound, or my defense against my wound. I am my journey.

James Hollis

And there is something else – something spiritual and mysterious about this journey.

For five decades I've been a part of one church or another. All of these churches have been on the "conservative" side of the Christian spectrum, to one degree or another. The underlying message of these churches is the preaching about right and wrong ... good and bad ... God's will and sin. Most of the sermons were overt in teaching the faithful that the key to a good and prosperous life was to do what is right – obey – behave. Then God will bless you. And if you REALLY want God's blessing, the answer is tithing. If you give to God (which meant give to the church) you'd be blessed beyond measure. After all, "you can't out-give God," we were taught.

This teaching was reinforced by connecting everything people saw as "good" with God's blessing; and everything people saw as "bad" with God's punishment (or the Devil in some circles).

Standing around in the church foyer, two friends might be talking about a raise one of them got at work, or a narrowly missed auto accident, or the good grade card one of the kids brought home. And a common response to such good news would be, "Well, God is blessing you," or "You must be livin' right, brother."

Conversely, if anyone (like those who were new to the group and had not yet learned the danger of this) dared to share some aspect of life that was less than perfect, the responses would be different. These confessions might be something like having gotten laid off at work or having had a car broken into or a child who got arrested. Now the common response one might overhear in the foyer would be something like, "The Devil's working overtime," or "God chastises them that he loves," or "Have you checked to see if there's sin in your life, brother?"

Subtly, or not, the message was, "God helps those who help themselves," or "Good things happen to good people and bad things happen to bad people." You might even get an out of context quote from Jesus, "A good tree cannot bear bad fruit …"

It's a clear form of what some might call "the prosperity gospel." The prosperity gospel is typically presented as a heresy in the circles I come from. It is a heresy that teaches that God will provide health, wealth and a trouble free life to those who "obey the Bible" fastidiously – and, by implication, God will punish those who do not. And though my circles would call this extreme example "heresy," our own practices reveal that we believe and embrace a less perfect form of the same doctrine.

It is with this backdrop that I began my journey to discover my biological family.

But as I read through these pages attempting to make the words communicate my story in a way that you will find meaningful – and perhaps healing – I see something stark and different about my life than the bumper-sticker clichés about "livin' right" that I grew up with, embraced and taught most of my life.

It is bigger than that. It is less dualistic than that. It is more mysterious than that.

I see a young Beverly, born into poverty and simplicity in rural Iowa, whose little life was likely damaged, overtly or covertly, by some kind of sexual abuse propagated by someone she'd encountered. We know, from her friend who witnessed it, about the explicit pornography to which she had been exposed in her preadolescence. This is clearly not a good thing.

In her teen years, Beverly made one bad choice after another, "going wild" by several accounts. She disregarded school and stable friends. She became promiscuous, hung out with older men, got pregnant at 16, lied and connived so that she could seal a forbidden marriage. These are clearly not good things.

She did not demonstrate "normal" maternal care for her first three children, all born while she was yet a teen. She chose rather to ignore, smother, abuse and abandon them on numerous occasions. These are clearly not good things.

It seems likely that this abuse led directly to the terror and uncontrolled screaming of Ricky, who would cry so desperately that he would turn blue, pass out and go into seizures. During at least one of these many episodes, he aspirated and developed pneumonia as a result. All of this led eventually to urgent medical care and an emergency run to the hospital in Fort Dodge, where Ricky was admitted and cared for during a week in late September of 1959. This was clearly not a good thing.

And while Beverly was in Fort Dodge, she left the hospital and the nine-month-old child admitted there and went out to socialize with old friends. As a result of that evening of reconnecting with an old school mate, she chose to disregard her marriage vows and seduced her friend in the back seat of that 1957 Buick Century. This was clearly not a good thing.

I believe that the guilt of that infidelity led Beverly to cast off what restraint there was and give herself to the fling with the Fuller Brush salesman – abandoning her children in the process. It is possible that she embraced this promiscuity so as to conceal, even to herself, the true identity of the baby (me) that was growing inside her at the time. This was clearly not a good thing.

After my birth, the ignoring, abusing and abandonment continued in central Iowa and then in the Des Moines area, until that day in late June of 1962 when she "stole the family car and disappeared." This was clearly not a good thing.

Following the disappearance Alvin, by all accounts, was gobsmacked and overwhelmed with the responsibility of three kids, all under the age of five. After three months of trying to do the right thing, he gave in to the panic within and left us kids behind, disappearing himself – out of state. This was clearly not a good thing.

All the family and friends of Beverly and Alvin passed up the opportunity to take in the abandoned children, relegating us to an orphanage, where we would be separated and institutionalized for over a year. This was clearly not a good thing.

During our stay in the orphanage, Beverly was living out of the car she stole with Jack, the man she ran away with. Apparently they drove from state to state looking for the happiness that had eluded her. Then she got pregnant with a fourth child along the way. This was clearly not a good thing.

Finally, there was a new husband, three decades her senior, and a fifth child, another abandonment and another flight toward an elusive happiness. This final attempt of hers to find a different life brought the wrath of an angry man and a bullet through her heart. Five orphans and a family of broken hearts remained of that life, now ended at age 25. It was a life that had found so much that was clearly not good.

Yet, here I am. I exist; and, more than that, I love my life.

I am reasonably bright, somewhat accomplished, loved and loving. I have a full life of true companionship with my wife and scores of deep friendships. I am not locked into a small world any longer, I am free to explore the boundlessness of an interconnected universe and a God far bigger, more loving and more gracious than I ever imagined.

And, I have learned that this God is seemingly FAR more comfortable with chaos and disorder than modern, American Christianity proclaims. I have learned that this God is able to create good not only as a result of the good that humans do, but also in spite of the bad choices that we make. The case for God is more difficult, in my opinion, if people always do what is good; for Jesus came as a physician not to the healthy, but to the sick. Healing isn't necessary in a world where everyone is always well. "Healed from what?" we'd likely ask. Yet, healing happens moment by moment in this real and imperfect life in which God seems comfortable. Healing is a daily reality in the mixed up world that led to me – and includes me still.

I am proof of that. The moral equation I've set forth above, a long series of "clearly not good," plus "clearly not good," ... has added up to *me* and my life. Mine is a life that I deem not only good, but very good. And what makes it so special, at least to me, is that it never should have turned out this way – but it did and I am grateful.

To personalize Walt Whitman's *O Me! O Life!*:
That I am here
That life exists and identity
That the powerful play goes on, and I will contribute a verse.

CPSIA information can be obtained
at www.ICGtesting.com
Printed in the USA
FFOW03n1017250915
17203FF